Psychological Economics

Recent Economic Thought Series

Warren J. Samuels, Editor
Michigan State University
East Lansing, Michigan, U.S.A.

This series is devoted to works that present divergent views on the development, prospects, and tensions within some important research areas of international economic thought. Among the fields covered are macromonetary policy, public finance, labor and political economy. The emphasis of the series is on providing a critical, constructive view of each of these fields, as well as a forum through which leading scholars of international reputation may voice their perspectives on important related issues. Each volume in the series will be self-contained; together these volumes will provide dramatic evidence of the variety of economic thought within the scholarly community.

PSYCHOLOGICAL ECONOMICS
Development, Tensions, Prospects

Edited by
PETER E. EARL
Senior Lecturer in Economics, University of Tasmania

Kluwer Academic Publishers
Boston/Dordrecht/Lancaster

Distributors

for the United States and Canada: Kluwer Academic Publishers, 101 Philip Drive, Assinippi Park, Norwell, MA 02061.

for the UK and Ireland: Kluwer Academic Publishers, MTP Press Limited, Falcon House, Queen Square, Lancaster LAI IRN, UK.

for all other countries: Kluwer Academic Publishers Group, Distribution Centre, P.O. Box 322, 3300 AH Dordrecht, The Netherlands

Library of Congress Cataloging in Publication Data

Psychological economics.

   Bibliography: p.
   Includes index.
   1. Economics — Psychological aspects. I. Earl,
Peter E.
HB74.P8P697   1987   330′.01′9   87-3050
ISBN 0-89838-234-3

PRINTED IN THE UNITED STATES OF AMERICA.

Contents

v

About the Contributors

Randall Bausor is an Assistant Professor of Economics at Thompson Hall, University of Massachusetts, Amherst, Massachusetts 01003, United States of America. He has written on methodological problems caused for economists by historical time and expectations, in journals such as the *Cambridge Journal of Economics* and the *Journal of Post Keynesian Economics*.

John L. Baxter is a Lecturer in Economics at the University of Sheffield, Sheffield, S10 2TN, United Kingdom. He has also worked as an economist in industry and at the OECD in Paris. His main research interest is in wage behavior, but he has also written a number of articles on youth unemployment and the problems of long-term unemployment.

Lawrence A. Boland is Professor and Chairman of the Department of Economics at Simon Fraser University, Burnaby, British Columbia, V5A 1S6, Canada. He is author of *The Foundations of Economic Method* (1982) and *Methodology for a New Microeconomics* (1986) and numerous articles on economic theory and methodology in such journals as the *American Economic Review,* the *Journal of Economic Literature, Philosophy of Science,* and the *British Journal for the Philosophy of Science.*

Michael A. Brooks is a Lecturer in Economics at the University of Tasmania, Box 252C GPO Hobart, Tasmania 7001, Australia, and his publications include articles in the *Southern Economic Journal* and *Public Choice* (forthcoming). His main research is on public choice, taxation, and subjectivist economics.

A. W. Coats is Emeritus Professor of Economic and Social History at the University of Nottingham, United Kingdom, and is now Research Professor of Economics at Duke University, Durham, North Carolina 27706, United States of America. He is the author of numerous articles on the history of economic thought, methodology, the sociology of economics and the role of economists in government. He has also edited a number of books, including *The Marginal Revolution in Economics* (with R. D. C. Black and C. D. Goodwin, 1970), *Classical Economists and Economic Policy* (1971), and *Economists in Government: An International Comparative Study* (1981).

Rod Cross is a Lecturer in the Department of Economics, University of St. Andrews, St. Andrews, Fife, KY16 9AL, Scotland, United Kingdom. He has published articles on unemployment and methodology and is the author of *Economic Theory and Policy in the UK* (1982) and editor of *Unemployment, Hysteresis and the Natural Rate Hypothesis* (1987).

A. M. Endres is a Senior Lecturer in Economics at the University of Auckland, Private Bag, Auckland, New Zealand. His main research area is the history of economic thought, and he has published in, among other places, the *Journal of Economic Issues* and *History of Political Economy*.

Ben J. Heijdra is a Lecturer in Economics at the University of Tasmania, Box 252C GPO Hobart, Tasmania 7001, Australia. His publications include articles in the *Journal of Interdisciplinary Economics* on methodology and economic history. His main research interest, however, is in non-Walrasian economics.

John D. Hey is Professor of Economics and Statistics at the University of York, Heslington, York, YO1 5DD, United Kingdom, and is Managing Editor of the *Economic Journal*. His publications include articles on choice under uncertainty and numerous books, among which are *Uncertainty in Microeconomics* (1979), *Economics in Disequilibrium* (1981), and *Data in Doubt* (1984).

Alan Lewis is Reader in Economic Psychology at the School of Humanities and Social Sciences, University of Bath, Claverton Down, Bath, BA2 7AY, United Kingdom, and is Review Editor of the *Journal of Economic Psychology*. In addition to numerous articles, he has also published *The Psychology of Taxation* (1982), *The Economic Mind* (with A. Furnham, 1986), and edited *Mental Mirrors* (with C. Antaki, 1986).

Roger S. Mason is Professor of Marketing and Chairman of the Department of Business and Management Studies at the University of Salford, Salford, M5 4WT, United Kingdom. He has the unusual distinction of holding degrees in economics, management, and marketing, and has published internationally on consumer behavior, market economics, and marketing management. His specialist research interest is in the market for status goods, and his output in this area includes *Conspicuous Consumption* (1981).

Jochen H. Runde manages to combine a career as a musician with a Lectureship in Economics at the (multiracial) University of the Witwatersrand, 1 Jan Smuts Avenue, Johannesburg, 2001, South Africa. His main research interest is in subjectivist economics, and he has also co-authored work on rational expectations and Keynesian economics in the *South African Journal of Economics*.

Malcolm Rutherford is an Associate Professor of Economics at the University of Victoria, PO Box 1700, Victoria, British Columbia, V8W 2Y2, Canada. He has published extensively on economic method and institutional economics in journals such as *History of Political Economy,* the *Journal of Economic Issues,* and the *Journal of Post Keynesian Economics*.

THE EDITOR

Peter E. Earl is a Senior Lecturer in Economics at the University of Tasmania, Box 252C GPO Hobart, Tasmania 7001, Australia. His publications include articles on monetary economics, economic methodology, and consumer theory, as well as four books on behavioral/Post Keynesian economic theory: *Money Matters* (with S. C. Dow, 1982), *The Economic Imagination* (1983), *The Corporate Imagination* (1984), and *Lifestyle Economics* (1986).

Acknowledgments

A number of publishers are due thanks for providing permission for Alan Lewis to use copyright material in chapter 13 of this book. First figure 13–2 is reprinted from *Personal Values and Consumer Psychology,* edited by R. E. Pitts, Jr. and A. G. Woodside (Lexington, MA: Lexington Books, D.C. Heath and Company), copyright © 1984 by D.C. Heath and Company. Second, figures 13–3 and 13–4 are copyright © 1975 by the President and Fellows of Harvard College, all rights reserved, having originally appeared in the *Harvard Business Review.* Finally, figure 13–5 is copyright © by the Directors of the Columbia Law Review Association, Inc. All rights reserved. This figure originally appeared as figure 2 of Hoffman and Spitzer, Experimental law and economics: an introduction, 85 *Columbia Law Review* 991 (1985).

I would also like to thank my colleagues, Michael Brooks, Harald Gatenby, and Ben Heijdra, for their assistance during my frequent encounters with word-processing problems caused by computer/printer incompatibilities and "user-hostile" designs. Once again, I am indebted to Sharon Axford for her knowledge of psychology, and for tolerating the domestic consequences of my addiction to working on a fresh book each year. However, computer problems aside, this work has been a much more relaxed enterprise than my previous solo ventures. For this, I must thank Warren Samuels, the contributors who gave their time and effort so willingly (and who, in the main, adhered remarkably well to my deadlines), and those at Kluwer who were involved in commissioning and producing the finished product.

Psychological Economics

1 INTRODUCTION

Peter E. Earl

There is no doubt that it is appropriate for a series on Modern Economic Thought to include a book on the recent development of economic analysis incorporating ideas from psychology. This book was designed to appear in 1987, 15 years after the publication of a now classic collection of essays in honor of George Katona (Strumpel et al., 1972), who throughout the fifties and sixties had been tirelessly trying to persuade economists of the virtues of an infusion of psychology into their work. In the intervening 15 years there has been a considerable growth of interest along the lines for which Katona had been arguing. Many psychology-based economics monographs have appeared; a specialist quarterly, the *Journal of Economic Psychology*, commenced publication in 1981, with 1985 seeing the first issue of the *Journal of Interdisciplinary Economics* as yet another addition to growing ranks of "psychology-friendly" journals such as the *Journal of Consumer Research* and the *Journal of Social Economics*; and recently, within psychology itself, symposia have been taking place with a focus on the economics/psychology interface — for example, see the entire June 1982 issue of the *British Journal of Social Psychology*. For someone like myself, strongly committed to a psychological approach to economics, a

1

problem of information overload and consequent ignorance of pertinent developments already looms large as a possibility.

This burgeoning of interest is, admittedly, confined as yet to a small minority of the total population of economists. Nonetheless, it does mean that there exists a ready pool of authors upon whom the editor of a book on psychological economics can call for chapters on its development, tensions within its field, and its prospects. Bearing this in mind, some readers may be somewhat surprised by the list of contributors to this book: most of them are well-known for contributions that have *not* tended to include significant psychological inputs. A much more "obvious" cast of contributors is to be found in the collections edited by Gilad and Kaish (1986) and by MacFadyen and MacFadyen (1986), books which I hope will often be read in parallel with the present one but which appeared too late to be taken account of within it. It might be tempting to conclude that the present editor was a bit slow off the mark and found the "obvious" body of contributors already fully committed with chapters for the Gilad/Kaish and MacFadyen/MacFadyen books. While tempting, such a conclusion would be totally inappropriate; for there is a carefully considered strategy behind my choice of contributors.

The strategy was devised as a way of discovering answers in respect of the subtitle theme "Development, Tensions, Prospects" that was suggested for the present book by Professor Warren Samuels, the editor of the series in which it appears. Given that a psychological approach to economics is still favored by only a minority of economists, I decided that it would be particularly instructive if I commissioned many of the chapters from economists whose normal areas of interest seemed to have an obvious interface with psychology which they had so far not tended to exploit. They would be invited to explore some of the unfamiliar literature (where necessary, with the aid of some guidance from myself) with a view to seeing to what extent it offers scope for aiding their problem-solving activities, and what might be the broader ramifications of this exploratory experience for their research programs. They would also be invited to comment openly on how they felt about the exercise and on the problems they encountered during it, either within the text of their own chapters or during correspondence with myself. (In the latter case, their remarks would surface, unattributed, during my closing chapter for the book.) In a number of cases, short reactive pieces would be commissioned from economists with overlapping interests who might be expected to draw very different conclusions.

Overall, this strategy promised to be a way of learning much more about previous developments (or reasons for the lack of them), tensions and prospects than if I merely commissioned chapters from people like myself with well established commitments to a psychological approach to economics. It would have been all too easy to put together a book that was little more than a series of synoptic chapters by authors of recent monographs: such a book would doubtless be useful, but not in the context of a series on the development and evolution of economic ideas. As an editor known to have something of an evangelical zeal for psychological economics, I felt that the strategy would not only help me guard myself against charges of presenting an unbalanced picture; there was also the distinct possibility that I might generate converts among some of the contributors and even even among readers who were impressed by what could be produced in a fairly short space of time by economists who had never before ventured into the territory of the psychologist.

The first five contributions to a greater or lesser extent all address the questions of what the economic model-builder should assume decision-makers to believe they know when they choose in a world of uncertainty, how decision-makers come to possess this knowledge, and how they learn (change their minds). These chapters reveal very different attitudes to the implications of empirical and theoretical work in psychology concerned with this core area of interest for the economist. This is hardly surprising, since the five authors differ greatly in their backgrounds and habitual approaches to economics: roughly speaking, we have, in order, a Post Keynesian, an institutionalist, and then three neoclassically inclined thinkers, the last of whom seems to be moving increasingly in the direction of a behavioral approach.

The first two of these contributions, chapters 2 and 3, happen to be the boldest examples in this book of economists' first-time attempts at coping with psychology. Both were also written by contributors whom I decided to approach after enjoying their contributions to a 1984 symposium on uncertainty and knowledge in the *Journal of Post Keynesian Economics*. In chapter 2, Randall Bausor contrasts the methodology of mainstream Walrasian economics with what seems to be implied by some of the "classics' of psychology. Despite their different perspectives, Bausor's psychological sources seem to hold a common implication for economists: equilibrium could be a highly misleading focus for attention in many contexts, for the minds of decision-makers change as their lives develop and sometimes these changes are highly discontinuous in nature. Psychology, in Bausor's case, leads to an enhanced enthusiasm for Shackle's "kaleidic" vision of economics.

In chapter 3 Malcolm Rutherford takes a careful look at the literature within psychology on judgment and learning, with a view to assessing its implications for economics. I must confess that this chapter is my personal favorite from the collection and also the one that I find most difficult to summarize: not only does it cover a mass of literature from psychology but, in considering alternative approaches to the rationality issue, it pulls no punches in trying to achieve a tight philosophical analysis. It does need to be said, however, that particular profit is to be had from reading Rutherford's chapter while bearing in mind that what he says concerning the modeling of learning by economic agents may be usefully applied to the modeling of learning on the part of economists themselves.

After the opening pair of relatively uninhibited forays into the psychological literature, chapter 4 serves as an abrupt reminder that more mainstream economic theorists may have far less accommodating attitudes towards the use of psychology in economics. I was not surprised by the sceptical reaction of Rod Cross to the contributions of Bausor and Rutherford (for my own reactions to a 1982 attack by Cross on the kind of position adopted by Bausor, see Earl and Kay, 1985). However, Cross does offer a constructive message as well as scepticism: in *some* circumstances economists may indeed need an infusion of ideas from other disciplines if they are to deal with anomalies, but the fact that economic choices result from the workings of human minds does not mean that psychology is the obvious discipline to look to for inspiration. Cross himself, in his recent work on unemployment theory, has been attracted by the physicists' concept of hysteresis.

Chapter 5 is the first of two chapters by colleagues of my own at the University of Tasmania, but readers should understand that in both cases these contributions arose as a result of controversy in our department rather than from Australia's well-known tendency toward "cronyism." Ben Heijdra and I have had many heated discussions about how one might usefully try to analyze decision-making under uncertainty, and my invitation to him to see what he made of psychologists' contributions in this area was extended in a somewhat guileful attempt to subvert his attachments to neoclassical modes of thought. The resulting chapter led me to see Heijdra as more of a "neoclassical imperialist" than a convert to the satisficing mode of thought, despite his quite enthusiastic reaction to the literature on the use of simple heuristics as means of coping with complexity: here is a neat case of what Remenyi (1979) has labeled the "absorptive reaction principle" for defending besieged research programs.

In chapter 6, John Hey examines prospects for using mathematics in psychological economics, and the result may surprise many readers. One way of tackling the issue would have been to review the kinds of formal techniques that have been popular with psychologists who have attempted to model phenomena of potential interest to economists, in journals such as the *Journal of Mathematical Psychology* and the *British Journal of Mathematical and Statistical Psychology*. However, Hey decided to focus on a much more fundamental issue than that of the kinds of techniques that might be appropriate, namely, the different kinds of methodological frameworks within which symbolic manipulations of whatever kind might be undertaken. Particular attention is given to the different attitudes of psychologists and mainstream economists to randomness, while tensions are readily apparent between Hey's views on the methodological implications of complexity in decision-making and those expressed by Heijdra in the previous chapter.

Chapters 7 and 8, by Jo Runde and Tony Endres, present between them a detailed case study of changing attitudes to the use of psychology within the Austrian economics research program. The Austrian school has been undergoing a substantial resurgence during the period that psychological economics has been gathering momentum. Given the well-known subjectivist perspective of Austrian economists, one might expect them to be natural bedfellows with psychologists, especially as one leading Austrian has produced a book-length contribution to pure psychology (Hayek, 1952). Things turn out to be far more complicated than that, as these two chapters show, with Hayek keeping his psychology so separate from economics that Runde and I agreed that it was best explored in an appendix. And, as Endres — an economist who also has a background in sociology — argues, neither can the ups and downs of the relationship between Austrians and psychologists easily be kept separate from that between Austrians and sociologists.

John Baxter's obvious enthusiasm for the work of the early Austrian Carl Menger, in a context that also leads one to look to sociology as well as psychology, makes it appropriate that his chapter should be placed next in line, as chapter 9. It also provides an obvious bridge to the chapter by Roger Mason. Whereas Baxter uses psychological material to argue the case for taking seriously concern among worker groups over wage relativities and then goes on to explore its possible implications, Mason, in chapter 10, looks at the development of the literature on conspicuous consumption, an obviously social and image-centered form of behavior. In both areas the potential for economists to make greater use of inputs from social psychology seems considerable. Baxter's chapter concerns just one area of a subdiscipline that is especially rich in possbilities for symbiotic work with economics and psychology. At least four other areas of labor economics and industrial relations are worth highlighting as territories that could be worth exploring with a psychological orientation.

First, one can note that there already exists an economics literature built around the theme that "The basic reason why strikes occur at all in conventional bargaining models is the misjudgment by one party of the other's intentions" (Siebert and Addison, 1981, p. 390). In other words, strikes are seen as psychologically rooted accidents, rather than politically rooted attempts to exert union power, and it would therefore seem that work aimed at understanding the judgmental processes commonly employed by the representatives of bosses and workers might be more valuable for policy purposes (for example, in advising on the creation and operation of conciliation authorities) than that which focuses on changing economic incentives against striking.

Second, worker immobility in respect of tasks and location despite changes in "economic" incentives may be more readily understood in the light of literature on motivation, hostility and anxiety. So too may Marxian arguments about workers becoming "alienated" due to the increasing use of automation-based, skill-depreciating production techniques (see Braverman, 1974). Suppose, for example, that one accepts the central proposition of Kelly's (1955) psychology of "personal constructs," that people may usefully seen as being essentially concerned with being able to predict and control their lives. Then one can easily see why experiences at the mercy of continuous-flow, management-paced production systems (of the kind so vividly depicted by Charlie Chaplin in his film *Modern Times*) may drive workers not merely to join trade unions but also to take desperate steps — such as deliberately throwing a spanner into the works — in order to try to keep intact the image that they are not totally at the mercy of events in their workplaces.

Third, there seems to be tremendous scope for making use of psychologists' contributions in the area of organizational behavior and human performance to shed light on international, interfirm, and interworker productivity patterns that fit in poorly with the predictions of neoclassical theory. For example, Lester Thurow's address to the 1986 meeting of the American Association for the Advancement of Science made great play on the attitudinal factors behind falling U.S. office productivity in the face of increasing office automation and the use of computerized accounting information systems. (One proposition was that if senior managers have poor keyboard skills and view secretaries with virtuoso keyboard skills as symbols of their own status, they will end up having word-processing devices merely used as expensive typewriters by their secretaries instead of suffering humiliation while learning word-processing and then coldly firing their secretaries.) More generally, it should be noted that a key message in Leibenstein's (1966, 1976) often-cited work on X-efficiency is that production functions have a significant psychological/sociological dimension.

Nelson and Winter (1982) appear to go even further and use the "tacit knowledge" concept of Polanyi to argue that production functions cannot be precisely pinned down in engineering terms and separated from the contributions of particular individuals with highly idiosyncratic acquired skills. Nor should we forget (and I am grateful to Stanley Siebert for a reminder) the psychological aspects of Lydall's (1976) "D-factor" — the extent to which drive, doggedness, and determination help, possibly more so than either cognitive ability or years of education, to explain productivity and earnings differences.

Fourth, and finally, it is to be hoped that economists will begin to acquaint themselves with some of the work that is presently being undertaken on the psychology of unemployment: the book by Jahoda (1982) contains many references but its text is somewhat disappointing and a much more inspiring starting point would be the excellent paper by Warr (1983). Given the images raised in some of this literature — of the crushed personalities of the unemployed and the feelings of lost control from which they often suffer — it would be particularly tragic if work by psychologists continued to be ignored by economists with monetarist inclinations who have so far rejected the Post Keynesian view that much of the unemployment of the past decade has been involuntary in nature.

The most striking thing about Roger Mason's subject area, conspicuous consumption, is the paucity of pertinent literature, psychologically oriented or otherwise, relative to the phenomenon's apparent importance in everyday life. It is easy to see why orthodox economists have kept well clear of the topic: conspicuous consumption behavior makes little sense if one habitually models consumers as if they are fully informed. Acts of conspicuous consumption are of their essence designed to emit signals — but in most cases to do so without appearing as though one is quite deliberately showing off. (*In*conspicuous consumption is a new variation on this theme, where, for example, the successful German businessman is anxious not to be seen, in these depressed times, as flaunting his wealth: he purchases a fairly innocuous looking but ultra-high performance BMW M5 and insists that the tell-tale trunk-lid badge is replaced with one from the much cheaper yet similarly bodied BWM 528i.) As well as having interesting motivational underpinnings, the guileful nature of much of this behavior raises questions, in my mind at least, concerning information-processing problems and judgmental heuristics. For example, there are many varieties of publicly consumed goods upon which one can spend one's wealth, so how does the conspicuous consumer work out the most effective *mix* of display activities in the eyes of his or her intended audience? (And we should not forget that a choice has to be made concerning how much to spend on display:

by spending little on his or her private life a person may be able to create a misleadingly prosperous public image, so long as privacy, and hence credibility, can be preserved.) It is possible to concentrate on a few obviously expensive items, or many cheaper ones; a person can also seek to exploit the ignorance of his or her audience by purchasing secondhand models of goods that look very similar to brand new models. (The slowly evolving styles of "prestige" automobiles facilitate this, but without the possibility that a consumer might impress poorly informed onlookers, who cannot tell, say, a well-kept decade-old BMW from a nearly new one, the used-car selling line of "prestige you can afford" would make little sense.) To judge from the minimal attention accorded to conspicuous consumption in the review of economic psychology provided by Furnham and Lewis (1986), little work has been done by psychologists on either the motivational or strategic aspects of conspicuous consumption. The reason for the psychologists' neglect of this area may well be one that would rightly worry any economist and may help account for the state of the economics literature revealed in Mason's chapter: the results of empirical investigations of guileful behavior are intrinsically open to question.

Chapter 11 emerged as a result of my reading Lawrence Boland's (1986) latest book on methodology around the time that chapters 9 and 10 were being finalized. Whereas Cross (chapter 4) and Heijdra (chapter 5) focus on equilibrium and on maximizing behavior, respectively, as core features of the orthodox research program, Boland gives special attention to the rule that neoclassical models must be based on methodological individualism. If it were not possible to reconcile this model-building rule with the kind of crowd behavior that is central to the chapters by Baxter and Mason, then one would not expect to see mainstream economists jumping to study these areas with the aid of materials from social psychology. Certainly, Coddington's (1983, chapter 6) famous essay on varieties of Keynesian economics must have led many to conclude that anything to do with crowd behavior is a "no-go area" as far as "reductionist" Walrasian model-builders are concerned, and is fit only for Post Keynesian "fundamentalists." Boland's short chapter attempts to clarify the nature of methodological individualism and, as might be expected from the discussion in chapter 3 of his views on psychologism, he attempts to keep well clear of social psychology. However, this does not prevent him from arguing the merits of incorporating insights from sociology in work on conspicuous consumption — just as Cross had a bigger enthusiasm to make neoclassical theory more multidisciplinary with the aid of concepts from physics. It can be argued, though, that Boland's broad vision of how one should conduct neoclassical economics is a lot closer to much modern work on the psychology of decision making than he wishes to suggest (see Earl, 1986c).

It seemed important that at least one chapter of this book should refer to material within the broad domain of public sector and welfare economics. My colleague Michael Brooks emerged as the "victim" to work on this area after I had given a departmental workshop on the methodology of behavioral economics. To put it mildly, the workshop had been a very lively event, and at the end of it Brooks kept asking what it all implied for thinking on public choice and public goods. (The fact that he had been more open)minded than some of our mutual colleagues may well be due to the subjectivist background provided by Buchanan and others for his graduate work at Virginia.) I was forced to confess that I had not yet found time to extend my thinking into that territory and suggested that he was better equipped to do so. Chapter 12 gradually emerged as a result, but it very soon became clear one would need an entire book, at least, to explore the area fully.

A possible deterrent to empirical work aimed at following up ideas raised in this book is that empirical work in psychological economics is by its nature incompatible with many of the quantitative techniques that economists conventionally employ (usually to process readily accessible "objective" data series). Chapter 13 is thus offered as a device to show would-be psychological economists some of the techniques they might need to learn. Its author, Alan Lewis, is best known as the leading pioneer of "fiscal psychology," but I approached him as the prospective author of the chapter more because of his experience in lecturing on research methods to students at the University of Bath's multidisciplinary School of Humanities and Social Sciences. Lewis' chapter uses a series of carefully chosen case studies to illustrate particular techniques for obtaining and processing data from the minds of subjects and also comments on the overlap between psychological economics and experimental economics.

In chapter 14, A.W. Coats begins to tie threads from the earlier chapters together as he examines the nature of the resurrection of psychological economics. His chapter is in a number of ways an obvious sequel to his case study of the failure of Veblen and others at the turn of the century to redirect economics with the introduction of psychological inputs (Coats, 1976) and his more recent paper on the revival of subjectivism in economics (Coats, 1983), prepared for the proceedings of a conference on the theme "Beyond Positive Economics?" In the latter paper, Coats had noted how subjectivists' attitudes to psychology were changing, and thereby he rather provided a basis for chapters 7 and 8 of the present book. I had also been struck by the success of the technique Coats had used to write that paper, literally during the conference (at the University of York, United Kingdom,

in 1981), in the light of the other papers as well as his own broader scholarship. Given the organic nature of this book as a whole, it seemed entirely
appropriate that he should prepare his overview in the light of chapters 2–
13 of this book, as drafts became available.

For the closing chapter of this book I decided to employ the reflexive
style of thinking with which I had experimented in an earlier paper on the
comparative lack of success of behavioral approaches to the theory of the
firm (Earl, 1983c), a paper that was originally written at a time (1980)
when I was not feeling optimistic about the payoff to pursuing a deviant
kind of research. Ultimately, the fate of psychological economics would
appear to depend not upon the existence of puzzles in economic analysis
that seem more amenable to investigation (if not to unambiguous solution)
with the aid of psychological constructs. Rather, the outcome hinges upon
whether economists with the capacity to make such contributions judge
that the efforts seem sufficiently likely to be worth their opportunity costs.
These costs will seem to vary according to the goals that the potential
psychological economists are setting themselves and the constraints against
which they believe they are working. My January 1987 examination of the
economics and psychology of attempting to win the games economists play
is a much more optimistic piece than I would have been able to write in
1980, but it is still replete with notes of caution.

Before readers proceed to investigate these chapters and form their own
mental images of prospects for the further development of psychological
economics, they should note that, unlike other books in this series, this
one features a single consolidated bibliography. At the end of each entry
it is indicated in which of the chapters citation occurs. I assembled it in
the hope that this would reveal something about the overlap in sources
among the independently written chapters, and that it would highlight the
existence of works other than those by particular authors referred to in
each chapter. On both of these counts, the results were quite satisfying:
many individual works receive citations in several chapters, and many
authors have a variety of their works cited. One begins to get a picture of
a network of possible key sources in this kind of research, and of scope
for synergy between what one might normally think of as disparate chapter
themes.

2 HUMAN ADAPTABILITY AND ECONOMIC SURPRISE

Randall Bausor

1. Introduction

We cannot understand society without understanding people. The ways in which humans behave, including their adjustments to each other and to their communities, contribute to the complex interactions from which all activity arises. Attempts to think coherently about economic phenomena must incorporate, at least implicitly, some image of human motivation and epistemics, and of the skills by which accommodation between people is achieved. Only then can one gain insight into the individual's emergence as a socially integrated creature responding to, and attempting to influence, events.

Most economists invoke a mathematically precise formulation of a person's economically relevant traits, and axiomatize a particular image of preferences and knowledge from which individually optimizing actions and socially equilibrated states emerge. Obviously, this implicit image of the nature of human affairs influences the resulting image of the nature of economic processes and performance.

In this chapter I critically examine the conceptual foundations of the economist's treatment of people, especially their dynamic aspects, and

11

assess this image's impact upon subsequent characterizations of social phenomena. The social sciences are lamentably fragmented, and the economist's description of individuals need not be compatible with that of a
colleague in a different academic department. My second purpose, therefore, is to consider how alternative conceptualizations of adaptability that
have arisen in psychology relate to the economist's depiction. These alternatives yield a rather different kind of economic analysis. In particular,
they permit entry of impulsive actions, and abrupt reactions to surprising
events. The resulting disarrangement of plans disrupts the economy, spreads
surprise, and foils equilibrating tendencies. Consequently, economic dynamics appears less like a sequence converging toward equilibrium and
more like a process of muddling through time in the face of ceaseless
response to surprise. We assemble, that is, a view akin to what G.L.S.
Shackle has called economic kaleidics.

2. The Walrasian Characterization of People

We take the Walrasian approach as paradigmatic of most economic analysis. Although not universal, it does predominate. Moreover, it rigorously
formalizes an elegant and powerful description of private volition that
simultaneously isolates attributes common to all agents while emphasizing
individual variation.

Walrasian economic models construct aggregate economic systems from
logically antecedent and exogenously established persons. The agent is
conceived as a rationally optimizing person whose existence precedes his
or her own economic consequences. Each is a bundle of motivating preferences, combined with some procedure to translate these preferences into
social acts. The models attempt to replicate the economy's behavior by
aggregating across individuals, and by examining the interdependence between personal action and market allocation. Since prices indicate exchange
opportunities, their values assume primary organizing roles for the economy by constraining the decisions of the people comprising it. A vision of
each person as socially autonomous from, and volitionally independent of,
his or her companions is essential to this view of systematic performance
as governed by the rationally motivated acts of individuals. Conceptually,
each person stands alone, and is, at least potentially, economically distinguishable from all others. Each is a mature agent competently following
his or her own judgment to satisfy his or her own preferences, given his
or her endowments and vision of the world. Analytically, therefore, the

agent is a social atom whose preferences, cognition, and initial endowment has been effectively established prior to entrance into the economy. This preserves the individualistic character of decentralized market economics. Although an agent's actually experienced state — the commodities acquired, hours worked, and welfare achieved — results from a constellation of economic factors, the defining attributes of the individual, especially preferences, remain inviolate. In one of the more abstract versions of the theory, that contained in Debreu's (1959) *Theory of Value*, for example, the model

> . . . consists of a certain number of agents, the role of each of them being to choose a complete plan of action, i.e. to decide on the quantity of his input or of his output for each commodity. Thus an agent is characterized by the limitations on his choice, and by his choice criterion (p. 37).

Consumers each possess complete, reflexive, transitive, continuous, increasing, and convex preferences defined over a commodity space taken as R^n, where n is the finite number of distinguishable goods and services in the economy. Given an initial endowment of commodities, and prices, an agent attempts to acquire his or her most preferred yet affordable commodity bundle. Agents rationally strive to optimize by adjusting the endowment of commodities they possess, but that optimizing process assumes that the individual's identifying personal characteristics (preferences) have already been formed, and are invariant with respect to exchange. Stigler and Becker (1977), for example, argue that cases in which preferences appear to change can be explained as the accumulation of human capital in the production of commodities from which utility is gained. One's ability to produce utility may change, but not one's preferences. Tobin and Dolbear (1963) note the antecedence of preferences to economic analysis, commenting that "economics looks to psychology to explain the formation of preferences' (1963, p. 679). Equilibrium occurs when every individual's acts socially accommodate everybody else's. It characterizes a powerful prereconciliation of plans in which individuality is manifested in a socially coherent pattern. Thus, although each choice reflects both individuality and the constraints shaping decisions, personhood remains independent of prices, endowment, trades, welfare, and both consumption and production decisions. Economic performance derives from autonomously constituted agents.

This model, prized for its generality, can be subjected to numerous variations, and descriptively enriched by the amendment of complicating features. In addition to the static perfect-information version of the theory, variations incorporating, first, dated goods and contingent markets, or, second, sequences of temporary equilibria have been widely studied. The first of these replaces timeless commodities with goods and markets identified with their particular date. The initial state (and thus its prices) is known to all, whereas future possibilities are contingent upon future happenings. Expectations are probabilistically articulated, and people trade in contingent futures markets. Although it introduces risk, analytically it treats marketing forward the same way it treats spot markets. All decisions are made prior to time's passage, and there is no learning. All markets, both spot and forward, clear in advance of trading, and time reveals only which contracts must be honored.

The second alternative introduces sequential decisions, which necessitates a more sophisticated statement of personal cognition. Here, the system proceeds through a sequence of "periods" during which individuals plan and transact, and then adjust their future plans according to current performance. Consequently, the economy is said to be in "temporary" equilibrium if each period's markets clear, and a "perfect" equilibrium if the sequence of temporarily equilibrated periods exhibits intertemporal continuity of plans. This notion of dynamics as a progression of temporarily cleared markets was introduced by J.R. Hicks in *Value and Capital* (1946), and although he has since voiced reservations about it (Hicks, 1979), its influence remains. Time's introduction necessitates formalization of the notion of "expectations" so that some plausible characterization of planning can be incorporated with either of these variations. In addition, sequential adaptation enters the latter model as adjustment of expectations. Therefore, the insertion of "time" into the economist's abstraction requires a richer and more complicated treatment of society's citizens. As becomes clearer, however, individuals remain fundamentally antecedent to the system's dynamic path, for their defining attributes remain invariant with respect to whatever trajectory results.

These models depict expectations probabilistically. This assumes the form, developed by Kenneth J. Arrow (1970), in which expectations tether choice. Each period is endowed with an exhaustive set of possible outcomes called *states*, of which each person is cognizant. This sample space includes all possibilities, including the one that, ontologically, will occur. Until the end of the period, however, nobody knows this "true" state. An *event* is a set of states (a subset of the sample space), and a person's expectations are represented by a probability measure, which maps every event into a real number between zero and one, inclusive.[1] A larger value for the probability reflects greater confidence that the germane event will pertain.

This model represents each person's cognitive (as distinct from volitional) identity by the probability measures. It captures what each agent thinks about possibilities, and individual epistemic variation is manifested through them. Whenever probabilities are interpreted as representing *subjective* beliefs, individual probability measures must reflect individual cognitive variation. Whenever they are taken as conforming to "true" distributions as, for example, in the assumption of Muthian rationality, then all cognitive individuality is suppressed. In financial capital market equilibrium, probability measures are also taken as the same for all people. Probabilistic statement of expectation becomes relevant to choice only if action influences a chooser's rewards and punishments. For each person in each period, the *consequence* is what he or she receives, and varies with the state that occurs. Although agents cannot affect the "true" state, they do have a power over the consequences to themselves of a state's happening, which is how action and choice come to matter. Formally, an *act* is a function assigning a consequence to the individual for every possible state of the world, and choice is the selection by the individual of that act he or she anticipates will yield the most favorable consequences on average. The famous "expected utility theorem" asserts that the rational person selects that strategy whose behavior yields the highest weighted average utility where the weights are the probabilities. Thus, one's preferences over consequences translate into preferences over acts, and choice in the face of risk becomes calculably determinant.

This analysis forges a viable explanation, however, only if people possess the sample spaces, and *know* that probabilistic calculation is justified. They must, that is, recognize that their sets of all possible states of the world are complete, and their attitudes about them must be coherently shaped so that they can be quantified by a probability measure. They must banish ambivalence. It is important to note that since every agent's sample space exhausts all possibility, there can be no variations of possibility across agents. Probability explicitly prohibits personal differentiation in terms of varied construction of sets of imagined possibilities. Each person employs the same sample space as everybody else, so that individual identity cannot be established through generations of possible outcomes, but only through evaluation of the same collection of possible states.[2]

In temporary-equilibrium analysis the sequence of periods yields a sequence of choice, and each person adapts to the new constellation of possibilities as time goes by. This adaptation assumes the form of an evolving probability measure via an "expectations-formation function," which, for each person, maps one period's ontological results onto its successor's probability measure. In a series of temporary competitive equilibria, for example, every market clears each period, and the market-clearing price vector then influences expectation of next period's prices.

The expectations-formation function may take any number of forms. It may incorporate classical rules of statistical inference, of Bayesian inference, or simply rules of thumb. It must, however, be defined prior to acquisition of experience. What seems crucial for sustaining temporary equilibration is that the expectations-formation function must be continuous. Similar results must yield "close" expected price vectors next time.[3] Without this continuity, the orderly progression from one period to the next may stumble as people's adaptation to events takes aberrant turns for which others cannot adequately plan. The existence of equilibrium then becomes doubtful.

Such a construction, which typifies much of Walrasian dynamics, retains a powerfully individualistic flavor. In general, the expectations-formation function, and therefore probability measures, remain individually identifying attributes. The person remains the logically and causally governing entity, and the economic interaction of autonomously constituted people remains the central conceptualization of economic organization and behavior.[4] The analysis begins with disaggregated "atoms" — autonomous people rationally following their own interests as best they can — whose behavior can then be aggregated to investigate the overall performance of the system.

The individual must be conceived as antecedent to the economy. Crucial aspects of individuality must be treated as constant and invariant with respect to both the current state and past history of the economy (for example, prices, quantities consumed, and quantities produced). First among these constant attributes are preferences. What a person desires, his or her own idiosyncratic tastes, cannot simultaneously act as economic sovereign, and emerge from the social phenomena they control. In addition, one's expectations are a fundamental part of one's personality. They sequentially evolve, but this cognitive adaptation to events is circumscribed and controlled by psychological processes unique to the person and exogenous to the economic processes examined in the model. Economic events influence the actual expectations adopted, but not the procedures determining those expectations — see, for example, Arrow (1963). The sample space around which an agent's cognition is said to operate is fixed and common to all. Presumably it corresponds precisely to some, perhaps innate, ontological notion. It cannot be a learned phenomenon, for to be acquired renders it contingent upon personal experience, and permits variation from always containing *all* possible states, which destroys its sample space status.[5] Ironically, if every agent possesses a sample space, he or she must all have the same sample space so that it cannot reflect individual variation. Further, since probability measures may vary, at the most general level, with experience, they symbolize personal cognitive differentiation. Each person has his or her own probability for the same event, and this probability (a number) suffices for individuation of opinion and attitude. Thus, it captures all epistemic variation across the population representable within the model. Preferences represent an additional volitional scope for variation.

Probability measures reflect idiosyncratic histories, and differences of information distribution and use.[6] One's cognitive state, therefore. can be said to change; people can be said to learn. This is learning only of "facts," however, for the expectations-formation function, which contains the rules by which an agent interprets information, is given in advance. Even though it may account for changing algorithms for estimating probability distributions, it remains one of the invariant properties of individuality. One's expectations may adjust to events according to clever rules of inference, but the conditions determining when to employ those rules remain unquestioned and unaltered. Basic cognitive processes, as well as the other psychological bases for choice, all remain essentially unmoved personal properties. The rules of thinking and of assimilating information do not change with experience even though the circumstances of their application do. Economic performance proceeds from them, and never they from it. Such preservation of individuality despite the vagaries of economic activity characterizes the Walrasian research program. This view of each human as independently constituted and fundamentally immutable to economic events is nothing less than the pedagogical basis for individualism.

It comes at some cost, however. Preferences are constant and immune to the influence of friends and status.[7] There is none of Jon Elster's (1983) *Sour Grapes*. Both sample spaces and the rules by which inferences about them can be made are similarly independent of economic activity. Thus, the "learning" of these models is almost like that of an invertebrate: each agent is fully programmed to respond, but there is no flexibility of response.

Individualism requires individuals, and for these individuals to rule as well as reign, they must arise exogenously to the processes they control; they must persist regardless of their choices, and they must not themselves be constructed by the phenomena they supposedly govern. Otherwise they can be seen as neither logically nor causally sovereign.

We now contrast this view of human nature and society with alternative depictions from psychology. It is not intellectually adequate, however, merely to demonstrate that different social scientists adopt different images of what people are and how they grow. In addition, we will show how these alternative psychological characterizations of more flexible and adaptive people lead naturally to a richer and more complex characterization of the economy.

3. Psychological Insights and Economic Man

Walrasian economics commences with a notion of society aggregated from atomic agents constituted antecedentally to economic processes. In fundamental ways an agent's identity is fixed with respect to economic outcomes. Preferences, probability measures, and expectations-formation functions all serve to identify individuals and characterize them. Each contributes to a distinguishing identity that remains oblivious to economic processes and therefore can be seen as causative.

Alternative views abound. Contrasting them with the Walrasian type proves fertile first because it hones one's consciousness of the assumptions implicit in the Walrasian paradigm, and second because it suggests ways in which economists might construct models based on ideas of human ingenuity embodying greater flexibility. It leads to an economics in which someone's scope for adaptation extends to alteration of the person as well as of the person's social acts, and in which apparently impulsive behavior is explained as a natural form of optimization.

One difficulty with endeavoring to gleen insights for economists from theories of psychologists is that so many distinct psychological theories have attracted adherents. One necessarily must be selective in pursuing them, but a common thread running through each of the following is an emphasis on the dynamic aspects of the person's life, and concern with problems of psychological growth and development. They vary in ascribing sources of that growth, and controversies between them continue to rage. Our task, however, is not to evaluate them critically, but to draw upon threads common to all in order to revitalize *homo economicus*. Our tactic is to describe briefly four alternative approaches to the analysis of human psychology, and then to contrast them with the three fixed aspects already isolated as central to Walrasian individualism.

3.1. Innatist Theories

For millenia — certainly since Plato — there has been a strong view that, at the deepest levels of human existence, ideas and emotions arise from attributes common to all individuals, and are innately part of being human. Indeed, these characteristics could be taken as defining properties of the species. To Plato such universals arose in the realm of perfect forms which were only imperfectly perceived in practice. The psychoanalytic theories of Freud (1950, 1953, 1960) or Jung (1959, 1964), in comparison, rely upon innately held internal, frequently unconscious, drives, desires, and tendencies rather than "ideas." These, however, are expressed symbolically, and are translated into concrete preferences only through obscure channels. Freud relied on such things as the "pleasure principle" and "death wish," just as Jung referred to the "collective unconscious" to explain widely varied aspects of behavior and superficially contradictory volitional systems. Although both theories invoke innate basic aspects of personality, those innate tendencies generate behavior through complex patterns of psychological association governed by personal experience, especially in childhood. Central to psychoanalysis is the assertion that such experiences can surface in behavior decades later. The adjustment of such patterns can be undertaken — and is the particular goal of psychotherapy — to reveal underlying motivation, and to channel it to consciousness in healthier ways.

Chomsky's (1957, 1965, 1975) structural linguistics also emphasizes innate attributes. Language skills arise spontaneously and trigger a genetically programmed "universal grammar" governing the "deep structure" of all human languages. He writes of the individual's inherent talent for lingual behavior as a species attribute possessed of everybody, rather like a cognitive organ. As with psychoanalysis, however, there can be no denying variation in content and expression from person to person. Using a language does not mean using the same language, or expressing the same things. These, of course, remain dependent upon individual exposure to other people's language use. Nevertheless, structural similarities among all human language impose a common innate background for all language and expression.

Thus, even in these most "innatist" theories, events play a fundamental role in the psyche's conscious manifestation of basic desires, and in the psychology of cognition. Current events may trigger deep associations, or suddenly realign the established mechanisms by which innate drives are felt; and as these shifts occur, abrupt and apparently illogical transformation of preferences and motivation may also occur. In Freud's famous case of the transference neuroses, for example, the focus of the disease may suddenly shift so that a long standing fear of one circumstance may settle on another circumstance.

3.2. Structuralism and the Psychological Equilibration of "Operations"

A different image emerges from the research of Jean Piaget (1970, 1981). Based on investigations of the development of intelligence, especially of spatial operations in the young, he built a psychological theory in which intelligence is reflected in the assimilation of reversible binary operations within an invariant field, precisely exhibiting the properties of mathematical groups. Reversible in this sense is analogous to a mathematical operation possessing an inverse. A famous example from Piaget's work with children involves recognition of the conservation of volume by a liquid. The same quantity of a fluid appears larger in a tall narrow container than in a short stout one. Very young children fail to accept the liquid's constant volume, even as they pour it back and forth between the two containers. Only after a certain age do children assimilate the volume conservation principle, which keeps the quantity of the liquid the same through reversible operations on it (pouring it from one vessel to another and back).

Through these operations, the individual acquires the capacity for mental manipulation, for logic, and for reason. In this way people construct universals, grasp abstract concepts of identity, and think in terms of relationships. Originating in sensori-motor functions, the capacity to acquire such operations comes slowly to the child, but it is present by the time a richly imaginative mind fully functions in adolescence. Which particular operations, and which integrated groups of phenomena a person actually employs, however, are a matter of personal experience, and of what Piaget calls equilibrations: adaptation and accommodation of the individual to his or her environment. Intelligence thus reflects the adjustment of the whole person toward apprehension of reality in terms of structures of reversible operations. Equilibration is the process of cognitive adjustment to establish an accommodation between the environment and thought:

> . . . intelligence, whose logical operations constitute a mobile and at the same time permanent equilibrium between the universe and thought, is an extension and a perfection of all adaptive processes. . . . Only intelligence, capable of all its detours and reversals by action and by thought, tends towards an all-embracing equilibrium by aiming at the assimilation of the whole of reality and the accommodation to it of action . . . (Piaget, 1981, p. 9).

In constructing a coherent psychological replication of reality, each person assembles structures of reversible cognitive operations, which constantly adjust in response to new events and new disequilibrating perceptions. Adaptation occurs in ways that may have cognitively far-reaching effects:

a disturbed psychological equilibrium may never reappear, and the person's sense of reality may be permanently, and unpredictably, altered.

3.3. The Psychology of Personal Constructs

George A. Kelly (1955, 1963) proposed a cognitive theory of personality in which each person

> . . . looks at his world through transparent patterns or templets which he creates and then attempts to fit over the realities of which the world is composed. The fit is not always very good. Yet without such patterns the world appears to be such an undifferentiated homogeneity that man is unable to make any sense out of it (Kelly, 1963, pp. 8–9).

These patterns, or "constructs," are used for "construing" the world. They are the channels by which we all compose a basis for behavior. The individual develops a repertoire of constructs and hierarchically organizes them to structure mental activity. One's repertoire, however, is constantly changing, as is the pattern of relationships between personal constructs. One adapts to events, discovers and experiments with new constructs or abandons familiar ones (see also sections 7 and 9 in chapter 7). Similarly, their hierarchical precedence can be rearranged as an adaptive strategy, which may yield a profoundly transformed person with fundamentally altered patterns of behavior. Not only may cognitively familiar mechanisms fade, but attitudes, and motivation, may be suddenly jarred in ways untraceable at the level of superficial external observation. The path of adjustment is revealed only by examination of the obscure system of personal constructs (see section 3 in chapter 13, and Earl, 1986b, chapter 6).

3.4. Behaviorism

Most closely associated with B.F. Skinner (1972, 1976), this approach insists on examining only the revealed facts of psychology: that is, behavior. Accordingly, adherents of Behaviorism explicitly avoid all causal references to mental states. For them, the question of why an organism behaves the way it does cannot be answered by reference to the way it "feels," or to what it "wants," but must be pushed further to ask why it "feels" the way it does. Answers can be found only in its past involvement with its environment, and in the subject's history of contingent reinforcement of certain kinds of behavior. The schedule of rewards determines which behaviors

we pursue. Motivation and desire are the consequence of past reinforcement, not the cause of action. Choice, in the conventional sense used by
economists, is simply irrelevant. Behaviorism sees human, indeed most
animal, behavior as wonderfully malleable in the forge of past experience,
and sensations of feeling, desiring, and wanting merely reflect behavioral
patterns previously reinforced. Motivation and preference symptomize, but
do not cause the behavior with which they are associated. Here we have
the exact reversal of the Walrasian position. The individual, through patterns of contingent reinforcement, adjusts to behave in particular ways that
have been rewarded in the past. Each wants to do what he or she does
because of past social experience — including experience of advertise-
ments. The individual's behavior is profoundly modified by social experiences, and it is only a mirage of clever self-deception that yields the impression
of an individual sovereign over choice. Alien as this view is to conventional
Walrasian analysis, for our purposes it is especially important to note that
behaviorists insist that individuals be seen as malleable and manipulable.
One's wants and preferences result explicitly from past reinforcing experiences and are not themselves behaviorally causal. Social life molds individuals so that individualism is seen, from the behaviorist viewpoint, as
nonsense. We can derive three connected stylized facts concerning human
psychology from these brief descriptions. They are compatible with each
of the four positions outlined. There may be controversy about relative
emphasis or interpretation, but the propositions themselves seem to be
widely accepted.

The first is that the events to which a person is exposed provoke responses (though Kelly — in contrast to the behaviorists — would note that
these will depend very much on how the events have been subjectively
construed), and that adaptive reactions, far from being exceptional, are
typical and occur frequently in every human life. Normally, but not always,
such adaptations are marginal and not reflective of profound psychic transformation. People, however, are not immutably static. There may be disagreement as to what adaptations will be prompted by what stimuli, and
concerning the mechanisms or extent of possible response, but it should
be clear that, in fact, individuals change in response to their environment.
This does not deny that in many cases such modification may encounter
resistance and that it may occur painfully slowly (indeed many clinical
problems reflect failure to adapt), but merely affirms that people may, and
frequently do, adapt and grow with their surroundings. The issue here is
not that people are erratic and that one's psychic condition is necessarily
ephemoral — clearly it can be difficult indeed for people to adjust psychologically (as the experiences of both psychoanalysts and Kelly show) —

but that the possibility for growth exists, and it may occur. For economics, this means that as a consequence to surprise, the person may, as Kelly might phrase it, come to ask new questions with new significance. A person is not simply an independent automaton from which society causally arises. Rather, individuals are constituted by their environment, to which they also contribute. A person in isolation is not the same person in society.

Second, adaptation can involve all aspects of the person, and of the person's relationship to his or her environment. The changes provoked may directly involve alterations of ostensive behavior, may incorporate new data, may reorganize the structure of cognition, and may even rearrange symbolic associations and identifications. Any or all of the above happen at various times, and may not be confidently anticipated by an external observer. Complex situations yield complex reactions for which controlled experiments need not have reliable predictive power.

Third, the complex mechanisms of individual psychological adaptation may abruptly lead to substantial alteration of mind, body, and behavior. Discontinuous and far-reaching changes from past behavior, past cognitive processes, and past bonds between conscious and unconscious aspects all may be unleashed as surprise invalidates customary practice. Such changes include, but are not limited to, religious conversions, sudden acquisition of intellectual insights, or the final acceptance of a close friend's death. They can involve basic emotional responses, unconscious associations, and cognitive processes. Even those who argue that the fundamental characteristics of every person arise innately from genetic sources do not deny that the practical manifestations of innate tendencies can suddenly jump from what has been.

4. A Psychological Assessment of the Walrasian Agent

With this background, we can now address a psychological response to the Walrasian image. Recall that it ascribes invariance to three key areas of personal identity. First, preferences are the cornerstone of individuality in Walrasian economics. They are the criteria according to which each person optimizes. They govern the operation of the entire economy through their expression as market excess demands. Efficiency, welfare, and rationality are all defined in terms of constant preference orderings. At the simplest level, an individually disaggregated system functions effectively only if people know what they want, and their desires do not capriciously shift. Can we be assured that preferences are stable over time and reflect an unchanging volition? In particular, can we justify feeling confident that the economic dynamic itself does not psychologically reorient individuals and their behavior? Apparently not, for human adaptability may extend beyond matters of learning to the social constitution of desire. Psychoanalysts contend that innate urges may be spontaneously manifested in consciousness through new channels or symbols that transform the direct means by which indirect desires are satisfied. Similarly, one could argue that adaptation of a scheme of personal constructs, in Kelly's terminology, or a reconstituted equilibrium in Piaget's sense, would reformulate one's sense of reality, and therefore one's expression of motivation. In any case novel preferences will command behavior, with impulsive economic acts as consequences. Spontaneously innovative strategies might be tried, and people may simply contradict their own prior behavior. What they *want* (regardless of what they *know*) may, given the same financial constraints, be different. From this we can generate more precise understanding of the mechanisms by which surprise modifies economic behavior. Impulsive acts need not be interpreted as the arbitrarily capricious deeds that demolish economic optimization, as seems to have troubled Coddington (1982), but as optimizing reactions to events in which psychologically creative alterations provide the individual with novel psychic options. Seen in this light, surprise and uncertainty do not entail "puzzled indecision," in Coddington's (1982, p. 485) words, but provoke adjustments in the basis by which self-interest emerges as choice. Normally, such adjustments are minor, as in spontaneously selecting a new brand of soap, but they may also be fundamental and profound, as in religious conversion. What might appear to an external observer as "impulsive" lapses into irrationality may be nothing more than revelations of preferences newly transformed by psychological adaptation. Behaviorists assert, moreover, that what is sensed as altered desire merely signifies, rather than causes, the behavioral change authentically caused by previous experience of the environment.

Regardless of interpretation, the significance of such characterizations of people lies for economics in the spontaneously impulsive disruption of traditional economic behavior. What would have been rational no longer is, and what is would not have been. Apparent intertemporal behavioral inconsistencies can now be interpreted as rational obedience to preferences regardless of whatever "learning" occurs. We shall see how deeply such impulsiveness matters for Walrasian economics when we consider the possibility that surprising behavior may generate surprising response in other people.

The second invariant property of an individual is explicitly cognitive. People are presumed to know all possible states of the world so that their expectations can be probabilistically analyzed. They must, that is, be endowed with sample spaces for each period. Where these sample spaces come from, however, remains an open question. A classical innatist might point to Platonic forms or to a "universal grammar," but this does not entail specific imagined possibilities. It is impossible unambiguously to identify the possibility that tomorrow's banana will be bruised with either the concept "yellow" or syntactical abstraction. Attempting to do so neglects the relation between the ideal and the real, between the general and the particular.

An alternative treats states of the world as constructions erected by the imaginative powers of the individual. Moreover, to be articulated, each state must be described, which involves linguistic aptitude as well as imaginative creativity. What, however, influences imagination, and does psychological displacement affect imagination? Psychological innatists might contend that imagination is influenced by genetically imprinted urges and instincts. Jungian imagery, for example, identifies archtypical forms repeatedly encountered in the dreams of people in widely different circumstances. Such images, however, only provide rough outlines for imagination, which can assume particular aspects in particular cases. Although the details of an imagined possible outcome (for example, that it might rain in Kew Gardens tomorrow afternoon, but not in Central Park) may be influenced by innate forms, they are not equivalent to innate forms. Similarly, references to either Piaget's psychology of equilibrated operations or Kelly's psychology of personal constructs can hint at how the psyche's organization might affect imagination by channeling the interpretive and cognitive processes of the mind, but they do not assign, in advance, the detailed content of imagination in any particularity. They only suggest ways in which psychological adaptability affects the sorts of things one is prone to imagine at different times. Moreover, they can help organize an analysis of how responses to the actual experience of surprise can thrust repercussion back onto future acts of imagining potential outcomes, and of anticipating the future potential for surprise. For example, if I experience surprise now, one aspect of my response to that surprise might be adjustment of my repertoire of personal constructs, in Kelly's terminology, or of my systems of cognitive operations in Piaget's. Both affect the kinds of things I might imagine in the future, as well as what I might consider potentially surprising in the future. Obviously, such reactions to experienced surprise dislodge accustomed patterns of economic behavior. (For example, an unemployed person might finally abandon the search for employment in despair, independently of any labor-market "information.") At the very least, such psychologies can suggest what mechanisms underlie the economic response to surprise.

Third, we consider the expectations-formation function, which assigns a probability measure in the succeeding period to each of this period's possible states. Given what happens in one period, this function determines the person's probabilities next period. It incorporates the dissemination and processing of information, and within the model is the mechanism by which any learning occurs. As noted earlier, it may represent particular statistical rules, such as in Bayesian, adaptive, or rational expectations, or it may reflect rules of thumb. More generally, it can indicate evolving patterns of interpretation and inference.[8] Walrasian analysis presumes that the function can map into any scenario of the agent's expectations — of shocked surprise as well as smug confirmation. This level of generality is purchased at a price, however, in terms of demonstrating the existence of competitive temporary equilibrium.

To investigate this, we consider the possible psychological adaptations of an agent who has pursued certain actions on the conjectured hypothesis that particular consequences will ensue. For example, a firm might have undertaken the manufacture of a commodity on the presumption that its output can be sold at a profitable price. A number of things might then happen. The anticipated consequences (sales at the expected price) may be perceived to have occurred, in which case the hypothesis will be psychologically confirmed, the inferential technique validated, and the behavior reinforced. If, however, the anticipated consequence has not been perceived (inventories accumulate as sales fail to materialize), the hypothesis will tend to be refuted. This refutation may or may not dislodge the inferential methods (including economic and marketing analyses) psychologically employed, depending upon the source and strength of attachment by which the person adheres to them. The person is surprised, however, and psychological invalidation can stimulate psychological reformulation in addition to the information-processing response of an unaltered cognitive edifice. We have already argued that such response can transform preferences and rearrange the possibilities imagined, but they may also shuffle the cognitive apparatus by which a person organizes sensation into a coherent image of reality. They may, that is, provoke profoundly novel insights, inferences, and notions of causation. Since the very psychological control of thinking adapts, thought itself adapts as well. For economic analysis, the issue extends beyond the experience of surprise to the recognition that it has been the operation of the economic system itself, feeding back into the psychological status of the agent, that is economically problematic. The issue is not that people evolve psychologically, but that their psychological development is provoked by their economic experiences.

Consequently their attitudes and preferences are not truly exogenous to the economic process but emerge as a fundamental aspect of it. Entrepreneurial enthusiasm derives from entrepreneurial success.

Piaget's argument that intelligence is the assimilation of group structures of psychologically reversible operations suggests one theory of the mechanism by which cognitive response to surprising events could be behaviorally expressed. According to this theory people might adjust the frameworks within which they organize thought, and these frameworks, which develop from sensori-motor neurology, embody the same structure as mathematical groups. The specific format of the resulting mental manipulation evolves from the particular evolution through which the individual strives to attain congruence between his or her sense of things and his or her environment. Similarly, in terms of Kelly's psychology of personal constructs, either one's repertoire of constructed forms, or their hierarchical arrangement, may respond to surprising evidence. Both conceptualizations provide a theoretical framework for modeling the economic agent's response to surprise. Both suggest that when surprise invalidates one's cognitive equipment, that equipment adapts, and the renovated structures can abruptly render new thoughts an inferences discontinuously removed from their immediate predecessors.

At the most obvious level, experience of surprise and subsequent cognitive invalidation provokes discontinuities in the Walrasian expectations-formation function. The very basis for thought is reshaped, which leads to aberrations of hypotheses and suddenly restructured expectations. This demolishes any intertemporal basis for economic planning, since the reactions of others, and indeed of oneself, may prove incompatible. Behavior at different times can be internally inconsistent and cognitively incoherent.[9] Even if temporary competitive equilibrium is sustained, perfect equilibrium, where people successfully persist with later phases of earlier plans, must be beyond hope. When the basis for behavior changes, what had been rationally optimal need no longer be.

Even more seriously, any grounds for generating, in advance, a well-defined expectations-formation function are eroded by the fundamental cognitive adaptations at issue here. First, as we have already demonstrated, sample spaces are themselves mental phenomena, and it is unclear how they can be anteriorly formulated, and even less clear how they can be identically adopted simultaneously by all people. When the psychological basis for cognition is reformed, previously unconstructible — literal intellectual impossibilities — may arise. Specification of all possibilities thus has no clear meaning transcending the particular state of mind from which it arose. Without antecedent sample spaces, however, an expectations-formation function cannot be defined, for its range incorporates reference to subsets of sample spaces.

Furthermore, one must question any meaning ascribed to "knowing" expectations-formation functions in advance. If the reasoning behind the function is to be known, and is itself taken as reflecting metamorphoses of the psychological foundations of cognition itself, then what, if anything, can be the basis for this "knowledge"? When the business of knowing is shifting, it cannot be presumed that any transcendent act of knowing can, in advance, express what happens. One cannot know that which is knowable only with an alien cognitive appliance. The assimilation mechanisms of mental manipulation vary, so that no single logical structure reflects all potential reactions; all learning in its most general sense. Thus, claims that these functions can be well defined with sufficient generality to itself encompass structural transformation of the foundation of cognition are necessarily illogical and meaningless. The class of these functions may achieve remarkable generality, but in the very nature of logic and cognition, it cannot represent all forms of learning. To include all possible cognitive adaptations, those paths must be knowable and known. To construct a truly general expectations-formation function, therefore, is to commit an act of knowing. Any such act transpires within a particular intellectual framework, however, and cannot escape its own foundations. No such foundations attain universality. Just as the small child cannot comprehend the conservation of a liquid's volume, an adult cannot conceive of phenomenal identity preserved through reversible processes he or she has not acquired. Moreover, nobody, in practice, can have personally mastered all operations, for their scope extends beyond any single conceptualization. Although expectations-formation functions may be capable of logical generality, they cannot be defined with the psychological generality necessary to contain all of the potential cognitive responses to surprise.

5. An Economics of Surprise

Walrasian economists have assembled a powerful theory for analyzing an economy sensitive to individual preferences and control. Focusing on the agent as a volitionally autonomous atom requires an image of human existence as independent from and invariant with respect to overall economic performance. This, in turn, imposes an essentially static characterization of the agent's identity, and allows only a limited capacity for adaptation. Introducing greater individual flexibility and wider responsiveness to economic conditions greatly refashions the consequent sense of how the economy operates. The following can only suggest how an economics of socially constituted agents might proceed.

Since much of what we have said deals with dynamic aspects of personal psychology, it follows that an economics reformulated in order to include that flexibility must incorporate a more flexible characterization of its agents. In particular, the identifying attributes of people must not be seen as antecedent to the economic process, but should be recognized as a fundamental aspect of that process itself. People respond to events in many ways, and their personal adaptation to the economic environment cannot be ignored as central to economic dynamics. Indeed, only when our models depict agents as both psychologically flexible and intellectually constructive can they yield a fully dynamic economics. This does not mean that economic analysis must first contain all of psychological analysis, but merely that it cannot ignore the psychological feedback onto individual behavior — through both preferences and expectations — of economic performance itself.

Fundamental to this new view is acceptance of acts of cognition as precisely that — as acts. Knowledge does not simply happen or magically come to a person, but must be constructively assembled. Acts of intelligence are positive efforts to organize and employ mechanisms — be they Kelly's personal construct systems, Piaget's reversible operations, or Chomsky's structural syntax — by which one can survive in, and cope with, a social existence. For the economist, to grasp the constructive role in cognition is to realize that the possibilities one apprehends are imagined, and not ontologically imposed. They are the products of creativity. One erects a collection of imagined possible outcomes which certainly reflects cognitive originality, and then uses it as a basis for expecting the future. Imagination need not be governed by logic, and certainly need not achieve the probabilistic ideal of "all" possible outcomes.

In Bausor (1985) it has been argued that the construction of sample spaces encounters conceptual and logical obstacles in precisely delineating the scope of all possible outcomes. Any person's mind engaged in accumulating a complete manifest of possible outcomes can never verify that the job has been accomplished. Without verification that it has, assurance that the "true" state has been included is absent, and probabilistic calculation is unjustified. Ultimately, the problem is that we can never know, in advance, whether or not any of our imagined outcomes will come true. Lacking such *knowledge*, probabilistic formulation of expectations fails, for sample spaces cannot be constructed. Instead, one can employ Shackle's (1955, 1969) measure of potential surprise, which quantifies a person's currently anticipated future surprise upon learning that a currently imag-

ined future possibility had occurred. In this construction it is always recognized that the outcome might not correspond to any previously imagined
possibility.

A psychologically rich economics must also be compatible with the varied possible reactions to events. More than the calmly continuous reesti-
mation of stochastic parameters, such a theory must address the consequences
of events that, in refuting particular hypotheses, invalidate the cognition
producing them. What happens, that is, when events disrupt one's psychic
equilibrium and provoke structural adjustments within the mind? A person
then seeks to establish new psychic composure. Literally, one's mind changes,
and with it so does the basis for choice and action. For our purposes as
economists, this fungibility is most significant. Reactions to surprise can
be oblique changes of course or sudden alterations in patterns of choice.
Reactions arise that could not have been anticipated by extrapolating from
past decisions. Impulsive behavior enters and, upon appearing, banishes
the basis upon which social planning and rational optimizing can confidently
lead to efficient organization and equilibration. One person's experience
of surprise may provoke responses surprising to others, whose own reactions may subsequently generate additional barbs at complacency. Surprise
can spread throughout the population like a contagion, building and re-
building upon itself in an unending process of surprising stimuli provoking
surprising responses.

This discussion elicits the outline of an economics accommodating psychological flexibility in response to surprise. It motivates the construction
of models which, by yielding an explanation of impulsive acts, enrich and
generalize economic analysis. To incorporate surprise and adaptability gen-
uinely into economics we must employ a construction in which the full
scope of interaction between agents is possible. Moreover, we must emphasize the distinction between potential surprise and actual surprise. The
former refers to a currently anticipated reaction to an imagined possibility's
occurrence, whereas the latter reflects the actual reaction to events, whether
or not they had been imagined. The former forges choices facing uncertainty whereas the latter may stimulate adaptation. Maintaining this distinction enables a formal analysis of the helical process by which current
preferences and expectations (reflecting imagined possible outcomes and
the potential surprise at their eventuality) mold choice of actions, the
outcomes of which may or may not provoke the experience of surprise.
Reactions to surprising events may, in turn, provoke psychological adjustments such that future decisions will be based on novel volitional patterns, as well as reformulated expectations. In such a scheme, preferences
as well as expectations emerge as dynamic components of the economic

process itself. In discrete time, such a model might take the form of a pattern of one period's expectations and preferences mapping into an agent's plans for that period's activities. Such plans for all persons could then map into outcomes, which then, through actual surprise or its absence, influence the next period's expectations and volitions. Such a model must specify both the cognitive response to events (expectations-formation) and the adaptation of preferences. A preferences-formation function might, for example, map current outcomes into a member of the family of preference orderings for the succeeding period which satisfy the postulates of demand theory. Such a device would retain well-defined, transitive, convex, continuous preferences over commodity space, yet permit their variation in response to surprising events. Such a model not only recognizes the importance of potential surprise in choice but organizes analysis of the economics of response to actual surprise as well.

With it, one might investigate the properties of the preferences-formation function much as temporary-equilibrium theorists have investigated expectations-formation functions. This is where psychology can constructively join with economics, for its evidence and understandings can inform the economist's theories of preference formation. One obvious contribution from psychology might address this function's continuity. For example, do small provocations yield small adaptations? Similarly, are there thresholds of surprise below which preferences are unaltered, and above which they change abruptly? If so, impulsive acts might emerge as unusual jumps in an otherwise continuous pattern. In addition, psychological insights might aid the economist in identifying crucial surprises. Crucial in this sense means that they are capable of fundamentally altering one's psychic composure and behavior.

Regarding such issues, Kelly's personal construct theory provides a systematic approach to uncovering the internal psychic structures manifested as preferences, and may be of particular help in understanding which particular surprises may cut more deeply to the heart than others. It may also help explain continued adherence to an existing scheme even in the face of apparently astounding events. Similarly, Piaget's work suggests structural attributes the mind obeys, forms issues of adaptation as one of psychological equilibration, and can help economists constructively grapple with the terrible questions of what happens to the surprised agent. Behaviorist models of reinforcement also suggest patterns by which behavior — including desires — can be conditioned by history.

Most economists would want to develop equilibrium concepts for such a model. Whereas economic equilibrium may require psychological stability (if not health), understanding the sources of emotional perseverance is of economic significance. Indeed, psychological resistance to adaptation may emerge as a source of economic equilibration. Historical reproduction of preferences might result from possessing a vigorous system of personal constructs, for example. Piaget's principle of psychic equilibration may also prove congenial to many economists' intuitions about optimization.

Analysis of equilibria, however, are unlikely to fulfill an economics of surprise and adaptation. Surprise remains a reaction to what had been unexpected. As such, it provokes reconsideration of behavioral patterns and may encourage implementation of novel and apparently impulsive acts. These, in turn, surprise other people, so that the calm of accomplished equilibration never occurs. The economy may bounce from surprising event through surprised adaptations to surprising event.

This, of course, is precisely what Shackle has described as a kaleidic economy. Shocks requiring response, psychological adjustment, and accommodation with one's economic environment typify such processes. The environment, however, is no more rigid than its components, for its components constitute it just as it constitutes them. Agents collide with one another in a constantly disrupting and disrupted dance. Similarly, the social-action approach of Levine (1977, 1978), and Levine and Levine (1975), conceives of individuals as fundamentally constituted by society, and mutually determined by it as it is composed of them.

Methodologically, considering individuals as continually adjusting, and never assured that the process is complete, degrades equilibrium depictions as the sole standard of normalcy. In the words of Shackle (1974, p. 74) himself: "the equilibrium method itself shows how things would be if they were perfectly adjusted, and says nothing about how they could become so." Alternatively, economics can pursue kaleidic explanations in which surprise discommodes conventionality. This method, pursued by Bausor (1982, 1984), Dow and Dow (1985), Earl (1983a), Earl and Kay (1985), Kay (1982), and Vickers (1978, 1979, 1985), involves establishing a taxonomy of possible macroeconomic tendencies and remaining sensitive to changes of mood in the economy. The point of such kaleidic analyses is not that equilibrium is conceptually impossible, but that it cannot be taken as typical. All social adjustments, including psychological accommodation, are never complete, for much of what it means to be alive is to be experimenting with new ideas and with new alignments of old ideas.

Acknowledgment

The author is grateful to Peter Earl, Donald W. Katzner, and Douglas Vickers for many helpful comments on this chapter.

Notes

1. Formally, the set of all events forms a σ-algebra, and a person's expectations are represented by a probability measure from the field of events into the closed unit interval of the real line.

2. Note how strongly the Walrasian and Austrian traditions clash on this point. Walrasian sample spaces leave no room for individual competence in generating possible states, whereas Austrian economists emphasize the entrepreneur's special talent for generating perceived opportunities. An interesting discussion of these ideas appears in Kirzner (1979) (see also section 8 in chapter 7).

3. For a more complete discussion of this function and its properties, see Grandmont (1977).

4. See Weintraub (1985) for a discussion of this focus on independently optimizing agents as a "hard-core" proposition of Walrasian economics.

5. For a more elaborate treatment of the conceptual limitations of using sample spaces and probability measures to model human expectation, see Bausor (1985).

6. The probabilistic scheme of representing expectations faces potential inconsistencies of interpretation when addressing matters of information distribution. On one hand, sample spaces contain unflawed perception of past and present, whereas probability measures may vary. They thus reflect different perceptions of past and present. An alternative interpretation may be that different people contrive different, but incomplete perceptions about the past.

7. This may be overstated, for there have been interesting attempts to introduce dependence of preferences on economic activity. Kalman (1968) put prices into the utility function, which leaves the function unchanged but one's attitude toward a commodity bundle varying with the price vector; Pollak (1970) devised a scheme in which the parameters of one period's utility function evolve with the previous period's commodity bundle; and Gintis (1974) examined the effects of education on preferences. Hey (1981, pp. 160–161) suggests that what is both lacking and needed is analysis of how one achieves a set of perceived possibilities, and what happens when an individual is surprised. Nevertheless, the predominant view, as articulated by Stigler and Becker (1977), remains the conviction that individual volitional adaptation to economic events is not a serious question.

8. An expectations-formation function, per se, does not require that individuals know any or all current states. Neither does it require that one's description of this period be ontologically "true" or exhaustive. Accordingly, variation in probability measures reflects variation in personal perceptions. Significantly, such variation never reflects on sample spaces.

9. Rationality in almost any dynamic sense need not be preserved. In the particular Muthian sense, however, it most assuredly vanishes, for the economy's operation will not obey any stable stochastic process. As responses rummage through alternative cognitive edifices, individual behavior will be erratic and so will phenomena aggregated from it. Consequently, the parameters of presumed probability distributions vary unpredictably, so that an equilibrium of "rational" expectations (where actual forecast errors are orthogonally distributed with mean zero) never arises. Past experience is systematically inadequate for anticipating future opportunity.

3 LEARNING AND DECISION-MAKING IN ECONOMICS AND PSYCHOLOGY: A METHODOLOGICAL PERSPECTIVE

Malcolm Rutherford

1. Introduction

It is, as Latsis (1976, p. 22) has argued, an established part of the "positive heuristic" of standard neoclassical economics to avoid explicit psychological content. In recent years, however, and particularly in the area of human judgment and decision-making, psychological research has been forcing its attention on economists. Simon's theories of decision-making and of satisficing behavior (1959, 1978, 1979) and work by Kahneman and Tversky on prospect theory (1979) and on judgmental heuristics and biases (Tversky and Kahneman, 1974) are very well known and have been widely referred to in the economics literature. The notions of heuristics and rules of thumb now appear quite frequently, and it is no longer uncommon to find economists other than institutionalists expressing doubts concerning the empirical validity of the concepts of rational behavior contained in the standard theories of the maximization of expected utility and Bayesian revision of subjective probabilities in the light of new information (Arrow, 1982; Schoemaker, 1982; Hey, 1983a).

More recently, a wider variety of psychological theories, many dealing with aspects of learning, have appeared in the economics literature. Reinforcement learning models can be found in the work of John Cross (1980, 1983); Akerlof and Dickens (1982) have utilized Festinger's cognitive dissonance theory; van Raaij (1985) has discussed the literature on causal attribution and its possible application to economics; Cohen and Axelrod (1984) have made use of research in artificial intelligence, in particular the heuristics to be found in A. L. Samuel's checker playing programs; and the personality theory of G.A. Kelly has informed the work of Brian Loasby (1983) and Peter Earl (1983a, 1983b, 1986a, 1986b).

This broadening interest in psychology is undoubtedly due to the fact that questions of knowledge and expectations, and the effects of experience on the knowledge and expectations of decision-makers, have assumed central importance in a number of modern research programs in economics (Boland, 1982). Oligopoly theory has always presented the problem of knowledge and expectations in unavoidable form, and modern game theoretic approaches have simply made it more obvious that in certain situations single optimal strategies may be difficult to identify or may not even exist (Simon, 1981). Rational expectations theory usually avoids explicit discussion of learning, but where learning mechanisms are specified they are usually Bayesian in nature and not infrequently accompanied by observations concerning the prodigious informational and computational requirements necessary to achieve a rational expectations equilibrium (Blume, Bray, and Easley, 1982). This in turn has led some economists to attempt to explain departures from such an equilibrium in terms of informational constraints or failures in rationality (Zarnowitz, 1985). That virtually all discussions of cycles and unemployment (classical, neoclassical, Keynesian, and rational expectationalist) rest on some more or less ad hoc modification of the idea of rational maximizing by all individuals has been argued by Simon (1984). In addition, work by Akerlof and Yellen (1985a) and Haltiwanger and Waldman (1985) indicates that in both micro and macro contexts even small departures from universal maximization can cause significant changes in the equilibrium positions achieved.

That economists should turn to psychological work on belief formation, learning, and decision-making is, therefore, not surprising. Unfortunately, what the interested economist finds is often not enlightenment but simply more confusion and difficulty. The problem faced by the novice or outsider on first approaching modern psychology is the welter of different explanations for each phenomenon discovered, combined with the fact that it is "almost impossible to compare theories because they are based on different sets of data, using separate constructs and terminology" (Eysenck, 1984, p. 359; see also Claxton, 1980, and Newell, 1973). In the case of the two areas to be covered in this chapter, learning and decision-making, the latter topic is somewhat more accessible, tending to make reference to a more or less common body of experimental and theoretical literature. The topic of learning, on the other hand, is far more difficult to come to grips with. What might be called the classic psychological literature on learning is to be found within the framework of "stimulus-response, behavioral associationism" (Bower and Hilgard, 1981, p. 17), but in the more recent work on cognitive psychology the issue of learning seems conspicuous only by its absence. Points relevant to the issue of learning are scattered throughout many literatures dealing with topics such as memory and the structure of knowledge, concept formation, causal attribution, cognitive balance and dissonance, deductive and inductive reasoning, problem solving and artificial intelligence. The lack of research within cognitive psychology dealing with learning as its central theme has been remarked upon (Claxton, 1980; Norman, 1981; Simon, 1981) and, as will be seen below, the omission is not without significance.

Partly because of these difficulties, this chapter does not attempt a review of all (or even most of) the relevant material. Good reviews of research in decision-making are readily available (Slovic, Fischhoff, and Lichtenstein, 1977; Einhorn and Hogarth, 1981; Pitz and Sachs, 1984), while a full review of the literature on learning would be a task beyond the constraints of time, space, and patience facing this author. Instead, what will be attempted here is an examination of some of the methodological issues raised by recent psychological research and the possible implications of this research for the future conduct of economics. This in turn requires an initial examination of the methodological predilections of both economists and psychologists.

2. Economics, Psychology, and Psychologism

It is certainly true that the standard research programs in economics exclude, quite deliberately, significant consideration of "hypotheses relating to decision rules, information gathering rules, learning procedures and psychological or social psychological theories which substantially concern the decision-making process" (Latsis, 1976, p. 17). What replaces such hypotheses in standard economics is, of course, the assumption of given preferences and goals and the rationality principle interpreted as a rule of maximizing behavior. It is, however, important to realize that although standard economics has excluded explicit psychological content it is, despite appearances, *psychologistic* in character. Psychologism here is defined in the manner of Popper (1961, pp. 157–158), Agassi (1975, p. 148), and

Boland (1982, p. 30; 1986, p. 11) as "the doctrine which teaches the reduction of social theories to psychology, in the same way as we try to
reduce chemistry to physics" (Popper, 1961, p. 157). This position leads
to a reductionist program in which only psychological and natural givens
are allowable exogenous variables (Boland, 1982, p. 30). The particular
combination of psychologism with the prohibition of more explicit psychological content has led to the interpretation of preferences and of rationality as given psychological attributes of individuals. In other words,
while the psychology used in economics is implicit, it nevertheless deeply
affects the nature of economic reasoning.

Given that people are to be regarded as psychologically rational, questions arise concerning the nature of the learning and decision-making processes that such people possess. That is, what *psychological* processes ensure
rationality? As far as questions of knowledge are concerned, both economists and psychologists have traditionally accepted the empiricist argument that a rationalist epistemology must be inductive. In this view,
knowledge, to be rationally held, must be capable of empirical justification.
Justifiable knowledge is knowledge that is based on, derived from, or
supported by a sufficiency of observation and experience. Psychologically,
the rational individual is seen as capable of learning from experience in a
very direct and unproblematic fashion, a theory which has been satirized
by Popper (1972, pp. 60–63, 341–361) as the "bucket theory of the mind."
It is however, exactly this bucket theory that lies behind stimulus-response
associationistic and behaviorist psychology, and even infests at least some
of the work that utilizes cognitive and information-processing approaches
(Popper, 1972, pp. 61–62; Neisser, 1976; Brehmer, 1980; Berkson and
Wettersten, 1984). It is also the standard theory of knowledge in economics
(Boland, 1982, pp. 66–78).

The problem with this point of view is very simply the argument made
by Hume and repeatedly reemphasized by Popper (1965, 1968, 1972): there
is no logical connection between the quantity (or quality) of observations
or experience that confirm a general or universal statement or theory and
that statement's truth or probable truth. General theories cannot be justified by observation or experience. It must be emphasized that probabilistic
versions of induction — that although a general statement cannot be proven
true, it can be confirmed to some degree of probability — do not overcome
the problem. Hume's own reaction to this finding was to abandon induction
as a logical thesis but *not* as a psychological one. Unfortunately, this leads
straight to irrationalism; to the view that our knowledge, although gained
through observed repetitions and the association of events, is no more than
an irrational belief. Equally unfortunately, the response to this has not

been to abandon inductivism and justificationism, but to retain the psychological theory of induction and either to ignore or to attempt to find some way around the problem of justification (Brehmer, 1980, p. 226). Examples of this can be found in the widespread (and in economics, growing) use of Bayesian inference as descriptive of learning processes, and in the argument recently put forward by Stitch and Nisbett (1980, p. 200) that an inductive inference is justified if it is based on an inferential rule which captures the "reflective practice . . . of the appropriate experts in our society."

Of course, many researchers recognize that people often fail to be fully rational in the sense outlined above. Indeed, a very significant part of modern psychology is centered exactly on such failures. This material is discussed below, but it should be noted here that the argument that people are not very good inductivists does not *necessarily* involve any abandonment of inductivism, justificationism, or (for economists) of psychologism. To the extent that the failings of human judgment and inductive learning are seen as being due either to subjective or psychologically given biases, heuristics, or information-processing constraints, or to the difficulty (or impossibility) of collecting sufficient data to induce correctly the nature of a complex environment, inductivism and justificationism can be retained. All that is being claimed in these arguments is that the processes of "correct" inductive learning are limited, distorted, or interfered with by informational or cognitive constraints and biases. Such ideas, too, can easily be incorporated into a psychologistic economics. Admittedly one has to abandon the much-cherished idea of full psychological rationality, but the assumption that (at least some) individuals are "naive" in the sense of possessing "limited capacities to process information" has been defended as an assumption which avoids the more ad hoc approach of introducing imperfections and rigidities into rational expectations models (Haltiwanger and Waldman, 1985, pp. 326, 336). What is meant by this argument is that the introduction of exogenous rigidities is incompatible with reductive psychologism, while assuming that some of the population are naive is, given the recent findings of psychologists, quite compatible with a psychologistic, reductionist program.

3. Psychology, Psychologism, and Rationality

From the above it would appear that as long as one accepts inductive learning as a part of the concept of rationality, psychological research which disputes the ability of individuals to learn in the appropriate inductive manner must force some weakening of the idea of rational behavior. Ingenious attempts have been made to avoid this implication, the most common being the argument that if information is costly to obtain or process, rational maximizing only involves collecting information (knowledge) up to some optimal point. Satisficing, or the use of decision heuristics, can thus be interpreted as maximizing subject to further constraints. The answer to this has been given by Winter (1964, p. 252) and is simply that to achieve an optimal information structure one needs information about that structure. As with most inductive arguments, one immediately finds oneself in an infinite regress. While, to some, this may appear to deal something of a death blow to the notion of rational maximizing behavior (Elster, 1984, p. 136), it should be understood that this is only the case if rational behavior is associated with a psychologistic and inductive view of learning processes. If the concept of rationality can be separated from such ideas its future becomes significantly less bleak. An attempt at this separation has been made by Popper and, in economics, by Boland.

Popper's views have been the subject of a voluminous literature, so much so that mention of his name has become almost passe, but surprisingly little has been written on his views on social science, psychology, and the rationality principle. The ideas are certainly not without their ambiguities and difficulties (Hands, 1985; Berkson and Wettersten, 1984), but it is worth outlining some of the major themes. Popper's anti-inductivism and his view of knowledge as conjectural and fallible is well known, but, unlike Hume, Popper's attacks on inductive ideas include the psychological theory of induction through repetition. Popper's argument is that no repetition is ever exact. Repetitions, then, are only repetitions from a particular point of view. The point of view, which may consist of a hypothesis or simply a problem, determines what we look for. Pure observation does not exist; observation takes place and experience is interpreted within a frame of reference. What occurs is that, in attempting to solve a problem or answer a question, people *jump to conclusions*, sometimes on the basis of only a single observation. These conclusions are conjectural. They are not empirically justifiable and they may be false, but they can be examined and criticized once they have been formulated (Popper, 1968, pp. 42–46). Rationality here lies not in the psychological processes involved in conceiving an idea, theory, or strategy, but in the *logical* processes of critical appraisal.

Of course, Popper's notion of critical rationality has its difficulties. Most obviously it seems to lack any very precise content. Popper does emphasize the role of refutations and disappointed expectations in bringing about a revision of theories, and this is an idea of great logical force. Nevertheless,

Popper can be found arguing for the functional role of at least some degree of tenacity — of not giving up theories too easily — and he also recognizes that, given sufficient ingenuity, virtually any refuting instance can be explained away (Popper, 1965, p. 50; 1968, p. 49). Explaining away refutations does have a cost in terms of the ad hoc modifications that must be made in order to save the theories in question, but exactly when a theory either will be or should be abandoned in favor of another is not clear, and Lakatos' (1970) efforts to distinguish progressive from degenerative problem shifts have done nothing to ease the difficulty.[1] Popper's principle of transference, the "conjecture" that "what is true in logic is true in psychology" (Popper, 1972, p. 6) simply leaves those questions unanswered in logic unanswered in psychology.

Popper has also been a staunch defender of the rationality principle in social science. He presents this principle as logical and not psychological in nature and as a necessary part of theorizing in the social sciences; theorizing which should run in terms of the "logic of the situation" (Popper, 1961, p. 158; Hands, 1985). Popper's situational logic does seem to owe something to his understanding of economic methodology, but it is not, despite Latsis' (1976) opinion, exactly equivalent to any of the more usual approaches to economics.[2] Popper's situational logic can be described as being based on the rationality principle defined as the presumption that an agent will act appropriately *given his own understanding of his situation and goals*. Rational action does not presume justified knowledge, only that action is consistent with the (possibly true, possibly false) knowledge the decision maker decides to act upon. Errors and failures are not evidence of irrationality but of opportunities to learn.

More recently, Boland has extended Popper's rationality principle to the area of methodology itself, arriving at what he calls "problem dependent methodology" (1982, pp. 188–196). In this approach Boland dispenses with the idea that Popper's own critical falsificationist strategy is necessarily the best methodology. If practical problems are of concern, then an instrumentalist methodology — in which theories are judged simply as tools — is appropriate, whereas if advancing knowledge for its own sake is the goal, then Popper's method of critically searching for refutations may be superior (Boland, 1982, p. 196). The significance of this is that, once this approach is accepted, the individual's understanding of his/her problem situation together with the principle of rationality can be used to explain the psychological states of individuals (Boland, 1982, p. 176); to explain their methodologies and how they might react to new information, errors, or disappointed expectations. In other words, there is no need to refer to any psychological givens at all in the discussion of learning or decision-making. The principle of rationality can be retained and inductivism, justificationism, and psychologism all entirely dispensed with.

Ideas taken from, or with similarities to, Popper's can be found in psychological literature. Popper's work has been used in the criticism of associationistic psychology (Brehmer, 1980; Berkson and Wettersten, 1984); ideas of hypothesis testing based on refutation can be found in models of concept formation (Restle, 1962); it has often been observed that it is surprise or the unexpected which is informative, attracting attention and "switching on" hypothesizing and information seeking processes (Bower, 1975, p. 70; Hastie, 1984); and strategies of disconfirmation have played an important normative role in research on hypothesis testing practice (for example, Wason, 1960). On Boland's problem dependent methodology, it is less frequently realized that an instrumentalist method is appropriate for goals involving short term success. The idea that scientist and nonscientist alike are interested in "prediction and control" is not an uncommon idea in psychology (G.A. Kelly, 1955, p. 6; H.H. Kelley, 1972, p. 22), but that these goals may be served by instrumental criteria, and that an interest in practical success may affect hypothesis selection and testing procedures has not been generally understood (for an exception, see Tschirgi, 1980).

While Popper's ideas do have relevance for psychology, a question does remain as to the relevance of psychology for Popper. The extent of Popper's antipsychologism and of his maintenance of the priority of logic over psychology is clearly an extreme position.[3] The Popperian research program for the social sciences would appear to involve the rejection of theories containing *any* given psychological propensities at all (and not merely the rejection of the argument that the *only* exogenous variables allowed are psychological and natural givens). The other side of this coin is Popper's insistence that the principle of rationality is necessary to social science and should be seen as metaphysical in nature (Popper, 1976). Thus, if faced with an apparent deviation from the principle, social scientists should presume that they have incorrectly specified the goals or situation of the subject (as the subject understands them), rather than that the subject is irrational or behaving in an inappropriate fashion. Of course, within the Popperian framework, irrationality is exceedingly difficult to demonstrate empirically, as irrationality is action that is inappropriate given the decision maker's own, and possibly incorrect, understanding of his/her situation. Nevertheless, the usual interpretation of the Popperian position is that the principle is indeed *potentially* falsifiable; it is just that a methodological decision has been made to treat it otherwise (Hands, 1985; Koertge, 1975, 1979; Boland, 1981).

A high degree of caution in accepting irrationality, or that psychologists have discovered any significant "givens" of human nature or of human learning or decision-making, is quite proper. Even among psychologists there are those who reject the notion that any human inferential procedures are "static" or "wired in" (Nisbett et al., 1983, p. 361), and others warn against uncritically assuming the notion that everything that "appears sub-optimal to us" is due to irrationality (Fischhoff and Beyth-Marom, 1983, pp. 257–258). Nevertheless, the Popperian position seems overly narrow, ruling out certain lines of inquiry and evidence on principle and tending to the opposite extreme of assuming that "there is a hidden method to any apparent madness" (Fischhoff and Beyth-Marom, 1983, pp. 257–258). What seems more appropriate here, and not outside Popper's own "Socratic" approach to learning, is the avoidance of both extremes and the mainte-nance of a critical attitude throughout. It is from this point of view that the psychological literature discussed below will be approached.

4. Heuristics and Biases

Within the last 20 years the psychologists' view of the logical and inferential processes of the layman has been radically altered. From viewing man as a good intuitive scientist or statistician, psychologists have come to see the layman (and often the expert and scientist as well) as relying on simple decision heuristics and prey to a large number of, sometimes serious, logical and inferential shortcomings (Slovic, Fischhoff, and Lichtenstein, 1977, pp. 2–3). Two of the most outstanding examples of this development are to be found in Nisbett and Ross (1980) and Kahneman, Slovic and Tversky (1982), but even these works do not provide a complete listing of all the various failures and biases that have been discussed in the psychological literature. By necessity only a selection of the relevant research areas can be dealt with here.

4.1. Deductive Reasoning

Research on deductive reasoning has concentrated on syllogistic reasoning tasks and on the deductive (falsificationist) testing of hypotheses. On the first issue it has been found that people make frequent logical errors. A number of different explanations of these failures have been put forward. The "atmosphere effect" hypothesis suggests that people respond to the overall impression of the premises rather than to their logic, but contradictory evidence has since been found (Eysenck, 1984, pp. 282–284; Gilhooly, 1982, pp. 67–72; Wason and Johnson-Laird, 1972), and an alternative explanation which runs in terms of "mental models" has recently been put forward by Johnson-Laird (1983). Mental models can be thought of as incorporating an analogical mode of reasoning. The events contained in the premises are imagined and this mental representation of the premises suggests the conclusion. The conclusion is then checked by searching for alternative models of the premises that might be incompatible with the conclusion. The difficulty of a syllogism depends on the difficulty of constructing a model of the premises, and the variation in performance over subjects is seen as due to differences in the degree to which a careful check of the conclusion is carried out, rather than to differences in the initial interpretation of the premises. A contrary, rationalist, interpretation has been given by Henle (1962), who argues that apparent logical errors stem not from failures in reasoning but from misinterpretation of premises, addition of premises, or failure to accept the task as a logical one. Some experimental evidence is available to support Henle's view, although among psychologists the mental model approach is often presented as the most promising, with the added advantage of consistency with research in other areas such as problem solving (Gilhooly, 1982, p. 84).

On the issue of deductive testing of hypotheses using *modus tollens*, the key work is that of Wason (1960; see also Wason and Johnson-Laird, 1972). On a variety of tasks Wason has found a failure to apply falsificationist strategies properly, the tendency being to look instead for corroborative information. In one such task, the card selection task, the subject is shown four cards, each card showing either a letter or a number; for example, an A, an N, a 6, and a 9. The subject is then asked to name the cards which must be turned over to test the statement: "If a card has a vowel on one side, then it has an even number on the other." Most subjects pick the A and the 6 to turn over instead of the A and the 9. Explanations of this tendency have run either in terms of a type of atmosphere effect (matching bias) or in terms of the possible misinterpretation of the task (Evans, 1980; Gilhooly, 1982, pp. 92–93). It has also been argued that performance is much improved when letters and numbers or abstract symbols are replaced by concrete material, but this finding has also been challenged, at least as a general result, and an alternative has been suggested which runs in terms of memory-cueing of general experience and reasoning by analogy (Cox and Griggs, 1982).

Wason has also experimented with a rule discovery task in which subjects are given a set of numbers consistent with the true rule — for example, 2, 4, 6 — and asked to discover the true rule by generating other number sequences and receiving feedback. In this experiment the true rule is usually highly inclusive — for example, any increasing sequence of numbers. The finding is that most subjects test their hypothesized rules by generating only number sequences that are consistent with them. Only when they are actually told their rule is incorrect will they try alternative hypotheses. Many other experiments also seem to indicate a "verification bias" both in abstract reasoning tasks and in the testing of hypotheses concerning social behavior (Snyder and Swann, 1978; Schustack and Sternberg, 1981).

It is the case, however, that calling the performance on the Wason rule discovery task an example of verification bias may be misleading. The problem is the highly inclusive nature of the true rule. Indeed, the tests that Wason's subjects performed were tests which could potentially have generated falsifying instances. This should be distinguished from verification bias in the sense of conducting tests which in principle are incapable of generating falsifiers. Many of the subjects in this type of experiment fail to see the need for a deeper level of critical test, but they do not approach their task in an entirely uncritical fashion[4], and once a falsifier has been generated most subjects behave in an appropriate manner, abandoning or revising their hypotheses and solving the problem reasonably quickly (Gilhooly, 1982, pp. 99–100).

4.2. Problem-Solving

The work of Simon and his colleagues on problem solving strategies has had wide influence in psychology. This is most noticable in Simon's argument that the operation of human intelligence is affected by certain invariants to be found in both "inner" and "outer" environments. The invariants of the inner environment are highly abstract and only constrain the "possible organizations of intelligent systems" rather than their "material substrates." They consist of such things as serial as opposed to parallel information-processing and a working memory of limited capacity. The invariants of the outer problem environments are that "they do not present obvious paths to attainment of a system's goals" and often contain "immense" numbers of possible alternatives, "only a small fraction of which satisfy the goal requirements." Given these constraints and the nature of the problem environments, the "principle mechanism of intelligence . . . is heuristic search" (Simon, 1981, pp. 18–19).

This heuristic search takes place in what Newell and Simon (1972) have called the "problem space," which can be seen as a representation of the task environment. Within this problem space the problem solver conducts a highly selective search for solutions. The general method employed is "means-end" analysis in which the problem-solver compares the goals with the starting state and attempts to develop subgoals and to find operators which will successfully solve each subproblem. If a goal cannot be achieved, the problem is broken down into further subproblems each with their own subgoals. Difficulties in problem solving can arise out of inadequate or inappropriate representation of the task in problem space or from the selection of inappropriate operators (Eysenck, 1984, p. 277). Although means-end analysis is a useful heuristic approach for many problems, it must be stressed that it "will not necessarily result in a solution, or the best solution, being found" (Sanford, 1985, p. 300).

A number of other issues are also relevant here. First, work by Simon and Hayes (1976) indicates that the problem space generated by problem-solvers is highly sensitive to the exact way in which the problem is presented. Second, performance on problems improves with experience. The exact processes of learning in problem-solving tasks have not been closely studied, but it is clear that experience may alter the problem space and the heuristics used within it. The possibilities of learning and adaptation have led Simon (1981, pp. 21–22) both to argue that "we must not imagine invariants where there are none," and to suggest that the proposition that "human cognitive programs are determined as much by social and historical forces as by neurology" be taken seriously. The latter point serves to link problem solving ability with the gradual advance of knowledge in general and to emphasize that the use of heuristics and satisficing instead of max-imizing are, for Simon, not species of irrationality but the result of "limits on knowledge and how to obtain it rather than on the ability to perform according to knowledge that has been assimilated" (Newell and Simon, 1972, p. 866). Finally, it should be noted that work on problem-solving has tended to concentrate on well-defined logical puzzles or on games such as chess. In these problems, "the initial state, the goal state, and the various permissible moves are all clearly specified," whereas real-world problems are usually much less well defined (Eysenck, 1984, p. 280). This raises the issue of how well people understand their environment.

4.3. Attribution

The literature on attribution deals with a broad range of issues concerning the manner in which people judge or attribute causation. A great deal, though not all, of this literature is social psychological and deals with perceiving the causes of behavior, both the behvior of others and one's own behavior. Within this literature the major issues of relevance here concern the misperception of covariation, the failure to utilize "consensus information" and the so-called "fundamental attribution error."

A great deal of work in attribution theory is derived from Kelley's (1967) idea of the lay attributor engaging in an analysis of variation (ANOVA). A significant amount of research, however, has argued that people have only a poor understanding of covariation, so that even when presented with all relevant information in the form of a fourfold presence/absence table (Figure 3–1) and asked to judge the covariation serious errors are made, particularly in overconcentrating on the present/present cell of the table (Nisbett and Ross, 1980, pp. 90–93). This can be seen as a type of verification bias.

These results have been called into serious question in recent years (Einhorn and Hogarth, 1985b; Crocker, 1982), but other problems arise when attribution is considered in less artificial circumstances. Kelley and Michela (1980) argue that "the perception of covariation can be greatly affected by subjects" preconceptions about cause and effect relations, even being rendered wholly erroneous." Prior beliefs are seen as adversely affecting the "intake and use" of relevant information. Nonexistent covariations are thought to exist and actual covariations are missed. This line of criticism obviously relies on highly inductive ideas concerning how people should learn. Other difficulties involve the much discussed issue of the failure to give sufficient weight to consensus information, information concerning how other people behave in given circumstances (Harvey and Weary, 1984; Wells and Harvey, 1977). Finally, the fundamental attribution error is a tendency to overestimate the role of dispositional factors and underestimate the significance of situational forces (Ross, 1977). Many studies have supported the existence of this tendency (Harvey and Weary, 1984), but considerable debate surrounds the issue of whether the attribution error is indeed an error (Harvey et al., 1981).

4.4. Probability Judgment

The literature on probability judgment covers a vast range of issues, but most involve a comparison of the actual practice of naive subjects with

		EFFECT	
		PRESENT	ABSENT
SUSPECTED CAUSE	PRESENT		
	ABSENT		

FIGURE 3–1. Fourfold presence/absence table.

some normative standard drawn from probability theory. The recent literature in this area has been dominated by the argument of Tversky and Kahneman (1974) that "people rely on a limited number of heuristic principles which reduce the complex tasks of assessing probabilities and predicting values to simpler judgmental operations." These heuristics often work well but can lead to "severe and systematic errors."

The major discussion concerns the representativeness heuristic, in which probabilities are evaluated by similarity; the availability heuristic, in which the frequency or probability of an event is judged on the basis of the ease with which instances can be recalled from memory; and the anchoring heuristic, in which the estimate of a value is arrived at by adjustment from some initial starting point or anchor. The major errors and biases associated with each are, for representativeness, an insensitivity to prior probabilities; insensitivity to sample size; misconceptions of chance or randomness; insensitivity to predictability; illusions of validity; and misconceptions of regression toward the mean. A number of these biases can lead to the use of sometimes elaborate causal explanations for events that could more easily be explained in probablistic terms. Availability can result in biases due to the differential retrievability of instances, which may depend on salience or familiarity or how recently certain events occurred; biases due to the effectiveness of a search set; biases of imaginability; and illusory correlation. Anchoring can lead to errors due to insufficient adjustment from the starting point; biases in the evaluation of the probability of conjunctive or disjunctive events, the former being overestimated and the latter underestimated; and to poor "calibration" of subjective probability distributions. Many of the points mentioned above in the discussion of attribution have also been interpreted as examples of the biases introduced by one or other of these heuristics (Nisbett and Ross, 1980; Kahneman, Slovic, and Tversky, 1982).

Criticisms of this pessimistic view of probability judgment are, however, beginning to accumulate. The two main issues appear to be the normative standards that are applied and the external or ecological validity of the experimental research. It has been noted that the concepts of probability and randomness are concepts which have been, and still are being, debated within philosophy and mathematics. For example, Kahneman and Tversky talk about misconceptions of randomness and failures to utilize base rate information, but the ideas of randomness they criticize are close to those suggested by Popper (Lopes, 1982), and problems also exist in defining the relevant population for calculating base rates (Einhorn and Hogarth, 1981). In addition, not only are a wide variety of interpretations of probability available (Cohen, 1979) but also any interpretation which sees a probability as a probability of truth, or even as a subjective level of confidence or degree of belief, runs into the Hume/Popper criticism that there are *no* logically or rationally defensible standards of inductive inference. Perhaps even more importantly, Hogarth (1981) has argued that judgment in fact takes place in a continuous environment which provides feedback, whereas the experimental literature deals only with discrete events. This leads Hogarth to emphasize the "continuous adaptive nature of the judgmental process," the importance of learning, and to suggest that many "biases" may in fact be the result of heuristics that although not normatively correct, are functional in continuous and dynamic environments. However, as Einhorn and Hogarth (1981, p. 58) have pointed out, there has been no serious consideration of "the distribution of tasks in the natural environment in which heuristics would work well or poorly," and the argument should not be thought to imply that all heuristics will be well adapted. Einhorn (1980) has shown that the feedback obtained from simply implementing a rule can be misleading even if the rule is false or instrumentally ineffective. More critical tests may be required, but the opportunities for carrying out such tests may be limited (Brehmer, 1980). The literature concerning verification bias has also been cited in this context (Einhorn and Hogarth, 1981, pp. 78–79).

4.5. Decision-Making

The work on problem-solving and that on probability judgment discussed above has made a significant impression on behavioral decision theory, particularly in terms of the criticism of normative models based on given preferences and Bayesian revision of probabilities. March (1978) has discussed the effect of uncertainty concerning preferences, while Bayesian models have also come under attack. A not inconsiderable literature (Edwards, 1968; Fishbein and Ajzen, 1975, pp. 176–187) suggests that people are too conservative in the way they revise their subjective probabilities, but Kahneman and Tversky (1982b, p. 46) go much further, arguing that "in his evaluation of evidence, man is apparently not a conservative Bayesian: he is not Bayesian at all."

Decision theory is now dominated by discussions of a wide variety of simple decision heuristics that are often presented as having been adopted because they reduce the cognitive load or information-processing costs of optimal decision rules. Kahneman and Tversky (1979) have put forward prospect theory as descriptive of decision-making under uncertainty; Tversky (1972) has argued for an "elimination by aspects" model for choices between multiattribute alternatives; and a very large number of other models and process descriptions can now be found (Payne, 1976; Svenson, 1979; Earl, 1986b, chapter 7). This variety of different models each with their own heuristics has given rise to studies which suggest a high degree of task and context specificity (Simon and Hayes, 1976; Payne, 1982). This specificity has, in turn, led to the argument that all that has been generated by this research is a list of heuristics without any theory of when any particular heuristic will be used (Pitz and Sachs, 1984). Payne (1982) has attempted to evaluate some possible alternative frameworks but has found that none seems unambiguously supported. In particular, the economic or cost-benefit framework does not appear to be able to account for the effects of even slight changes in context on the strategies chosen.

The finding of task and context specificity has also been used to argue that "decision tasks do not tap a few simple and basic processes" and that rather than attempting to explain task and context effects "by assuming the existence of all sorts of cognitive limitations and biases, one might think of people as continually shifting their strategies to meet the demands placed upon them by contrived decision tasks" (Ebbesen and Konečni, 1980, pp. 25, 37). A slightly different interpretation of specificity is that of learning, but of the learning of rules which are applied only to particular tasks and contexts (Einhorn, 1980). More general optimal rules are likely only to have been learned through instruction or much abstract study of problem situations. The abstract nature of optimal rules requires, for their appropriate use, an ability to discern the general nature of the problem and the relevance of the rule, which is itself a difficult task (Brehmer, 1980).

5. Implications and Conclusions

The conclusions that can be drawn from the research reviewed above depend upon how the implications for the concepts of psychologism, inductivism, and rationalism are assessed. Within the economic and psychological literature four positions can be discerned. First, the traditional position which uses a psychological and inductive concept of rationality. Second, the position on the opposite extreme with respect to rationality but which retains psychologism and also retains inductivism as a normative standard. Here people are seen as utilizing psychologically given heuristics which lead to serious errors and shortcomings. This appears to be the position of Tversky and Kahneman (1974). Third, a less extreme version of the above, which sees people as behaving rationally but within bounds given by certain information-processing constraints. These constraints are only "gross" in nature and do not determine which specific problem spaces or heuristics will be used. In this position the full psychological rationality of the traditional view is still taken as the standard and as necessary for optimal behavior. Thus, the constraints that place limits on the quantity of information that can be processed are presented as making optimization virtually impossible. On the other hand, adaptive learning may well result in strategies that work reasonably well. This, of course, is the position expressed by Simon and which has now become quite common among decision theorists. Fourth, there is the antipsychologistic, antiinductivist, and rationalist position of methodologists such as Popper and Boland that has already been described.

There can be little doubt that the psychological literature casts most doubt on the first of these positions. If anything is clear it is that people have neither any intuitive understanding of standard probability concepts nor any innate psychological ability to learn directly through experience to characterize their environments accurately or arrive at optimal problem solutions. The truth is not manifest, and people do make systematic errors due to their misconceptions, but all of this is only surprising or disturbing if one begins from a psychologistic or inductivist point of view.

The attempt to save the traditional position by arguing that heuristics are simply a balancing of the costs of gathering and processing information against the benefit of reduced probability or error fares little better. Not only does this cost-benefit argument require the acceptance of the inductive idea that the probability of error will decline with the quantity of information collected and processed, which can be subject to telling logical criticism, it also runs counter the the anti-Bayesian findings of empirical work. In addition it is far from clear that the choice of heuristics responds only to relevant economic variables such as task complexity (Payne, 1982), or that the heuristic devices utilized are always cognitively less burdensome than optimal ones (Nisbett et al., 1983). The most promising conclusion is that the use of heuristics arises not from some rational calculation of costs and benefits (or its evolutionary equivalent) but from a simple *lack* of relevant knowledge. One cannot use probabilistic concepts or optimal strategies unless one already knows of them and recognizes their applicability (Brehmer, 1980).

The second position does at least have the advantage of recognizing that individuals are not possessed of full inductive psychological rationality. The problem with this position is, however, substantial. The presumption is that the heuristics people utilize are given, that they are either psychologically given or the necessary outcome of psychological or neurological constraints. While some such constraints may exist, particularly limitations

on short-term or working memory, serial processing, and, possibly, in the
way information is coded into long-term memory, it is difficult to see how
these factors can be thought of as very closely constraining or determining
inferential or problem solving heuristics, particularly where external memory aids and resources are available.

While Tversky and Kahneman (1974), as noted above, argue for this
highly psycyhologistic position, Nisbett et al. (1983) take the view that
there are "few grounds" for the presumption that inferential heuristics are
fixed, a position which is supported both by the wide variety of heuristics
that have been found, and by the possibilities of learning, whether through
formal instruction or feedback.

Simon's view, that rationality is "bounded" by information processing
constraints, stands between the position just discussed and that of Popper
and Boland. Simon's emphasis on the task as the decision-maker perceives
it and on the possibilities of learning results in similarities with the Popperian view of rationality. On the other hand, Simon maintains psychological inductivism as his standard of full rationality and also that it is the
discovery of the invariants of intelligent and adaptive systems that is the
basic task of research in cognitive science (Simon, 1981). These invariants,
however, are not seen as closely determining human behavior, and there
seems little point in denying that invariants of the type Simon has in mind
may exist. On the other hand, his notion of bounded rationality does have
some difficulties, particularly to the extent that it suggests full rationality
is necessary for the discovery of optimal solutions (if they exist) and that
the problem of induction is simply a matter of the difficulty of processing
sufficient information. Also, despite recognizing its importance, Simon has
not devoted much attention to the processes involved in learning.

The final position is the only one that entirely avoids inductivism in both
normative and positive roles. The purely situational definition of rationality
given by Popper and Boland turns into an irrelevancy much of the criticism
of human inferential and decision-making abilities found in the psychological literature. Nevertheless, some problems do exist. First, some of the
information-processing constraints mentioned by Simon may be significant
in certain types of situations. This is not to say that these constraints are
so close as to uniquely determine the strategy used, but where external
memory and other decision-making resources are unavailable they may
well rule out certain possibilities. To accommodate this point might necessitate the abandonment of the very strict antipsychologism of Popper
and Boland, although Simon's position is consistent with the rejection of
the idea of a complete reduction of social science to psychology. Second,
a lack of feedback or the possibility of misleading or uninformative feed-

back suggests that learning, even, in a Popperian fashion, is much more problematic than might at first be thought. Thus, in analyzing behavior, one must specify not only the situation as the actor himself perceives it but also the feedback that will result and (following Boland) how that feedback might be interpreted. It is important to understand that Popperian learning will not necessarily result in optimal or even in well-adapted or effective rules or instruments, although it may well have that result.

Finally, and most importantly, the Popperian arguments for a logical and critical concept of rationality might be challenged by the psychologists' findings concerning logical reasoning and verification bias. As argued above, Henle (1962) provides a possible rebuttal to the charge of illogic in human reasoning, but the question is still open. On the issue of verification bias, it is unclear what normative standard should be applied to judge whether a bias does exist. Given that people are likely to be more interested in practical success than in discovering the truth, Boland's point concerning the appropriateness of a less critical instrumentalism is particularly important. The behavior of Wason's subjects on his rule discovery task can be interpreted as instrumental in nature. Indeed, the whole idea of the use of heuristics can be seen in instrumental terms, and such a viewpoint could lead to a useful reinterpretation of the literature on adaptive learning. It is also the case that the experimental literature generally lacks the social dimension mentioned by Simon and which is also present in Popper's discussions (Gilhooly, 1982, p. 102). Most knowledge concerning the nature of the world and of abstract problem-solving techniques is developed by specialists and gradually disseminated to the society at large. Each individual does not create the world anew. Furthermore, most criticism, even in science, is not self-criticism but criticism of the work of others, and clearly particular institutional arrangements can help or hinder such criticism. The situation of the decision maker includes his or her institutional situation in the sense of both the general state of knowledge and its dissemination in the society in question and the particular institutional incentives and constraints he or she faces.

The final conclusion of all this is that the traditional psychologistic and inductivist notions of rationality are open to serious empirical (and not merely logical) criticism. This is not to deny the unsettled nature of psychology, but despite the debate and disagreement many behavioral phenomena have been found which do not appear to be easily reconcilable with traditional notions of rationality in economics. If economists are to be more than dogmatists, or wish to pursue more than a purely normative discipline, empirical psychology demands some response. The technically simplest response, and the one most often met with, is to retain a reductive psychologism and to substitute some heuristic or binding cognitive constraint for the rationality assumption. This has the effect of abandoning rationality in virtually any form, denying or severely limiting the possibilities of learning, and could merely lead to as many different models as there are heuristics. It might be presumed that the various inferential and decision-making heuristics arise out of some "basic" cognitive or psychological processes, but this is a most questionable hypothesis.

The only other alternative is to adopt either the position associated with Simon, or that of Popper and Boland, or, what is perhaps most promising, some combination of the two. This is not an alternative to which economists have given much attention as yet, and much remains to be done. It will require a concentration on processes of (noninductive) learning, and it is also an alternative that will involve breaking the close attachment economists have developed for models that reduce to a few natural and psychological givens. Whether such a program can be successfully developed remains to be seen, but the choice that modern psychological research leaves to us appears to be between abandoning reductive versions of psychologism or abandoning the rationality principle itself.

Notes

1. In the opinion of this author, Feyerabend's (1970) criticism that Lakatos' methodology is, in fact, a position of "anything goes" has considerable merit.

2. This is due to differences in the treatment of knowledge. Popper's treatment is neither inductivist nor a priorist nor subjectivist. Popper's view of knowledge is that it is conjectural but *potentially objective*. Knowledge is objective to the extent that it has been expressed and is available to be criticized. Latsis' (1976) inclusion of Popper in the Austrian camp is certainly questionable (Hands, 1985). Boland (1982, pp. 174–187) has indicated how ideas from Hayek and Popper might be combined.

3. Not without justice Berkson and Wettersten (1984, p. 31) claim that Popper's point of view is not merely antipsychologistic but antipsychology.

4. The definition of verification bias sometimes appears to be such that it would include the case of an individual testing his hypothesis that his car stopped running as it was out of gas by first looking at the fuel gauge. Particular confusion over what a falsificationist testing strategy implies can be found in Tschirgi (1980).

4 ON PSYCHING UP ECONOMICS

Rod Cross

Can you know anything but illusion? If once illusion were destroyed you would never dare to look back; you would be turned into a pillar of salt. For the Last Time Psychology!

— Franz Kafka, from *Reflections on Sin, Pain, Hope and the True Way*, translated by Willa and Edwin Muir (London: Secker and Warburg, 1946).

1. Introduction

If an "internalist" account of the development of economic thought is adopted, empirical anomalies and logical inconsistencies mark the points at which existing theories are modified or new theories emerge. At the time of mutation or birth there are no signposts dictating the avenues along which economic theories must develop. The Duhem-Quine thesis, in its weaker form, points out that there is not any sure way of knowing which of the axioms, lemmas, initial conditions, boundary conditions, measurement specifications, hypotheses, and so on which constitute a particular theory are to blame when a fault is detected: the content of the theory arises from the juxtaposition of the aforementioned ingredients, and while

55

there might be a tendency to blame individual players, it is the team that has lost and no one can be sure that a particular positional change would have led to a different result. At various times when faults have been detected in economic theories it has been suggested that economists look beyond the bounds of their subject, narrowly defined, when modifiying existing theories or producing new ones: the team performance might improve if players from biology, physics, politics, psychology, social anthropology, sociology, and so on were to be introduced. "Introduced" here means introduced into "mainstream" theory — that is, neoclassical theory — given that there are already in existence theories and even special journals which attempt to harvest for economics the insights to be gained from the disciplines mentioned above.

The problem is that most of the economists whose coin is mainstream economics have to date resisted the temptation, or exhortation, to modify in any noticeable way the aspects of their theories which have, in the context of the complaint lodged in this book, discernible psychological innuendoes: many have been called, but few if any of the modifications labeled "psychology" have been chosen. The point of this chapter is to ask, in the light of arguments of the kind employed by Randall Bausor and Malcolm Rutherford in this volume, whether this is a just, or otherwise justifiable, state of affairs.

2. Mainstream Theory Versus Bausor and Rutherford

Mainstream theory in this context is taken to mean neoclassical or Walrasian theory (after Walras, 1874/1954), whose hallmark at inception was, arguably, the formalization of Adam Smith's synergistic concept of the invisible hand (see Schumpeter, 1954, for this argument). This theory provides conjectures about economic behavior at two levels: the market and the individual. The heuristic employed insists that market or aggregate outcomes be traced back to individual choices — hence the adjective "reductionist" which is often applied to this theoretical structure (see Coddington, 1983); in reverse the heuristic insists, rather clumsily, on being able to derive market behavior from some aggregation procedure mapping from the individual to market level, often requiring the use of simplifying devices such as "composite commodities" or "representative" individuals or firms. At the atomistic level — if you will excuse the loan from physics rather than psychology — the main conjecture is that people maximize some objective function determined by "preferences," "psychological factors," or other aspects of the individuals which the theory takes as given:

although, as Rutherford notes, the term "psychologism" is sometimes used to describe this short circuit, "keep psychology out" might be a more appropriate description. At the market level, the main conjecture is that no net profits remain in equilibrium, all advantageous trades — defined in terms of individual objective functions — having been exploited.

In this book Bausor and Rutherford both argue, in their different ways, that the account of economic behavior given by neoclassical theory is severely flawed, and that the "psychologistic" axiom of given preferences needs to be abandoned if the problems encountered by neoclassical theory are to be resolved. But before moving on to consider their arguments, it is worth noting as an aside that several nonmainstream theoretical systems already exist in economics that do without the notion of preferences, assuming fixed or exogenously shifting coefficients in consumption and production (for example, see Pasinetti, 1981).

Bausor's argument is that "alternative psychological characterizations of more flexible and adaptive people lead naturally to a richer and more complex characterization of the economy" than that contained in neoclassical theory. After reviewing a wide variety of theories of human behavior, decision-making, and learning, ranging from Plato, Freud, Chomsky, Piaget, and Kelly to Skinner, Bausor argues that individuals (in the form of their objective functions or preferences, in the neoclassical parlance) "change in response to their environment," and that the complex reactions are areas for which "controlled experiments need not have reliable predictive power." The prescription is that "the identifying attributes of people must not be seen as antecedent to the economic process but should be recognized as a fundamental aspect of that process itself." The vision is one of an economic analysis where Kellian personal constructs are substituted for neoclassical preferences, these constructs being modified through the medium of surprise events, the systemwide manifestation of which is a kaleidic economy, as depicted by Shackle.

Rutherford focuses more specifically on accounts of rational behavior and learning to be found in expected utility theory and Bayesian theories. He notes the severe doubts cast on the theories by experimental evidence and the increasing interest in psychological theories of learning evident in the economics literature, but points out the problems faced by economists looking to psychology for inspiration, in the form of "the welter of different explanations for each phenomenon discovered," and the incommensurability of many of the experimental results. His complaint about neoclassical theory concerns not only the "psychologistic" characterization of individuals but also the inductive theory of learning which, he argues, is involved. Following Popper, Rutherford argues that induction is not a "rational" method of learning. After reviewing the psychological literature on learning which stresses the role of heuristics and biases, Rutherford concludes that economists can: either retain psychologism as a short circuit, substituting some alternative to induction from the wide variety of inferential and decision-making heuristics which have been proposed; or abandon psychologism and retain a rational method of learning such as those suggested by Popper and Simon. An unnecessary source of confusion arises here from a rather uncritical acceptance of Boland's claim that neoclassical theory is based on an inductive theory of learning. The confusion is between the conjectural and meta-conjectural levels of discourse: a statement that individuals generalize from specific instances does not imply the statement that neoclassical economists believe in induction (see Birner, 1985).

3. Which Psychology?

The temptation is to expect a state of certainty characterizing knowledge in other disciplines which does not pertain in your own discipline: in other contexts people tend to believe newspaper accounts of events of which they do not have direct knowledge, despite the discrepancies between newspaper and their own accounts of events of which they have knowledge. Hence the temptation is to look to sociology for clear guidance if you suspect that some social forces at work in wage determination explain why the points are off the curve predicted by some species of the Phillips curve genus; or to look to psychology for clear guidance if you think that some psychological mutation explains why people shorten their subjective estimates of the odds on their chosen horses winning after placing bets; and so on. For many economists, the process of theory amendment stops at this point: anomalies arise, the magic words *sociology*, *psychology*, or even *biology*, *social anthropology*, or *physics* are invoked and the anomalies are explained away, leaving the underlying *economic* theory intact, fit to face further battles. In such circumstances, the unpopular task of the more reflective is to invoke the perhaps less magical term *philosophy* in order to point out that the amendment is ad hoc, tautologically conflating that which is to be explained with the explanation, so reducing the content of the theory, the range of phenomena about which the theory speaks.

For some economists the process goes further, the question, in the context of this book, being one of what light psychological theories can throw on how the anomalies can be explained in a non ad hoc fashion. At this point the unsuspecting economist can experience the shock of realizing how uncomplicated the task of distinguishing wheat from chaff is in economics, compared to psychology. To quote one not entirely unsympathetic to "psyching up" economics: "economists to my mind have been over respectful of what psychology is supposedly able to tell us. . . . while rich in data, at the theoretical level psychology remains a confusing clamor of competing categories: there is no integrating theoretical structure" (Hirshleifer, 1985, pp. 61–62). Those whom the gods love die young, without having studied psychology.

Both Bausor and Rutherford are aware of this "confusing clamor," and do, as far as an ignorant outsider can judge, a good job in organizing the queue of psychological theories. The problem of which psychological theory to adopt can vanish into an infinite regress of choosing a psychological theory of choice between competing psychological theories of choice, learning, and decision-making. Would economists not sleep happier in their own beds, and still be able to perform as well in their theoretical tasks, without worrying how to spell psychology? This would be an unduly arrogant response: why rule out a possible source of illumination? Perhaps there is a fruitful marriage to be arranged between the psychologist's account of the heuristics adopted by people in specific problematic circumstances and the economist's account of the optimal behavior patterns which might be adopted given sufficient experience? The suggestion of Rutherford and others that the heuristics postulated by psychologists be seen as tentative conjectures regarding optimal behavior, which are subsequently revised in the light of errors, along Popperian lines, offers a promising avenue of research.

4. Fecundity

Given an "internalist" interpretation of the development of economic thought, psychological specifications of choice heuristics would be attractive to economists if it could be demonstrated that their adoption would account, in a non ad hoc manner, for the empirical anomalies encountered by economic theories; or if their adoption would resolve problems with the logical structure of economic theories. In an earlier episode, in the United States from the 1880s to the 1920s, repeated efforts were made to discredit the subjective theory of value underlying the theory of demand formulated during the "marginalist revolution," a good part of the ammunition being provided by the physio-biological, behavioral and instinct theories propounded in psychology by James, Watson and McDougall, respectively (see Coats, 1976, for a review). This earlier attempt to persuade economists to modify their theories in the light of experimental results in psychology failed: as Coats (1976, p. 58) observes, "despite the scientific status of the new

empirical findings in psychology, that discipline was still in a highly unsettled state, and the efforts to infuse psychology into economics at that
time were over-ambitious, premature, sometimes confused, and generally
lacking in persistence and clarity of focus."

Are the problems faced by theories in economics either more severe,
or is what psychology has to offer more compelling, so that the attempts
at infusion will be more successful this time? It is beyond the scope of this
chapter to assess whether mainstream economic theory is in a more parlous
state than at the turn of the century, or to discuss the range of wares which
psychology now has to offer. What can be said here is that mainstream
economists are more likely to be influenced by concrete demonstrations
that the infusion of psychological theories into economics generates extra
content in the form of resolved anomalies, the prediction of "novel" facts
and other forms of insight, rather than by highly abstract discussions of
what psychology *might* have to offer.

In Bausor's contribution to this book, for example, it is argued that
psychological theories would help provide a "richer and more complex
characterization" of economies than that provided by the Arrow-Debreu
general equilibrium model. However, it is not clear that there are good
grounds for preferring more complex, or even richer, theories. The Arrow-
Debreu model was designed to investigate whether it was possible to prove
the existence of an equilibrium solution for a competitive economy. An
existence proof was provided, which served not only to clarify an old debate
but also to throw light on the characterizations of economic behavior which
were, and many of which have been, found necessary in order to demonstrate the existence of a general equilibrium solution: the nonexistence
of futures markets, for example, violates existence proofs (see Arrow and
Hahn, 1971). This mainstream, psychologistic, keep-psychology-out activity served to focus attention, albeit indirectly, on what would happen if
existence (or stability or uniqueness) proofs could not be provided. The
problem for the mainstream economic theorist of explaining disequilbrium
as well as equilibrium behavior is reasonably clear, even though the way
to resolve the problem may be opaque. If Bausor provided a psychologically
based theory of how people behave in disequilbrum situations, which had
clear, refutable content, many mainstream economists would be attracted.
Instead what seems to be presented is a menu of possibilities: it may be
true that the issue of "personal adaptation to the economic environment
cannot be ignored as central to economic dynamics," but it is not very
instructive if all we are told amounts to little more than that "people
respond to events in many ways." Shackle has been saying this, lucidly,
since 1945 but with little impact on mainstream theory.

Economists in the mainstream are more likely to be attracted by the fruits of introducing psychological factors into economic theory rather than by the menu of possibilities. Akerlof's work shows what can be achieved by piecemeal engineering, in which the consequences of replacing standard neoclassical assumptions with psychology-based specifications are carefully examined. Indeed, Akerlof (1984, pp. 3–4) notes that "the very absence of psychological, anthropological and sociological factors in economic theory allows a whole new field of potential interest today. . . . (Their) very absence . . . allows the economic theorist to ask what the consequences of these behaviors will be for the usual economic results. . . . In what way will the introduction of these factors alter the tradition equilibrium? . . . will such factors explain unemployment? . . . will such factors explain the nature of discrimination in a way deeper than blaming it on "tastes"? . . . perhaps these tastes will be endogenously explained?" Akerlof's (1984, chapter 7) paper on cognitive dissonance, for example, shows how the infusion of this notion from psychology can explain otherwise anomalous aspects of economic behavior and generate novel and surprising content. Akerlof himself, however, notes that despite the fact that he "would like to think that psycho-socio-anthropo-economics is at the beginning of a period when many people will be working in this area . . . this field has not reached the stage where there is a set of problems with a natural research agenda" (1984, p. 6). By their fruits shall ye know them.

5. Which Vehicle?

An issue that is not always clear is whether those who would infuse psychological theories into economics are advocating the modification of mainstream, neoclassical theory to deal with empirical anomalies or logical inconsistencies; or whether they are arguing the case for alternative research programs, such as Austrian or Post Keynesian economics, which might draw on psychology in their specifications of the heuristics or biases involved in the cognitive processes underlying economic behavior. An assessment of alternative research programs is beyond the scope of this chapter.

If the task is to modify neoclassical theory to deal with anomalous observations thrown up by experimental evidence (see Kahneman and Tversky, 1979, and Kahneman, Slovic, and Tversky, 1982, for discussion for such studies), or to deal with logical problems regarding the explanation of behavior outside of equilibrium (see Arrow, 1959), then the possible paths of development would be constrained by the heuristics which serve to identify neoclassical economics: market or aggregate behavior is to be traced back to individual behavior, and in the equilibrium situation of no net profits individuals are constrained maximizers of their objective functions. The role of psychology here would be one of attempting to explain short-run, disequilbrium behavior in a manner which would be consistent with convergence to a long-run, no net profits equilibrium. Otherwise neoclassical economics would lose that part of its content which refers to equilibrium behavior, the hallmark of the research program. A crucial issue here is whether the cognitive theories of rational behavior, contained in the psychological literature, and which might be employed to explain short run disequilibrium behavior, can be married with the neoclassical economist's account of rational behavior. The latter would then be relegated to the task of explaining long run, equilibrium behavior.

A clear distinction between these two specifications of rational behavior is provided by Simon (1976), who terms the neoclassical account "substantive" rationality, and the psychologist's account "procedural" rationality. On substantive rationality, Simon (1976, pp. 130–131) writes that "behavior is substantively rational when it is appropriate to the achievement of given goals within the limits imposed by given conditions and constraints. . . . The rationality of behavior depends upon the actor in only a single respect — his goals. . . . Given these goals, the rational behavior is determined entirely by the characteristics of the environment in which it takes place." Whereas in the case of procedural rationality Simon (1976, p. 131) argues that "behavior is procedurally rational when it is the outcome of appropriate deliberation. . . . Its procedural rationality depends on the process that generated it. . . . When psychologists use the term rationality it is usually procedural rationality they have in mind. . . . Conversely behavior tends to be described as "irrational" in psychology when it represents impulsive response to affective mechanisms without an adequate intervention of thought."

After surveying the literature on risk perception in psychology and economics, one of the coauthors of the Arrow-Debreu neoclassical model of general equilibrium concludes: "I hope I have made a case for the proposition that an important class of intertemporal markets show systematic deviations from individual rational behavior and that these deviations are consonant with evidence from very different sources collected by psychologists" (Arrow, 1982, p. 8). The question is one of whether the heuristic devices which psychologists postulate to explain procedurally rational behavior could be incorporated as devices whereby people grope toward substantively rational behavior. Or does the postulated existence of such heuristics rule out substantively rational behavior? The challenge here seems one of explaining why certain heuristics are adopted, of explaining how heuristics are modified in the light of experience, and of discovering whether such heuristics permit convergence toward substantively rational behavior.

Unless, or until, such convergence theories are forthcoming, it would seem pointless to advocate the infusion of theories of procedurally rational behavior into neoclassical economics: any increase in content arising from the ability to explain the procedures involved in economic decision-making would be at the cost of loss of existing content with regard to the explanation of the systemwide implications of substantive rationality. One of the features that distinguishes psychology from economics, insofar as an outsider can judge, is the lack in psychology of analysis of the system-wide implications of the various decision-making heuristics postulated. This is perhaps a major obstacle to achieving more than a shotgun marriage between neoclassical economics and the various psychological accounts of cognitive processes. The challenge for those who would infuse psychological theories of behavior into mainstream economics is to provide a theory that allows the aggregate phenomena which are of great interest in economics to be explained in terms of individual cognitive processes.

6. Two Problems

There are no logically compelling reasons why economists should have to turn to psychology for insight in the face of empirical or logical difficulties with their theories; equally well, there is no logically compelling reason why they should not. Economic theories have content with regard to both individual and aggregate behavior. Consider examples of the difficulties which have arisen with regard to the ability of economic theories to explain these two aspects of behavior: the Allais paradox in expected utility theory, where individual preference reversals appear to occur; and aggregate unemployment, where there are long epochs in which unemployment appears to have persisted way above — or below? — neoclassical equilibrium levels. Should economists look to psychology for guidance, as is advocated in this book?

In the Allais paradox, individuals are asked to choose between outcomes A and B, which consist of sums of money to which probabilities are attached: most prefer A to B, but when asked to choose between C and D, which in terms of the expected utility index can be rewritten as A and B, a majority prefer D to C (see Allais, 1953). Does the economist look to psychology in order to explain the cognitive processes involved, and abandon expected utility theory? On the surface it would appear that the paradoxical result violates the independence axiom of expected utility theory, which states that preferences are linearly defined over probability distribution functions for outcomes. Given the problem raised by the Duhem-Quine thesis, however, there is no sure way of knowing whether it is not one of the other constituent parts of expected utility theory — relating to the existence and continuity of probability functions, for example — which is to blame for the anomalous evidence. There are many responses possible from within the expected utility framework to the paradox: the domain of the theory could be expressed so as to exclude "artificial" experiments; the theory could be reformulated without the independence axiom (see Machina, 1982); the specification of probability functions could be changed; and so on. Such reactions retain the psychologism of neoclassical theory and keep psychology out without necessarily reducing the content of the theory. The alternative accounts of behavior in the face of risk offered in the psychology literature, surveyed by Schoemaker (1982), seem to be too specific to specific situations, sometimes to the extent of being descriptions rather than theories of behavior, to offer serious competition to expected utility theory in terms of content (however, see Levi, 1986, for a somewhat different view).

Turning to the case of unemployment, a major problem for neoclassical or theories of an otherwise classical persuasion is to explain why aggregate unemployment follows approximately a random walk in many countries (see Blanchard and Summers, 1987, for example). A random walk is a process whereby the current value of a variable equals the previous period's value plus a white noise error term (plus a constant in the case of a random walk with drift). This is a problem for theories of a classical persuasion because such a walk possesses no mean, and hence no tendency to return to a mean value: classical equilibria would have to be remarkably footloose for this property to arise. Here again there might seem to be an obvious prima facie case for introducing psychological theories of how individuals "change in response to their environment" (Bausor), the unemployment environment changing the individuals concerned and so changing unemployment in the next period. The task would be to provide a theory of the cognitive processes of the unemployed, of those responsible for hiring them, and so on. Again, however, psychological accounts of cognitive processes appear to be too specific to specific circumstances to be able to account for what happens at high unemployment as well as low unemployment, in different times and countries, and in the context of systemwide interaction between unemployed individuals, employers, and institutions, to be capable of explaining the apparently pervasive random walk path of unemployment. Given that theories which do not invoke psychology at a formal level are capable of generating random walk paths for unemployment, the case for psychological infusion is not compelling. In the insider-outsider account of labor markets, for example, insiders are postulated to maximize an objective function defined over the real wage and the probability of being employed. If the unemployed lose their "insider" status immediately on losing their jobs — that is, become "outsiders" — this modifies the criteria in the objective functions of the remaining insiders so — given, of course, other specifications of behavior — generating a random walk for unemployment (see Blanchard and Summers, 1987, for this model). Here the environment of unemployment changes the probability that insiders will become unemployed, so changing the optimal behavior of the group of insiders. Hence the environment affects behavior without the economist having to invoke accounts of cognitive processes from the psychology literature. In providing this account of unemployment, economists have borrowed the concept of hysteresis from physics (see Cross and Allan, 1987, for an account), which gives a lie to the argument that economists are isolationists who are loathe to trade with other disciplines.

7. Conclusion

Perhaps economists have not traded more with psychology because of the limited gains in content to be had from the trade, especially given the threatened obliteration of content which their existing theories contain with regard to the systemwide implications of behavioral patterns.

5 NEOCLASSICAL ECONOMICS AND THE PSYCHOLOGY OF RISK AND UNCERTAINTY

Ben J. Heijdra

1. Introduction

The prospect of writing a chapter on the psychology of uncertainty and its potential implications for the economics of uncertainty left me at once excited and worried. The excitement was prompted by the fact that the psychology of economics has a direct bearing on the hard core of the neoclassical research program. The apprehension was related to effectively the same thing. The dilemma that I was faced with is the following: can one do psychology of economics (or more specifically, uncertainty) without at the same time giving up the neoclassical research program? Or is it necessarily true that *de gustibus non est disputandum* in neoclassical economics?

A by no means exhaustive search through the recent literature on uncertainty in economics and psychology quickly provided me with a perception of a binding constraint of the following kind. The psychological literature on behavior under uncertainty is massive, and to compound the problem, ". . . no systematic theory about the psychology of uncertainty has emerged from this literature" (Kahneman and Tversky, 1982b, p. 32). It is clearly impossible for a nonpsychologist to read and assimilate this literature in a relatively short period of time. I therefore concentrate in this chapter on those authors from the psychology discipline that *themselves* have indicated the potential relevance of their findings to the economics of uncertainty. Furthermore, only the most recent literature is dealt with here. A tacit belief in the monotonic progress of scientific knowledge is all that can be offered in defence of this latter strategy.

The chapter is organized as follows. In section 2, I present my reconstruction of some recent psychological findings in the field of behavior under uncertainty. Section 3 contains a simple sketch of some criteria by which neoclassical economists' reactions can possibly be judged. In section 4, a number of recent contributions from the economics literature are examined as to their psychological foundations. Finally, in section 5 the main conclusions are summarized.

2. The Psychology of Uncertainty and its Relevance to Modern Neoclassical Economics

Perhaps the most famous contributors to the psychological literature on behavior under uncertainty are Amos Tversky and Daniel Kahneman, whose work, and that of close associates, has recently been collected in one volume (Kahneman, Slovic, and Tversky, 1982). Since they themselves have advocated the relevance of their findings to economics (Kahneman and Tversky, 1979), their work is a good starting point for the purposes of this chapter. According to Kahneman and Tversky, subjects in laboratory style experiments tend to use heuristic principles that may lead to biases that the decision)makers fail to detect themselves. This is in stark contrast to Estes (1972) who surveys the pre-Kahneman-Tversky literature on the learning of probabilities. Contrary to Kahneman and Tversky, he concludes that "laboratory analyses have abundantly confirmed the impression gained from everyday life that human beings are adept at learning the probabilities of uncertain events with considerable accuracy" (Estes, 1972, p. 98). In section 4 of chapter 3, Rutherford has already discussed in some detail the biases identified by Kahneman and Tversky and associates. For present purposes the message seems to be that subjects in laboratory situations appear to violate various statistical axioms.

As Levi points out, however, it is difficult to the outsider to get an accurate understanding of the different heuristics since they tend to be "defined" implicitly only, mainly by the use of illustrative examples (1985, p. 332). Furthermore, these examples tend to be entirely unrelated to the kinds of problems that neoclassical theory postulates economic agents to face under uncertainty. The adjustment and anchoring heuristic, for example, is illustrated as follows:

> Two groups of high school students estimated, within 5 seconds, a numerical expression that was written on the blackboard. One group estimated the product
> $$8.7.6.5.4.3.2.1$$
> while another group estimated the product
> $$1.2.3.4.5.6.7.8.$$
> To rapidly answer such questions, people may perform a few steps of computation and estimate the product by extrapolation or adjustment. Because adjustments are typically insufficient, this procedure should lead to underestimation. Furthermore, because the result of the first few steps of multiplication (performed from left to right) is higher in the descending sequence than in the ascending sequence, the former expression should be judged larger than the latter. Both predictions were confirmed (Kahneman and Tversky, 1982a, p. 15).

It is very difficult to relate this example to an economic setting. Are Kahneman and Tversky to be interpreted only as saying that economic agents have limited calculating ability, because the subjects in this example couldn't come up with the correct answer in 5 seconds? If the answer to this question is affirmative, then economists have been exposed to these kind of phenomena through the work of Simon for several decades (see Simon, 1979). Mainstream neoclassical theory has reacted to Simon's work by building models that recognize the importance of information costs, rather than by abandoning the maximization hypothesis as Simon suggested. Undoubtedly, the work of Kahneman and associates as interpreted here would undergo a similar fate.

It must be stressed that I do not claim to disprove the work by Kahneman and associates. The object here is to propose that there is little in the Kahneman and associates (1982) volume that would strike a neoclassical economist as immediately impinging on his domain of research. That is why the search now turns to Kahneman and Tversky (1979), a paper that was explicitly aimed at the economics profession. The object of their paper is to criticize explicitly the traditional expected utility approach underlying much of neoclassical theory under uncertainty (see Schoemaker, 1982, for an excellent survey of expected utility theories). Expected utility theory, according to them, is deficient in view of a number of empirical violations of its axioms and predictions found in laboratory situations. The first violation they label the *certainty effect*, according to which subjects underweight probable outcomes compare to certain outcomes (Kahneman and Tversky, 1979, pp. 265–267). The *reflection effect* consists of a preference reversal when gains are replaced in the experiments by losses. This implies that subjects are risk-averse in the positive domain and risk-seeking in the negative domain (p. 268). These two effects seem to suggest some kind of anchoring type behavior on the part of subjects: the anchor is the present level of wealth, and utility is defined on gains and losses rather than the level of wealth. In this sense the analysis is reminiscent of Markowitz who explicitly defines the utility function over wealth with the level of "customary wealth" as the reference point (1952, p. 155). The only difference with Kahneman and Tversky's "value function" is that the latter do not include a risk-neutral section around the reference point, and the branch defined on losses is steeper than that defined on gains (1979, p. 279). It thus seems to me to be an argument about slopes, and all that Kahneman and Tversky have done is to argue in favour of their value function on the basis of their "empirical" observations.[1] Kahneman and Tversky differentiate their product further: "[Markowitz's] treatment . . . retains the expectation principle; hence it cannot account for the many violations of this principle" (1979, p. 276). A third effect that Kahneman and Tversky discuss is the *isolation effect* according to which subjects can be fooled into behaving in an inconsistent manner when the same two prospects are presented in two different manners. They argue that this inconsistency is caused by the subjects' tendency to discard components that are shared by (in this case) both prospects under consideration (1979, p. 271). This effect, if it exists, is, of course, much more damaging than the previous two effects to the expected utility approach specifically and the neoclassical theory of choice in general. Indeed, if we were to base economic theories upon a theory of choice which is not independent of the order and manner in which alternatives are presented it is hard to imagine if any testable hypothesis would be derivable from it. We would have bought supposed realism of the assumptions at the (for economists) prohibitive cost of unfalsifiability. I return to this issue below.

In the positive part of their paper, Kahneman and Tversky propose what they call prospect theory as a more robust theory of choice under uncertainty. Instead of using probabilities (P_i), subjects are assumed to use decision weights, defined as a function of probabilities, that is, $W(P_i)$. These decision weights are assumed to satisfy $W(P_i) > P_i$ for low values of P_i, and $W(P_i) < P_i$ otherwise. Furthermore, the $W(P_i)$ function is assumed to be discontinuous at very high (near certain) and very low (near impossible) probabilities (events) (Kahneman and Tversky, 1979, p. 283). The value function, $V(X_i)$, is defined over prospects X_i, and agents base their decisions on $\Sigma W(P_i)V(X_i)$. It is therefore no surprise that Schoemaker (1982, p. 538) classifies prospect theory as just one more variant of the expected utility model — and, as Loomes and Sugden (1982, p. 817) point out, one which requires a "complex and somewhat ad hoc array of assumptions."

The only feature that really distinguishes it from the subjective expected utility model of Edwards (1955) is the fact that the decision weights, $W(P_i)$, are not constrained to add up to unity, and indeed should not be interpreted as probabilities at all according to Kahneman and Tversky (1979, p. 280; Schoemaker, 1982, p. 537).

Thaler (1980) argues that prospect theory is well suited to form the basis of a descriptive theory of consumer choice. He argues that traditional expected utility theory is normative (that is, it describes how people *should* choose), and that economists have erroneously assumed it to be positive as well (1980, pp. 39–40). Aside from the methodological problems associated with such a statement (see section 3), Thaler relies mainly on examples and anecdotes to support his claims. It is thus rather difficult to assess how useful prospect theory is to economics. Consider his example of supposed breakdown of the normative theory is the presence of complexity:

> Consider the famous birthday problem in statistics: if 25 people are in a room what is the probability that at least one pair will share a birthday? This problem is famous because everyone guesses wrong when he first hears it — nearly everyone guesses too low (Thaler, 1980, p. 40).

What this shows is that people make mistakes. But what if a person loses $500 because he had the wrong answer? The natural reaction of neoclassical economists would be to argue that next time this problem comes up he will at least attempt to improve his performance. This is merely one example of what I discuss in greater detail in section 3 below: economics has important reverse implications for (experimental) psychology. Unfortunately, neither Kahneman and Tversky (1979) nor Thaler (1980) report the results of any sequential experiments to find out if "undetected biases" remain undetected for long. As the psychologist Klayman (1984) points out, his colleagues may have painted too bleak a picture of the learning ability of people in the face of feedback.

Elsewhere, Russell and Thaler (1985) relate the findings of Kahneman and Tversky to the debate about rationality. They argue that rationality is often simply assumed and that the psychological literature has shown that this assumption is often violated. Quasi rational behavior is defined by them as any "regular yet non rational behavior" (Russell and Thaler, 1985, p. 1072). An example of quasi rational behavior is embodied in the distortion of probabilities through the decision weight function discussed above $(W(P_i))$. They admit that their approach is not the only one: "It is true that for every real world example of quasi rational behavior we can offer, rationality cannot be ruled out. This, however, in no way rules it in"

(Russell and Thaler, 1985, p. 1073). This statement betrays a confusion on Russell and Thaler's part of the status of the rationality postulate in neoclassical economic theory: as long as subjects think they are maximizing they are rational. (I return to this issue in section 3 below.) As an example of quasi rational behavior, Russell and Thaler utilize a simple Lancasterian consumption model. There is an objective mapping from goods to characteristics that is (in)correctly perceived by (quasi) rational consumers. The two types of consumers have identical preferences over the two characteristics. With the aid of this model, Russell and Thaler show that there exist equilibria that are not rational if there are (relatively) too many quasi rational consumers (1985, pp. 1074–1076). They go on to discuss conditions under which rationality would be restored in a competitive market. These conditions are, in my view, mere "red herrings": by showing them to be unreasonable and unlikely to be fulfilled in reality they are used as rhetoric devices to "prove" that quasi rational behavior is common. It seems, however, that the analysis is really a semantic one only. Some agents are called quasi rational by Russell and Thaler because they don't correctly perceive the objective characteristics technology. With the same justification one could consider such agents as merely having a different preference set. (What I expect will be a comfortable chair for me may be one which you would expect to be extremely uncomfortable for you; am I quasi-rational or just different?) Coining a new and laden term therefore adds nothing to what we already know.

Even if we accept Russell and Thaler's classification, there is another problem. In their introduction they claim that ". . . the knee-jerk reaction of some economists that competition will render irrationality irrelevant is apt only in very special cases, probably rarely observed in the real world" (1985, p. 1071). This seems to be a vast overstatement, at least as far as the case of irrational producers is concerned, and it is precisely this case that is the subject of the classic studies by Alchian (1950) and Winter (1964, 1971).

Another topic that seems a favorite in the psychological literature on choice under uncertainty is the problem of ambiguity. Economists were made aware of the problem by Ellsberg (1961), but have chosen to ignore it ever since. Ambiguity is described by Hogarth and Kunreuther as "uncertainty about one's uncertainty" (1985, p. 386). Einhorn and Hogarth (1985) propose a theoretical framework for probability assessment in the presence of ambiguity. Judged probability, $S(P_A)$, is assumed to be subject to the anchoring-and-adjustment process mentioned above. The initial guess (or anchor) is denoted by P_A, and "could be the best guess of experts, reflect one's previous information about the topic, or it could simply be a number that is salient in memory" (Einhorn and Hogarth, 1985a, p. 436). The adjustment factor is determined as the outcome of a mental simulation of different values of P on the part of subjects. Its net value is determined by three different factors: (1) the level of P_A: since $0 \le S(P_A) \le 1$, the direction of change is constrained depending on the value of P_A; (2) the amount of perceived ambiguity: this is captured by the parameter t ($0 \le t \le 1$) where t increases with amibiguity and equals zero if the situation is unambiguous; (3) the person's attitude towards ambiguity: parameter b captures the hypothesized asymmetry between simulations of P above and below P_A, respectively ($b \ge 0$). On the basis of these three effects, Einhorn and Hogarth derive the following expressions for the judged probability (1985, pp. 436–437):

$$S(P_A) = P_A + t\,(1 - P_A - P_A^b).\tag{5.1}$$

The first term on the righthand side of equation (5.1) is the initial anchor, and the second term represents the *net* adjustment. Einhorn and Hogarth show that (5.1) may be rewritten as follows:

$$S(P_A) = (1 - t)\,P_A + t\,(1 - P_A^b).\tag{5.2}$$

Thus $S(P_A)$ can be interpreted as a weighted average of P_A and $(1 - P_A)^b$. Superficially these judged probabilities resemble the decision weights discussed by Kahneman and Tversky (1979). The interpretation of the two is vastly different, however. In the Kahneman-Tversky decision weights, the true probabilities are fully known to the subjects. The decision weights differ from the probabilities because of distortion, by the subjects, of known probabilities, not because these probabilities are unknown. In Einhorn and Hogarth's case the probabilities themselves are unknown. In that sense, their analysis is (potentially) the more useful of the two. Also, the ambiguity model may be a good alternative to Bayesian updating procedures when dealing with low probability events such as the ones typically analyzed in relation to disaster insurance (Hogarth and Kunreuther, 1985, p. 390). In such situations there may be "limited opportunities for learning over time" (p. 390). A Bayesian, however, would argue that all relevant past information useful to estimating a probability is represented by the prior (in this case, the anchor P_A). The mental simulation experiments hypothesized by Einhorn and Hogarth are of course also distinctly un-Bayesian.[2]

The two parameters in this model, b and t, are likely to be affected by individual and situational factors. Einhorn and Hogarth test their model empirically using experimental data relating to both inference tasks and choice tasks. In general their model seems to fit the data reasonably well.[3]

In their general discussion they bring up some points that are of interest to economists working with the rational expectations hypothesis:

> Although the conditional nature of uncertainty has been implicitly recognized, ambiguity results from its explicit recognition, that is, by realizing that the "model" is itself subject to uncertainty. . . . Furthermore, even if a process is well-defined at a point in time, the parameter(s) of the process can change over time, resulting in ambiguity as well as uncertainty (Einhorn and Hogarth, 1985a, p. 455).

The theory of rational expectations has come under attack from within the economics profession exactly because of its neglect of the process by which agents discover the parameters and the structure of the economy (DeCanio, 1979; Friedman, 1979). As is pointed out by Blume, Bray, and Easley (1982), the literature on learning and convergence to rational expectations can be divided into roughly two groups. The first of these assumes that agents possess correct information on the structure of the economy, and only need somehow to estimate the coefficients. As is indicated by Blume, Bray, and Easley, this approach "embodies fully rational learning, but is extraordinarily demanding in terms of the information, understanding, and calculating ability of agents" (1982, p. 314). In a sense this method does not add much to the simple (rhetoric) thought experiment that is usually offered in defence of the existence and uniqueness of rational expectations equilibria. This thought experiment usually proceeds along the following lines: (1) any equilibrium in which potential gains from trade are left unexploited cannot be a "true" equilibrium; (2) in a rational expectations equilibrium there are no unexploited gains from trade; (3) ergo, from (1) and (2), the only true equilibrium must be a rational expectations equilibrium. Apart from the purely logical error this kind of reasoning contains, another criticism against it is that "the situation seems here to be that before we can explain why people commit mistakes, we must first explain why they should ever be right" (Hayek, 1937, p. 34). In other words, without an explicit theory of expectation formation and adjustment, this thought experiment cannot be very convincing. Blume, Bray, and Easley also show that in models of this category, convergence to rational expectations follows directly from the asymptotic properties of Bayesian estimators (1982, pp. 314–315).

The second, more interesting group assumes that agents do not possess the correct model, but instead learn on the basis of a misspecified representation of the economy. The main examples are Blume and Easley (1982), Bray (1982), and DeCanio (1979). The main drawback from a theoretical point of view is that in this approach the learning process itself is not rational in that agents do not use statistical procedures to test whether their personal models of the economic process are correct (Blume et al., 1982, p. 314).

As Blume, Bray and Easley (1982, pp. 315–316) point out, there are two different approaches to expectations formation within the second group. In the first approach, agents are seen "as if" they use a deterministic forecasting rule based on initial estimates of the parameters. At the same time they run ordinary least squares regressions of the same form as the forecasting rule. When the parameters of this regression have reached the probability limit then these new parameters are instead used in the revised (deterministically treated) forecasting rule. This process of periodic revision converges to a unique rational expectations equilibrium under certain conditions (Bray, 1982, p. 325). The problem with this approach is that it requires an infinitely long period of time before such convergence is completed — which is rather like saying that biases persist, as the psychologists would say.

In the second approach, exemplified by Blume and Easley (1982), agents use a collection of models, one of which being the correct rational one (in equilibrium). The models are weighted using a prior distribution that is updated each time new observations become available. The weight of any model that performs better (worse) than the average model is increased (decreased). Blume and Easley describe this learning process as "a boundedly rational version of Bayesian learning" since agents do not take into account the fact that their (and other agents') learning affects the outcome of the model (1982, p. 341). In other words, what is the "rational" model depends itself upon all the different models that the individuals use. Blume and Easley show that rational expectations equilibria are locally stable but that there exist nonrational expectations equilibria that are also locally stable: "[t]he learning process may get stuck at an incorrect model because all of the admissible models are incorrect away from the [rational expectations equilibrium]" (1982, p. 350).

Psychologists would find the Blume-Easley view of people as if being in several weighted states of mind a very curious way of modeling "normal" thought processes. Blume and Easley themselves as economists do not seem to be trying to learn about convergence processes by using weighted insights from, say, Marxian and Post Keynesian, as well as neoclassical, theories. Even when they mention the behavioralist notion of bounded rationality they do so apologetically. An alternative approach would be to keep Blume and Easley's notion of multiple models, but to assume decision makers to be committed to only one model at a time — rather like scientists and economists tend to be. This is essentially what Loasby (1986) argues, integrating Lakatos' theory of the growth of scientific knowledge (as discussed in section 3 below), with the "man-the-scientist" psychology of Kelly (1955) (discussed by Bausor in section 3 of chapter 2 and by Runde in section 7 of chapter 7). Loasby also makes the very important observation that *the* correct rational model is not a well defined concept: "[t]hese models cannot be derived from the phenomena by some natural principle of selection and adaptation, since an integrated universe embodies no such principles: *they are human inventions*" (1986, p. 45; emphasis added). The point is, of course, that subjective elements must be part of any credible economic theory of choice under uncertainty and learning. From an economic point of view the use of choice heuristics could be justified in a subjective manner: individuals use them because they *perceive* the costs of using more sophisticated learning processes as prohibitive. The existence of self-fulfilling equilibria (see, for example, Azariadis, 1981) may well imply that there is no (or insufficiently clear) feedback information available to signal to the agents using these rules that their perceptions are "incorrect."

It would seem to me that the research of psychologists and economists both point in the same direction in this case: namely, that more research is needed to find out how people learn in an uncertain environment. In this respect economists might find it useful to follow the lead of psychologists and find out which different heuristics different people actually use. The predictive performance of neoclassical theories might then be improved by the incorporation of empirically prevalent decision rules and principles. For example, one could segment the population of agents approximately according to the particular decision rules that they adhere to, rather than deriving aggregate predictions on the basis of the "representative" agent. If this caused the models to be more complex without at the same time increasing their predictive power, then of course neoclassical economists would rapidly reach for Occam's Razor.

3. Neoclassical Economics and the Psychological Evidence

In the previous section I have explored the potential interface between some of the work by psychologists and neoclassical economists on expectations and uncertainty. In this section I discuss different ways in which economists (of the neoclassical persuasion) could possibly react to the psychological evidence. The following categories can be distinguished:

A. The psychological evidence is essentially correct:
  1. Economics of uncertainty must be rebuilt on explicit behaviorist foundations (for example, Thaler, 1980);
  2. Economics of uncertainty need not be revised because of an *as if* type argument (see my earlier remarks about the use of Occam's Razor);
  3. Economics of uncertainty can be modified in a relatively easy fashion to incorporate the findings (for example, Machina, 1982; Loomes and Sugden, 1982).
B. The psychological evidence is essentially incorrect or inconclusive.

It is my guess that most neoclassical economists would probably refer to either (A2) or (B) and carry on.

Position (B) is not as antiintellectualistic as it seems at first sight. Economists have traditionally expressed great scepticism with respect to psychological findings. This is mainly because of the nature of the experimental method that is used almost exclusively in the psychological literature that I consulted. (Friedman, 1953, is of course the other main reason.) As John Cross points out, payoffs to human subjects in laboratory experiments are typically quite small. But this is exactly when deviations from rationality are not very costly, so that laboratory experiments are bound to find these deviations quite frequently (Cross, 1983, pp. 185–186). Although experimental methods have now entered the economics literature (Smith, 1982; Hoffman and Spitzer, 1985; and the discussion by Lewis in section 6 of chapter 13), many economists feel that the "economics of experiments' needs to be settled before we can believe the "experimental economics." Until that is achieved, experiments using real people and real payoffs, such as the ones performed by Binswanger (1981), will have far greater impact. Even better would be to ensure that the subjects used in the experiments are *unaware* of the fact that they are subjects. Ethical considerations may make such experiments impractical, however.

An alternative, more fundamental way to analyze the manner in which some economists have already reacted to some of the psychological findings is by means of Lakatos' (1970) methodology of scientific research programs (MSRP).[4] Although MSRP is by now well known to many economists (and presumably psychologists), it is nevertheless useful to outline briefly its main features. According to Lakatos, a research program is made up of two primary subgroups of hypotheses. The first of these is the *hard core* which is considered irrefutable and is protected from any kind of empirical or logical challenge. The hard core is protected from *modus tollens* refutations by what is called the *negative heuristic* of the research program.

The hard core is surrounded by a *protective belt* of auxiliary hypotheses which are continually confronted with observational statements and refuted or altered in accordance with any anomalies that may be identified. The *positive heuristic* of the program provides suggestions as to how the protective belt hypotheses should be modified in such a way as to produce the maximum amount of support for the hard core propositions. Research programs as a whole are evaluated in terms of their progressiveness relative to competing programs. A theoretically progressive *problem shift* occurs when the protective belt is augmented in such a way as to yield additional predictions. This implies that *content increasing* auxiliary hypotheses have been added to the protective belt. When some of the excess empirical content is corroborated, then a research program is called *empirically progressive*. In general terms, a program is progressive if it explains novel facts. On the other hand, it is *degenerative* if the hard core is continually "shored up" with protective belt amendments that serve only to reduce the number of predictions and hence the empirical content of the theory. As a rational reconstruction of the history of science, the Lakatosian MSRP predicts that degenerate research programs will tend to be replaced by progressive programs, although it is recognized that any one program may display phases of degeneracy within a globally progressive trend. It may be rational, therefore, for scientists to adhere doggedly to a degenerate program, especially if its only rival is an infant (albeit progressive) program with as yet minimal empirical content. Although it is by no means clear that Lakatos himself considered MSRP to be applicable to economics or psychology (see, for example, Lakatos, 1970, p. 176, footnote 1), I will use this framework below to examine how and to what extent economists have reacted to the psychological findings discussed in section 2 above.

According to Boland (1981), the neoclassical maximization hypothesis (NMH), of which maximization of (subjective) expected utility is only one special case, is nontestable (neither verifiable nor falsifiable) but not a tautology (it is *conceivably* false). He prefers to call it metaphysical. Elsewhere (Heijdra and Lowenberg, 1986b), I have argued that the NMH can be seen as the hard core of *the* neoclassical research program: that is, while there is a variety of styles of economics built around the NMH, it is this axiom which distinguishes all of them from "non-neoclassical" approaches such as behavioral theory. Without embracing the Lakatosian MSRP, Boland argues that criticizing the NMH is futile. He distinguishes between two main levels of criticism: (1) logical — can NMH be true? and (2) empirical — is NMH true? The first of these, as exemplified by Shackle (1972), argues that maximization is impossible because agents cannot possibly acquire all relevant knowledge. Boland counters this criticism by arguing that maximization does not require *true* knowledge — as long as the agent perceives his knowledge to be correct, maximization is possible. The second level of criticism that Boland discusses is exemplified by Simon (1979) and Leibenstein (1979). They argue that NMH is falsified by empirical evidence. Boland argues that this criticism must also fail because NMH is an "all and some" statement like: "For all decision makers there is something they maximize" (1981, p. 1034).

If one accepts this interpretation of the NMH as the hard core of neoclassical economics, then the psychological evidence discussed above is not at all inconsistent with the neoclassical approach. In effect, Kahneman and Tversky's prospect theory is under this interpretation merely an elaborate argument for a different maximization program. Instead of maximizing (subjective) expected utility, agents maximize the sum of decision weighted values of different prospects. Hence we can say that the role of the psychological evidence, if it is used by neoclassical economists at all, is as a means of falsifying or corroborating rival theories of *what* and *how* subjects maximize, but *not whether* they maximize. The future will tell if theories based on prospect theory outperform the ones based on (subjective) expected utility theory. Potential criteria include predictive ability, simplicity, and generality. Since both kinds of theories share the same hard core, this fight will have to be fought out in the protective belt. With Boland's interpretation there is thus no question of the hard core ever being under attack from psychologists. Indeed, if we interpret the NMH in the way Boland suggests, then the question of progressiveness or degeneracy of the neoclassical research program cannot be determined on the basis of economists' reactions to the psychological findings at all: if the hard core is not under attack, then no core protecting belt adjustments are made either. As I understand them, the psychological findings may turn out to be "manna from heaven." Something similar was expressed recently by the ultraneoclassical Robert Solow, with respect to sociological findings and their relevance to the labor market:

> Far from advocating that we all practice sociology, I am pleasantly impressed at how much mileage you can get from the methods of conventional economic analysis if only you are willing to broaden the assumptions a little (1980, p. 3).

Other famous examples of the potential fruitfulness of entertaining new assumptions are, of course, Becker (1976) and Akerlof (1984). The former, however, has strongly argued against opening up the black box of tastes (Stigler and Becker, 1977). I interpret Stigler and Becker as saying that economists should do their utmost to explain economic phenomena by shifting constraints, rather than appealing to differences in agents' preferences. This does *not* mean that economists should *never* use psychological variables in their explanations. As Hirshleifer puts it, "ultimately, good economics will also have to be good anthropology and sociology and political science and psychology" (1985, p. 53). In the next section I present a selective survey of some recent economic theories that have tried seriously to address some of the issues raised by the psychologists.

4. Recent Economics of Uncertainty

It is neither necessary nor possible to review the neoclassical literature on choice under uncertainty here. Excellent and exhaustive surveys are available, such as Lippman and McCall (1981), Hirshleifer and Riley (1979), and Radner (1982). These surveys reveal an extremely wide range of application of probabilistic methods to economic phenomena. Many of the applications make use of the (subjective) expected utility model, as surveyed by Schoemaker (1982), and it is exactly this model which seems to have attracted the harshest criticism from the psychologists discussed above. It is therefore of great importance to determine if and how the economics profession has (so far) reacted to the attacks on this popular theory of decision making under uncertainty. These can be divided into roughly three groups that: (1) change the maximand (the utility function); (2) change the constraint set (transaction costs); and (3) introduce rule-of-thumb behavior.

In a number of recent pathbreaking articles, Machina (1982, 1983a) has investigated whether expected utility analysis is possible without the independence axiom (implying linearity in the probabilities), which he admits to be refuted convincingly by the empirical data. Among the refutations of the independence axiom are the Allais paradox, the oversensitivity to changes in small probabilities, and the certainty effect that have all been mentioned above by either myself or other contributors (Machina, 1983a, p. 264). He shows that the validity of expected utility analysis does *not* depend on the validity of the independence axiom, but rather on the smoothness of preferences (Machina, 1982, p. 279). Rather than having the preference functional linear in the probabilities, Machina assumes that it is differentiable with respect to the cumulative distribution function (1983, p. 268). Using this generalized expected utility analysis and a simple refutable assumption about the shape of the preference functional he is able to explain a large number of phenomena that were previously thought to be unrelated (1982, p. 279). Among these are the Allais paradox and the Markowitz (1952) effect according to which utility functions shift when wealth changes. He therefore concludes that there is no need to discard theories based on expected utility maximization:

> . . . while the independence axiom, and hence the expected utility hypothesis may not be empirically valid, the implications and predictions of theoretical studies which use expected utility analysis typically will be valid, provided preferences are smooth (Machina, 1982, p. 279).

This is because for small enough changes in the probabilities the preference functional is *locally* linear in the probabilities so that agents can be seen as local expected utility maximizers (1982, pp. 294–295).

Machina thus chooses to react to the psychological evidence in a manner consistent with Boland's interpretation of the NMH. He uses the evidence in a positive fashion and generalizes the theory of expected utility maximization in a prediction-increasing and falsifiable way. John Cross criticizes Machina's approach (incorrectly, in my view) as follows:

> The independence axiom proved to be one aspect of modern utility theory that was subject to direct testing. Having failed that test, it is to be replaced by a more elaborate characterization of the form of the (essentially untestable) utility function itself (Cross, 1983, p. 62).

This criticism clearly misses the mark. Cross seems to accuse Machina of advocating a degenerative problem shift, yet it is clear that the opposite is true: Machina's theory can predict all that expected utility theory can predict *plus* some that the latter cannot predict. In fact, Cross seems to fall victim to the Friedman (1953) trap in the sense that he is arguing about the "realism of the assumptions," whereas it is well known that such an argument fails because of a methodological "second best" problem: all assumptions are unrealistic so that the "first best" model is not achievable.

Sugden (1986) reviews the group of literature that reacts to the psychological findings by arguing about the shape of the utility function. This includes regret theory (Loomes and Sugden, 1982; Bell, 1982) and disappointment theory (Bell, 1985; Loomes and Sugden, 1986). Regret "is a route by which the utility you derive from a particular consequence of one action may be influenced by a consequence of a *different* action" (Sugden, 1986, p. 16). Disappointment, on the other hand, is defined as the feeling one experiences "when 'what is' compares unfavourably with 'what might have been' " (p. 16). The future will tell which one of these taste-changing theories proves most useful. My guess is that Machina's analysis will prevail in view of its generality and the small amount of "disruption" it causes to the neoclassical research programme.

This changing of preference functions is clearly not the only strategy one can adopt in reaction to the psychological evidence. Indeed, as already seen above, Stigler and Becker (1977) would refrain from "arguing about tastes" and instead search in the realm of the constraint set for possible explanations. This avenue has recently been followed by De Meza and Dickinson (1984) with respect to Kahneman and Tversky's prospect theory. They argue that an expected utility model with transaction costs (in the form of liquidation costs for durable assets) can account for many (but not all) of the empirical results reported by Kahneman and Tversky in support of prospect theory (1984, p. 223). Since De Meza and Dickinson really only present an example of how transaction costs could "help out" expected utility theory, while Machina's theory is perfectly general, the latter seems preferable to the former. Both, however, present viable reactions to the Kahneman-Tversky results.

A third manner in which economists have reacted to the psychological findings relates to the apparent existence of rule-governed behavior. As was discussed in section 2 above, psychologists argue that subjects in laboratory experiments seem to rely on a limited number of simple heuristics (rules of thumb) that serve to reduce the complexity of the task at hand. Although Baumol and Quandt argued some two decades ago that ". . . rules of thumb are among the most efficient pieces of equipment of optimal decision-making" (1964, p. 23), these information cost-saving devices have been regarded with great suspicion by neoclassical theorists. This was presumably a result of the concurrent development of the rational expectations approach (Muth, 1961) and the search approach (Stigler, 1961), both of which attempt to extend the optimality criterion to situations of risk. In the absence of information costs and with perfectly known probability distributions it is indeed hard to defend the optimality of rule-of-thumb behavior. When information costs exist, or when learning occurs, then rule-of-thumb behavior is more acceptable. Indeed, as I pointed out in section 2, the literature on the stability of rational expectations equilibria is saying exactly that. Recently, Hey has argued that ". . . the Economics of Uncertainty must abandon its pre-occupation with optimal rules of behavior, and concentrate instead on reasonable rules of thumb" (1983b, p. 139). Akerlof and Yellen (1985b) have shown, for example, that some very interesting macroeconomic results can be derived in a model with some agents using rules of thumb that are near-rational (in the sense that the opportunity cost of using the rule is small). Again, if one is willing to posit information costs, then the rule of thumb can be modeled as a rational device. By far the strongest defense for the use of rules of thumb in economic models in my view is the fact that most situations in the real world are not related to risk but rather to nonreplicable uncertainty or even ignorance. Lucas (1981, p. 224) correctly points out that "[i]n cases of uncertainty, economic reasoning will be of no value."[5] He is incorrect, however, in building models that ignore uncertainty (as distinct from risk) altogether. The psychologists have shown us that subjects use rules of thumb (*even in situations of risk*). The least that economists can do is include rules of thumb in situations of uncertainty. I maintain that we can do this *and* retain the neoclassical research programme.

5. Concluding Remarks

Selten summarizes his reactions to the recent psychological evidence as follows: "The experimental evidence on human behavior shows what is wrong with present day economic theory, but it does not yet show how to improve on it" (1983, p. 410). My impressions differ in many respects. I summarize them in point form:

1.   The psychological evidence is almost invariably based on laboratory experiments. Economists have severe reservations with respect to this kind of evidence, and therefore pay too little attention to the psychological findings. A recommendation to psychologists desiring to influence economists would be to study ordinary people in everyday situations of uncertainty.
2.   The psychological evidence does not so much show what is wrong with current economics; rather it suggests alternative assumptions that could be entertained within the confines of the neoclassical research program. For example, the psychologists argue strongly in favor of simple heuristic rules. Especially in the realm of uncertainty these rules of thumb show great promise for adventurous economic theorists.

Jungermann (1983) is, in my view, quite right when he argues that the difference between economists and psychologists really lies in the fact that the former are optimistic (biases are in the research; people are rational — in the sense of not taking systematically wrong decisions — if you take all costs into account), whereas the latter are pessimistic (biases are in people). Nevertheless, I am optimistic enough to predict that some of the findings of the psychologists will turn out to be quite useful to economists.

Notes

1. The reason for the quotation marks will become evident in section 3, where I briefly examine the experimental methods that psychologists of uncertainty tend to use. Economists have traditionally treated experimental data with great suspicion, which is one of the reasons why psychological research has had virtually no impact on mainstream economic theory.

2. Sahlin (1983) refers to literature that extends the Bayesian decision theory to take account of higher order probabilities. He makes the astute observation that ". . . in the realm of second order estimates we are dealing with 'unverifiable' events . . . , i.e. we don''t know, and will never know, which first order estimate is the 'true' one" (1983, p. 97). Even this Bayesian theory is ad hoc in its treatment of the infinite regress problem caused by third, fourth and higher order probabilities (1983, p. 96).

3. There are some econometric queries relating to their empirical work. First, in fitting their model to individual subjects they find that 5 out of the 32 subjects behave in a manner inconsistent with the theory. In the final preferred results these 5 "recalcitrant" subjects have been omitted which would seem to suggest that the estimation is somewhat "cooked" in favor of acceptance of the model (see Einhorn and Hogarth, 1985a, p. 444, and their table 3, p. 446). Second, although they explicitly acknowledge the dependence of the parameters b and t on individual and situational factors, they fail to model this dependence for example by using a varying parameter model (see Maddala, 1977, chapter 17). Therefore it is impossible to judge how well the model fits the data overall. Inspection of their table 3 (p. 446) furthermore reveals that the parameters b and t do vary enormously across individuals, so that the results reported in their table 1 (p. 444) that ignore these differences are not very revealing.

4. This section relies heavily upon Heijdra and Lowenberg (1986a). The MSRP has been applied to psychology and its relation to economics by Coats (1976) and Simon (1976), among others.

5. See, for example, Green (1977) and Grossman and Stiglitz (1980) for a discussion of existence problems in models with perfect competition and costly information. The reason for the nonexistence of a competitive equilibrium is quite simple. By definition, in a competitive equilibrium, arbitrage opportunities are exhausted. This implies that arbitrageurs buy costly information without getting a return; clearly not an equilibrium situation. A major defect of the rational expectations concept is the multiplicity problem. This and other problems are discussed in Azariadis (1981) and Frydman and Phelps (1983). A survey and further discussion of these matters can be found in Lowenberg and Heijdra (1985).

6 PROSPECTS FOR MATHEMATICAL PSYCHOLOGICAL ECONOMICS

John D. Hey

1. Introduction

Economists and psychologists share an ultimate aim: to predict human behavior. Being economists and psychologists — rather than mathematicians, chartists, computer scientists, or whatever — they also share a penultimate aim: to explain human behavior. Both aims imply a belief that there is *something* systematic about human behavior. This, in turn, implies that there must be *some* role for mathematics in modeling that behavior. The only question that remains, therefore, is what role?

It is here that fundamental differences and disagreements are revealed, both within each of the two disciplines and between them. To explain these disagreements, it is instructive to begin by examining one striking difference that clearly separates the two disciplines. This revolves around the treatment of *randomness*. One needs only to browse through the respective specialist journals to note the following striking fact: in psychology it is the *model-builder* who incorporates randomness into the model of human behavior; in economics, however, it is *not* the theorist but rather the applied *econometrician* who puts in the randomness.

Partly this reflects the rather unfortunate trend within economics to separate theory and practice, and, probably equally unfortunately, the prevailing view in psychology that it is almost totally an empirical discipline. But it mainly stems from fundamental methodological differences between the two disciplines on the modeling of human behavior. In a nutshell: the economist regards behavior as deterministic, while the psychologist regards behavior as stochastic. Thus, in economics, it is left to the econometrician to introduce randomness — thereby taking into account the rather embarrassing fact that there appears to be randomness in real-life data. This seems to leave open the question: is the randomness in the data due to randomness in behavior, or has it come from somewhere else?

2. The Underlying Methodology of Economics

Let us delve a little deeper. When an economic theorist wants to analyze some particular aspect of human behavior, the theorist will set up a stylized model of that behavior, abstracting from features that the theorist considers inessential, and concentrating on those features the theorist considers crucial. This should — if the theorist is skilled in setting up models — lead to a well-defined problem with (more importantly) a well-defined solution. This solution (apart from those in a relatively small set of models involving strategic behavior) will have one remarkable property: it will be deterministic. The theorist will then perform comparative static (or "comparative dynamic") exercises on the solution, thereby yielding predictions which are then handed over to the applied econometrician (who, in a few instances, may actually be the same person) for confrontation with data.

Let us be more specific about precisely what it is that is handed over. It is: a list of variables (maybe just one) to explain; a list of explanatory variables; a specification of which variables are functions of which others; and usually a statement of the theoretical sign of the various partial derivatives of these functions. The applied econometrician presumably has some data on the relevant variables. (Presumably also, there are more observations than variables) The task is now to confront the theory with the data (and vice versa).

Unfortunately, this cannot be done immediately, since there is a gap between the theory and the data. First the applied econometrician must specify the *functional forms* of the relationships between the various variables; very rarely is this done in the theory. In principle, one could always specify functional forms which completely closed the gap between theory and data — in the sense that appropriate parameter values could be chosen so that the theory (with specified functional forms) fitted the data exactly.[1]

In practice, this is never done (by economists). Instead, simple functional forms (often linear or log-linear) are used, and the gap between theory and data closed by the incorporation of a *residual term* in the various relationships.

Of course, economists recognize that this reconciliation of theory and data is tautologically trivial if no constraints are put on the residual terms. So some structure is assumed for them: usually they are normally distributed "noise" (that is, independent, constant variance random variables). At the end of the day, therefore, the economic relationships that are empirically investigated by economists have randomness in them. But the randomness is put there by the applied econometrician, not the theorist.

What is the justification (other than that discussed above, which is far from satisfying) of this random term? Where does it come from? The theorist will respond by pointing out quite correctly that all the predictions of the theory were qualified with the words *ceteris paribius*; whereas real-life data were generated in a world where *ceteris* was manifestly not *paribus*. Hence the need for the random residual term. Moreover, since the things that are not *paribus* in the real world are multitudinous and diverse, one can safely rely on the Central Limit theorem to guarantee that the residuals (which catch all these multitudinous factors) will be normally distributed noise. Hence etc., as they say.

Two questions naturally arise. How does the theorist know all this? What precisely is the theorist saying about human behavior?

There are basically two attitudes that can be taken in trying to answer these questions. Recall the procedure adopted by the economist in generating the predictions of the theory: first, a stylized model of the problem facing the human decision-maker was set up; then it was solved; then the solution was manipulated to yield the comparative static (or dynamic) predictions. Now note that in the real world, wherein the real-life data were generated, the actual human decision-makers did not operate within the stylized model. Rather, they operated within a more complicated model — which, for the sake of argument, can be assumed to contain the stylized model as a special case.[2] So behavior in the real world will be different from that in the stylized model. The economic theorist (or the applied econometrician) says that the difference will be normally distributed noise. But why?

As noted above, two attitudes could be taken. The first builds on the implicit premise that actual human decision-makers are more sophisticated than the economic theorists that model them — in that they (the actual humans) actually set up and solve the *real* decision-problem that they face. They solve it deterministically,[3] which implies that their actual decisions are deterministic functions of the myriads (say N, which is a very large number) of variables which are relevant to the real-life problem. However, the economist, being a mere plodder by comparison, displaying severely limited imagination and mathematical incompetence, has solved the problem for just a few (say n, which is a *very* small number) of the relevant variables. So when the economist comes to investigate the relationship(s) built on just n variables, by definition the remaining $(N-n)$ relevant variables are necessarily excluded. At this point there must be a leap of faith by the economist: to argue that the n included variables explain a very large part of the variables(s) to be explained, and that the omission of the residual $(N-n)$ simply leads to an unimportant bit of noise — normally distributed, of course — in the equation(s). How is this known?

Let us leave this question hanging in mid-air, while the alternative is considered. This builds on the premise that human decision-makers follow the same procedure as the economic theorist does when modeling their behavior: that is, that they first set up a stylized model of the real problem facing them; that they then solve (deterministically, of course) this stylized model; and that they then "adjust" the solution in some way to take account of the fact that the real world and the stylized model differ. Indeed, one might even argue that this adjustment is necessarily white noise — maybe even normally distributed white noise — because (1) the humans have no *logical*, or computationally feasible, way of calculating an optimal adjustment, and (2) there are a large number of other factors ($N-n$ to be precise) which "ought" to be taken into account.

This alternative seems to be far more satisfactory; but it also leaves a number of questions hanging in mid-air: how do we know that human decision-makers take decisions in this way? If they do, why do they do it? How do we know that the stylized model chosen by the human beings is the same as that chosen by the economic theorist? And, how do we know how they adjust their solution to their stylized model — to take into account the fact that the model and the real world differ — in the way described above?

Economics does not have an answer to these questions; indeed, it *cannot* have an answer. Ultimately it must be an act of faith.

3. Experiments and Evidence

But faith is built on evidence, and it is here that the tensions in economics are revealed most clearly. As a crude summary, it is fair to say the following: at a sufficiently aggregate level the comparative static (or dynamic) predictions of much of economic theory seem to fit the facts quite well; however, at an individual level (particularly using experimental data) there seem to be systematic violations of the fundamental assumptions underlying most of the economic theory.

This brings us back to the underlying methodology of economics, and back to the point where economists and psychologists most obviously differ: interestingly, though, it does not really begin to address the issues discussed above, nor to offer a solution.

The fundamental assumption underlying 95% (or more) of (published) economic theory is that human decision-makers, within stylized models, are expected utility maximizers. Moreover, within the stylized model, the "rules of the game" are fully specified. Thus the decision-maker has a well-defined objective function, well-specified constraints, and well-defined probability distributions (albeit subjective) over any uncertain parameters. They are also perfectly capable of solving the implied constrained maximization problem. This inevitably means that the solution is a well-defined deterministic function of the parameters of the problem (including those of the relevant probability distributions). This is so even in a dynamic model.[4]

The reasons for the popularity of expected utility theory in economics are not hard to find. First, it provides a simple, very general approach to modeling behavior. It therefore provides a unified approach, which, for example, psychology manifestly lacks. Second, as has been noted above, it provides predictions which, at an aggregate level, perform reasonably well, at least in comparative static terms.

Unfortunately, as earlier chapters in this book have already noted, the theory does not appear to perform particularly well at an individual level — especially when using experimental data. There is now a large number of studies which show that subjects in experimental trials consistently exhibit behavior that is inconsistent with expected utility theory (for useful surveys, see Machina, 1983b, and Schoemaker, 1982). Now it may well be the case that subjects behave differently in experiments — even in well-structured experiments — from how they would in real life (for example, their objective may be to "beat the experimenter," or complete the experiment as quickly as possible, or whatever), but this evidence does raise the possibility that even in well-defined problems, human decision-makers do not behave in the way that economic theorists assume they do. It may be the case (as mentioned above) that the subjects are playing different games from that specified by the experimenter; it could be that they are acting "rationally," but in a different sense from that perceived by the economic theorist; it could be that they find the decision problem too difficult to solve; or it may be that they simply do not understand the experiment.

Whatever the reason, it might appear important the the economist tries to discover the reasons for the departure of actual behavior from "optimal" behavior even in apparently simple, well-specified problems. Indeed, over the past five years or so considerable efforts have been expended to try to specify more general approaches than expected utility theory which explain the experimental evidence yet, at the same time, have some usefulness in that they are *testable*. Among the more successful efforts are those by Kahneman and Tversky (1979), Loomes and Sugden (1982) and Machina (1982). Machina's theory, "expected utility without the independence axiom," is of particular importance, as it not only explains a large part of the experimental evidence but is also testable and, most interestingly, implies predictions (of aggregate economic behavior) which are in general identical — in comparative static or dynamic terms — to the predictions of theories based on ordinary expected utility. Therefore, many economists can breathe a sigh of relief.

On one level at least: all these studies relate to fairly simple experiments which attempt to verify, or otherwise, either the axioms or simple implications of expected utility theory or one of the new theories. As noted above, the new theories seem able to explain a large part of such experimental evidence (although testing is still ongoing). But there is also a set of experiments (a number of which have been carried out by the author of this chapter) which attempt to test the implications of expected utility theory in the kind of stylized models that economic theorists adopt when making predictions. One set of such experiments relate to simple search models (see Hey, 1982); another set relates to dynamic consumption models (see Hey and Dardanoni, 1987). It will be found instructive to examine the latter.

A very famous paper by Hall (1978) set up a stylized model of a dynamic consumption problem with uncertain income. As is typical in economic theory, this was very much a "stripped-down" model of human behavior: as the focus of interest was on the amounts consumed (and saved) out of income each period (month, quarter, year, or whatever), and on the influence of the uncertain income on that consumption, a stylized model was set up by Hall portraying a sequence of discrete periods (with a random end-point) in each of which the decision-maker received an income (which was, ex ante, random) and in each of which the decision-maker had to decide how much to consume and how much to save. Consumption yielded utility; saving yielded interest.

The decision-maker was assumed to be an expected utility maximizer. This enabled Hall to employ standard dynamic programming techniques to derive the optimal consumption strategy. One of the implications of that strategy is that consumption would follow a random-walk with trend. When tested using aggregate data this prediction performs remarkably well.[5]

This fact, combined with the earlier-expressed fact that the foundation stone of the prediction (namely, expected utility theory) did not appear to be supported by experimental evidence on individual behavior, tempted us to test experimentally the Hall model directly. To do this we set up an experimental problem with exactly the same structure as the Hall model, and with a payment scheme directly related to the analogue of expected utility in the Hall model. The results are described in detail in Hey (1986) and Hey and Dardanoni (1987), but they can be briefly summarized here.

In terms of the *absolute* levels of the decisions taken by the subjects, the decisions were quite clearly *not* taken optimally (in expected utility theory's sense of the word) by the majority of the subjects. Nevertheless, and this is the interesting thing, the *comparative static implications* of the actual behavior seemed to agree with the comparative static implications of expected utility theory. For example, expected utility theory predicts that if expected income rises, then the amount consumed increases. In our experiments, we found that those subjects for whom income was high "consumed" more than those subjects for whom average income was low.

This suggests a reconciliation of the aggregate empirical tests and the individual experimental tests: individuals do not behave optimally, but the comparative static implications of their actual behavior tend to agree with the comparative static implications of optimality theory (though there is still a lot of noise floating around the actual behavior). This confirmed a similar result that we had found in our search experiments.

It could be pointed out that comparative static tests of the predictions of economic theory are fairly weak tests, and that the same predictions could be generated by any number of alternative theories. Indeed this seems to be why our consumption experiments yielded comparative static predictions close to those of optimality theory. For example, one simple rule of thumb used by some of the subjects in our experiments was to consume a particular fraction of the wealth they held at the beginning of the period. For subjects who followed such a rule it seemed to be the case that the fraction they employed was related positively to the mean of the income distribution, and negatively to the discount factor, the rate of return, and the standard deviation of the income distribution. Thus for such subjects the comparative static predictions of optimality theory would hold.

A rather more surprising example can be found from our search experiments. One of the rules of thumb that subjects appeared to be using was one based on the strategy of keeping searching while it was paying off, but quitting when the payoff was negative. (More specifically, the "modified one-bounce rule," as we termed it, said: keep on searching while the gain from searching exceeds the search cost; otherwise quit. For details, see Hey, 1982.) This is a rather strange rule in that it imbues the order of a random sequence of observations with some significance. Nevertheless, this rule has three clear comparative static predictions: search increases as the distribution (from which the individual is searching) shifts rightward; as the distribution gets riskier (in the Rothschild and Stiglitz sense); and as the search cost falls. These predictions are identical with those of the optimality model.

There are two ways one could respond to these findings. First, one could ask the question, for each comparative static prediction: what is the minimum set of assumptions that one needs to generate this prediction? Often one will find this set much smaller than the set required for full rationality in the usual economic sense. Alternatively, one could ask: what are the minimal requirements for "reasonable" (as distinct from unreasonable) behavior? and then explore the implications — in terms of comparative static predictions — of these minimal requirements. In some cases the answers to these two questions may be the same. In essence they are both exploring the robustness of comparative static predictions.

This seems a fruitful route to follow. Moreover, it continues the tradition within economics of axiomatizing, and theorizing about, behavior. Nevertheless, it will leave unsatisfied those who want to know precisely which rules are governing human behavior, and why.

It is in this area that economics, mathematics, and psychology can usefully work together. Psychology has some useful mathematical models of behavior in any number of special cases; economics has a general mathematical model. The problem will be to get the two to work together. Of prime importance is to incorporate into economics the psychological notion of randomness of human behavior. This will not be easy: for reasons already explained, economics views decisions as deterministic. This point is emphasized by the new theories of decision-making under uncertainty that have been constructed over the past five years: like their predecessor, expected utility theory, they are deterministic.

4. Randomness, Complexity, and Choice

Let us explore how economics might introduce randomness into its basic model of human decision-making. The simplest way would appear to be the adoption of the assumption that tastes are random. Economists tend to fight shy of this — mainly for the reason that it could imply intransitive behavior. ("Now I prefer A to B to C; a second ago I preferred B to C to A; in a second I will prefer C to A to B.") A more palliative way would appear to be the adoption of the assumption that not all human beings are equally good decision-makers: some are better than others; some are perfect, some are lousy.[6]

To bolster this line of argument, one can simply argue that some of the decision problems that human beings face are *complex* decisions — certainly those in the consumption and search experiments that we performed were complex problems. To an economic theorist, skilled in setting up dynamic models, and solving them in *general* (that is, comparative static) *terms*, the problems are reasonably complex — but ultimately solvable if they have been set up appropriately (and definitely solvable if a paper based on that model has been accepted for publication in an academic economic journal!). But, even to the theorist, and especially so to the "man in the street," the actual computation of the *specific* solution to a specific problem may be very difficult, even insoluble. Indeed, the motivation for our carrying out the search experiments in the first place was the realization that although it was possible to write down the mathematics of the solution to a particular search problem, it was impossible — even on our mainframe computer — to calculate numerically the actual solution. In our consumption experiments, we could compute the optimal strategy, but this still required a considerable input of programming and computing time.

Our belief is that the vast majority of human beings are simply incapable of carrying out the complex calculations necessary to compute the optimal solution. True, a minority could have reproduced *our* computations in the consumption experiments, but this would have required a sizeable investment in programming and computation. (In any case they did not choose to do this.)

The easiest way for economists to take this on board is simply to recognize that "it hurts to think," or, in economic jargon, that there is a cost to decision making. To some economists this is a satisfying way of accounting for the awkward fact that actual human behavior does not appear to be optimal: one could argue that when one takes into account the costs of decision-making, actual decisions are indeed optimal. That is, it is optimal to use a rule of thumb because the costs of working out the optimal strategy would exceed the benefits of so doing (cf. Baumol and Quandt, 1964, and the discussion by Heijdra in section 4 of chapter 5).

Although superficially attractive, this line of argument begs the question altogether: how can the decision-maker know that the costs of working out the optimal strategy exceed the benefits? In some instances it will be obvious: for example, when the maximum possible benefit of behaving optimally is miniscule compared to the costs of thinking for even one second about the problem. (This would be the case where someone could earn $36 an hour, was searching for low prices of a particular make of television, and had already found a perfect example selling at the remarkably low price of one cent!) But most instances are not so clearcut.

In such cases, it is not obvious that there can be an optimal decision. For before deciding whether to act optimally or not, the decision-maker must first decide whether it is optimal to calculate whether it is better to decide optimally or not; but before deciding this, the decision-maker must first decide whether it is optimal to calculate whether it is optimal to calculate whether it is better to decide optimally or not; and so on. It is an infinite regress with no obvious end-point (cf. Winter, 1964, and the discussion in Elster, 1984, p. 135).

It would, therefore, seem impossible for economists, within their *present* (neoclassical) paradigm, to take on board the fact that it hurts to think. Doing so would destroy the central concept of optimal behavior which drives so much of economics.

The question remains: should economists try to take this on board? Interestingly, this question is of the very same structure as that posed earlier with respect to the economic agent (cf. Earl, 1983c, pp. 94, 102–103). At present, the economist makes predictions of varying precision. By investing in intellectual effort of unknown cost, it may be possible to improve economic theory in the sense that the precision of predictions would improve. But whether this would be a worthwhile investment is impossible to say — for exactly the same reasons that the economic agent is unable to say whether it is better for him or her to try to behave optimally (when there is a cost to decision-making). At the end of the day, it must be an act of faith.

Nevertheless, there seem to be certain areas of economics where intellectual efforts to reformulate its base appear to be particularly worthwhile. These are the areas where one feels embarrassed to be an economist: for example, in trying to explain and predict exchange rate movements, changes in stock prices, pattern of capital formation, changes in stockbuilding, and so on.

To improve economic explanations and predictions in these and other areas, it would seem important to take on board the fact that it hurts to think; that some human find some decisions very complex and some simply impossible to solve optimally. It is here that psychology should prove useful.

5. New Avenues for Research

It seems likely that progress can be made on two fronts, one theoretical and one empirical. The theoretical front could start from the general proposition that human decision-makers *try* to do as well as they can. This statement may appear simply a restatement of the conventional proposition that decision-makers optimize, but there is a fundamental reorientation implied. Conventional (optimality) economics requires — by its internal logic — that decisions in a dynamic context are taken by backward induction. In other words, decision-makers are supposed first to imagine that they are on the horizon (end-point) of their decision-problem; that they then work out the optimal strategy in the ultimate period of their decision-problem, conditional on the previous evolution of their problem; that they then imagine themselves in the penultimate period, in which they work out the optimal strategy conditional on the previous evolution of the problem *and* on the presumption that they will act out the optimal strategy (which they have already worked out) in the ultimate period; that they then imagine themselves in the last-but-two period . . . and so on. Clearly, in a complex world this is impossible.

The key to the theoretical reorientation is the replacement of the use of backward induction by the use of some form of "forward inference." By this, we mean a process in which the decision-maker tries to infer from what has happened in the past (and from what effects particular decisions have had in the past) what might happen in the future (and what might result from particular decisions in the future). One fairly general way to model this is to posit that decision-makers hold in their minds "a model of the world" (or, at least, a model of the relevant world — relevant to the problem to hand, that is). This could encompass optimality theory in the sense that the "model of the world" could coincide with the real model of the world, but it also allows for more simplified models.

One would then need to specify: how the model of the world is formed, how the model changes (if at all), and how the decision-maker uses the model in reaching decisions. As a general rule, one would suppose that the degree of sophistication of the model, and the speed and sophistication of its revision, would depend upon the degree of sophistication of the decision-maker and upon the complexity of the decision-problem, as would the sophistication of the use made of the model by the decision-maker. However, it is difficult to see at this date how far one could go in theorizing about such matters. (One possible fruitful avenue is that currently being explored by computer scientists in trying to measure the complexity of programming tasks and the sophistication of computers.)

To improve theorizing on such matters, it would seem essential to use empirical evidence, of the kind gathered by economists and psychologists in experimental situations. In such situations one can control the environment surrounding the decision-maker and carefully monitor the decision process. Verbal and written protocols can be used to supplement the raw data (on protocol analysis, see Waterman and Newell, 1971, and Hunt, 1982).

Two main avenues can be explored with such experimental data. The avenue currently most favored by psychologists is to use the data to build up a picture of the mental models of the world held by the decision makers. The alternative, more favored by economists, is to use the data to try to explain decisions in terms of past observations. This avenue, as typical of much of economics, chooses not to delve inside the "black box" of the actual decision-making *process*. Whether one needs to or not is again an act of faith. Many feel that economics has denied itself much by not so doing. The argument that convinces us is that delving inside the black box may well be the only route to an alternative to optimality theory that is just as general.

It would seem inevitable that the types of descriptions of behavior which emerged from such experiments would be stochastic (random). Indeed this is probably the reason why there are so many stochastic models of behavior in psychology.

A good example of the kind of model that can emerge from studies of this kind is that provided by John Cross (1983) in his book *A Theory of Adaptive Economic Behavior*. In it he postulates a fairly general model of adaptive (learning) behavior and applies it to a number of economic examples. Surprisingly — given the general nature of his theory — his book has not attracted the attention it appears to deserve.

The model put forward by Cross is a stochastic model. Apart from the stochastic element, the structure of the model and the model representation are of a type familiar to economists: it is algebraic. This is typical of many psychological models of behavior. However, there are a significant number which employ different model representations, of a type alien to most economists. For example, some models have discontinuous (possibly lexicographic) decision rules based on various subsets of the variables characterizing the environment. To economists, used to nice continuous and differentiable decision rules, these are strange indeed.

One set of models displaying this strange structure is that set based on the productions systems approach, pioneered by Simon and others at Carnegie-Mellon University (see Newell and Simon, 1972, and Hayes-Roth and Waterman, 1978, the latter being the more technical source). Almost of necessity these models are computer-based: with the model structure represented in the form of a computer program and with model simulation performed by running the program a large number of times. Of course, economists are already familiar with the use of computers for model simulation, particularly with macroeconometric models and large scale general equilibrium models, but it is the model representation of the production systems approach that is unfamiliar. Possibly the models could be represented in algebraic form, but whether this would be an advantage is unclear.

One area in which conventional economic modeling has produced relatively few results is the study of *strategic* behavior (see the discussion in the survey by Plott, 1982). In a sense this is hardly surprising in view of the structure of the problem. Interestingly, though, this is one area in which psychologists and economists have worked together. Paradoxically, perhaps, this is an area in which economists have worked with stochastic models (derived from mixed strategies), while psychologists have worked with deterministic models. The striking feature is the proliferation of solution concepts and the lack of emergence of an obviously superior solution, despite (or perhaps because of) the extensive use of experimental evidence.

6. Conclusion

This chapter, though addressed ostensibly to the prospects for the use of mathematics in psychological economics, may appear to have avoided the issue. In a sense this issue is semantic, as it depends on what one means by mathematics. If one means any symbolic model representation, then the issue is trivial. But first one needs to clear up a confusion about the meaning of the phrase "the use of mathematics in psychological economics." One can be referring *either* to the use of mathematics by the model-builder to describe the behavior of human being or to the postulated use of mathematics (possibly in an *as if* sense) by human beings to solve their decision problems. In conventional economics these go hand in hand, indeed conveniently so for the model-builder.

Most objections to the use of mathematics, or to the use of a particular kind of mathematics, in economics relate to the second of these. This is the issue to which much of this essay has been addressed. We have argued that economics can, and must, modify its view as to how people make decisions; that the level of mathematic sophistication assumed for economic agents must be modified. We have suggested ways how this might be done.

But this does not relate to the use of mathematics by economists to model the decision processes of individual, though there is obviously some connection. If economic agents do not smoothly optimize over well behaved functions, then the model describing their behavior may not be well behaved: the *type* of mathematics used to model behavior will obviously depend on that behavior. This indicates that economists ought to be prepared to consider alternative models or mathematical representations. We have suggested some alternatives in this chapter.

It remains to dispose of the argument that there is no role for any kind of mathematics in economics. The nihilists are one group who would so argue, but we can safely leave them at home, contemplating the futility of everything. Of more serious concern is that group of economists who argue that the world is so complex that any attempt to mathematize it is doomed to exclude the relevant bits. This line of argument is usually bolstered by the observation that mathematics necessarily implies measurement, which in some instances is simply impossible. In our view, this is simply tilting at the wrong windmill: it is not the use of mathematics that is wrong, it is the use of a particular kind of mathematics. We admit, though, that there is a problem if the right type of mathematics does not yet exist, and possibly even more of a problem if the wrong kind of mathematics is used instead. This leads to mathematics determining the economic problem, rather than the other way around (cf. Blatt, 1983).

If economics can be formulated in words, then it can be mathematized. Whether the mathematical version provides more insight depends on the problem at hand. Those, such as Karl Menger (1973, especially pp. 41–42), the mathematician son of the Austrian economist Carl Menger, who argue that the mathematical version says less than the verbal version (or indeed that mathematization introduces distortions) are simply pointing out that the wrong kind of mathematics has been used. It remains to use the right kind.

Notes

1. If the theory simply postulated a relationship between a variable Y and another variable X, and if one have n observations on (X, Y), then a polynomial in X,

$$Y + a_0 + a_1X + a_2X^2 + \ldots + a_{n-1}X^{n-1},$$

of order n could be made to pass through the n data points exactly, by appropriate choice of a_i ($i = 0, 1 \ldots, n - 1$). Note, however, that this method would not *guarantee* validation of any comparative static prediction.

2. In other words, for the sake of the current argument, it is being assumed that the economic theorist is able to identify *relevant* features of the real-world problem — and not introduce irrelevancies. But even this assumption may be wrong. We will return to this point in due course.

3. For reasons mentioned above and elaborated on below.

4. The decision at time t will appear uncertain at time $(t-1)$, because it will be conditional on information that is to be revealed between $(t-1)$ and t; but by the time t has been reached this information will have been revealed, and the decision t will be a deterministic function of the information available *at that time*. So, on the presumption that the economist can observe that which the decision-maker observes, the empirical relationship should be deterministic. Of course, this is not true if certain variables cannot be observed by the economist; this suggests a further possible alternative — though one not often heard — for including a random term in empirical relationships.

5. One should qualify this statement in certain respects, though its broad thrust stands.

6. This is a useful antidote to those who argue that the predictions of economics are *as if* predictions. "Okay, so Ivan Lendl does not know the laws of physics, as they concern tennis playing, but he plays *as if* he does." True, but not everyone can play tennis as well as Lendl.

7 SUBJECTIVISM, PSYCHOLOGY, AND THE MODERN AUSTRIANS

Jochen H. Runde

1. Introduction

Most Austrians are likely to say that economics and psychology are separate disciplines and should remain so. This position stems from a reliance on their version of the rationality postulate — that means are purposefully applied to arrive at certain ends — to account for action. But an emphasis on purposefulness and reason may alone no longer be sufficient to keep Austrian economics distinct from psychology. The Austrians have long stressed the influence of time and uncertainty on human action, something which has culminated in their acceptance of many of the views of Shackle. Shackle (1972) draws attention to the fundamental antagonism between time and reason. Should this result in the rationality postulate being abandoned, the door to alternative accounts of choice and action is opened. Austrians interested in pursuing these questions will find it increasingly difficult to keep psychology at bay.

As we are largely concerned here with decision-making, we begin with an overview of praxeology, the Austrian logic of choice. This is followed

101

by a review of Austrian views on mixing psychology and economics. Menger, Boehm-Bawerk, and Wieser are considered first, followed by Mises, Robbins (of the *Essay* [Robbins, 1932/1984]), and Hayek. We then examine some modern Austrian views regarding praxeology, which indicate that its applicability in creative decision-making situations is limited. We argue that if the latter topic continues to be considered worth pursuing, matters commonly relegated to psychology enter as a matter of course.

The chapter concludes with a brief discussion of some recent developments in modern Austrian thought regarding the problem of choice, and the "originative" decision-making of Shackle in particular. Here we compare and match some of the ideas of Kelly's (1955, 1963) theory of personality with Kirzner's (1978, 1979, 1982) view of the entrepreneur, and with the radical subjectivism of Lachmann (1977, 1986) and O'Driscoll and Rizzo (1985).

In what follows, *psychology* refers both to everyday matters of psychology — valuations, volitions, expectations and so on — and to the discipline itself. To avoid confusion, we follow Boehm-Bawerk and refer to the latter as "pure" psychology. With regard to pure psychology in the pages that follow, we also make use of Mises' distinction between "naturalistic" psychology and thymology.

2. Praxeology

Praxeology has been taken as the "distinctive methodology of the Austrian school" (Rothbard, 1976, p. 19), both by Austrians, as well as by non-Austrian commentators (Blaug, 1980, pp. 92–93; Coddington, 1983, p. 61; Caldwell, 1984b). But Austrian views on questions of methodology have diverged for almost as long as they have been debated (Hutchison, 1981) — a tendency that prevails among modern Austrians. Despite the varying degrees of importance that are nowadays attached to praxeology, we have two reasons for reviewing it: first, more recent Austrian attitudes toward the role of psychology in economics can be traced to the influence of the praxeological point of view; second, the scope of praxeology is now seen in some quarters as limited, which provides a more fertile ground for possible alternatives.

Mises regards praxeology — the science of human action, of which economics is "the most highly developed part" (Mises, 1949/1966, p. 3) — as a logic to elaborate on human action. It is a *theoretical* alternative to historicism and empiricism in the social sciences. Mises argues that since the regularity of natural phenomena cannot be matched in the social world, experience cannot teach us general laws. Methods of the natural sciences are thus ruled out. But the differences between the social and natural sciences extend beyond mere degrees of complexity. They are fundamentally different: "Reason and experience show us two separate realms, the external world of physical, chemical and physiological phenomena and the internal world of thought, feeling, valuation and purposeful action" (Mises, 1949/1966, p. 8). This position is one of *methodological dualism*. Since human action cannot be traced to external facts, the psychic and psychological factors that give rise to it, action must be considered as the starting point of the analysis, the "ultimate given."

While the natural scientist must rely on causal explanations, the social scientist may make use of the fact that human action is goal-directed. Human action is purposefully directed at substituting a more satisfactory state of affairs for one that is less satisfactory. Purposefulness implies that human action is rational, that is, that individuals consistently and consciously pursue their own purpose in selecting means to attain their ends: "Action and reasoning are congeneric and homogenous; they may even be called two aspects of the same thing" (Mises, 1949/1966, p. 39).

That means are purposefully applied in order to arrive at certain ends is the fundamental axiom of praxeology. On the basis of this axiom, the praxeologist deduces theorems relating to action in different situations. This is done by verbally tracing the logical implications of this axiom, as well as of subsidiary axioms such as "individuals differ" and "individuals regard leisure as a valuable good" (Rothbard, 1976, p. 19). The purposefulness that underlies the action makes the construction of praxeological theorems possible. By resorting to his or her own reason, the praxeologist may explain actions taken by individuals using their reason to attain their goals.

The epistemological status of praxeological axioms has aroused some debate. For Mises, a Kantian, purposeful action is prior to experience because it "refers to the essential and necessary character of the logical structure of the human mind" (Mises, 1949/1966, p. 34). Consequently, the propositions and statements of praxeology, like those of logic and mathematics, are not subject to verification or falsification on the basis of experience. They are self-evident. The only possible source of praxeological error is mistakes in the logic used in the construction of praxeological theorems.

Rothbard (1976, p. 25), on the other hand, who refers to himself as an Aristotelian, prefers to view axioms as derived from the experience of reality. But he qualifies this, arguing that as axioms are based on everyday experience they are self-evident and are not falsifiable in the accepted sense. In addition, the axioms, and in particular the action axiom, are derived from introspection (universal *inner* experience) as well as from external experience and are therefore prior to historical events. Kirzner (1976a, pp. 180–181) maintains that economics should resort to experience to ensure that it remains in touch with matters that do require explanation. (Mises, 1949/1966, p. 65, expresses similar views.) But he stresses that observation alone is not enough. Explanation requires subjecting the observed data to praxeological reasoning, and this is independent of the "facts." Kirzner notes that this is "the contribution of human logic and reasoning alone. In this sense the theorems of economics, closely though they refer to concrete reality, are described as a priori."

While praxeology provides knowledge valid for all instances in which conditions match those implied in its assumptions and inferences, it is restricted to the formal and general, without reference to material content and the particular features of the actual case. Yet praxeology "conveys exact and precise knowledge of real things" (Mises, 1949/1966, p. 39).

The role of psychology in Austrian economics has gone through three phases which coincide with Lachmann's (1984a) three-tier view of the history of subjectivist thought. (Hayek, however, is considered separately below.) The first stage of subjectivism was a subjectivism of wants. Here we find that, according to Menger (as well as Boehm-Bawerk and Wieser), there is some overlap between economics and psychology. There is, however, no such overlap in the second stage of subjectivism (praxeology). As praxeology is a logic of *given* means and ends, it effectively excludes psychology. In the third stage of subjectivism, emphasis shifts to questions related to expectations and learning. Here, we argue, matters of psychology reenter Austrian thought.

3. Menger, Boehm-Bawerk, and Wieser

The first stage of subjectivism coincides with the marginal revolution of Walras, Jevons, and Menger. To the extent that Menger and his disciples Wieser and Boehm-Bawerk were concerned with stating and refining the subjective theory of value, they seem to have been unable to avoid at least some reference to the determinants of individual wants. Consequently we find references to psychology or, at least, to "psychological aspects."

In his *Principles*, Menger (1871/1976, p. 77) notes that "needs arise from our drives and drives are imbedded in our nature. An imperfect satisfaction of needs stunts our nature. Failure to satisfy them brings about our destruction. But to satisfy our needs is to live and prosper." The generality of this statement would seem to indicate that Menger is avoiding all but the most basic psychological questions. In his presentation of the theory of value, Menger (1871/1976, pp. 122–128) investigates the source of "differences in the magnitude of importance of different satisfactions," which derive from the individual's ordering of needs. While he considers this a "difficult and previously unexplored field of psychology," he resorts to facts of everyday experience in his explanations and does not advocate going beyond this. (According to Hayek, 1976, p. 32, Menger developed an interest in pure psychology later in life.)

Boehm-Bawerk (1889/1973, pp. 86–92) considers the questions of "trespassing freely, cautiously, or not at all, over the border between economics and psychology," and concludes that the economist should "quietly but carefully step over the boundary line." But this amounts to no more than an appeal to use experience and "facts," such as Gossen's law of diminishing enjoyment, to clarify theoretical arguments — and this primarily for purposes of exposition. Boehm-Bawerk emphasizes that this does not require an extensive inquiry into pure psychology, and that the essential consequences of value theory are in any event independent of particular psychological premises.

Since he was a noted advocate of the "psychological method," one might expect Wieser to favor an overlap between pure psychology and economics. But Wieser's position on this issue turns out to be remarkably similar to that of Menger and Boehm-Bawerk. His views are clearly stated in a critical review of Schumpeter (Wieser, 1929). Wieser's psychological method is a method of introspection (*innere Beobachtung*). The scope of economics is the consciousness of economizing individuals. As this consciousness derives from everyday experience, it may be grasped by introspection. The theorist is thus not forced to resort to specialized disciplines (Wieser, 1929, pp. 15–16). Hence, economics (and this includes the psychological method) remains separate from pure (*wissenschaftliche*) psychology, the tasks of which are different from those of economics.

For Menger, Boehm-Bawerk and Wieser, economics does border on psychology. But they use the word psychology in its everyday sense, to refer to such things as expectations, valuations, and volitions. As these are simple facts of experience, no specialist knowledge is required to make use of them. They do not advocate an overlap between economics and pure psychology. If anything, they indicate that economists have more to offer psychologists than the other way around (Boehm-Bawerk, 1899/1973, p. 87; Menger, 1871/1976, p. 128).

4. Mises and Robbins

At the second stage of Lachmann's history of subjectivist thought, ends are taken as given and the analysis proceeds by asking if the means are sufficient to attain these ends. Emphasis shifts from a subjectivism of wants to one of means and ends. Action rather than valuation becomes the object of analysis. While Lachmann associates this stage primarily with Mises, we include Robbins (1932/1984) in this category. Mises and Robbins stress that the theoretical science of economics (praxeology) is independent of particular psychological premises. But they nevertheless allow that reference to psychological matters may provide an "understanding" of economic phenomena.

The Mises/Robbins position on psychology in economic theory is probably best summed up in Robbins' (1932/1984, p. 86) dictum that economists regard "the things which psychology studies as the data of their own deduction." The logic of choice is based on the proposition (axiom) that individuals act. It deals with the logical implications of the purposeful application of means to ends. The economist deals with given ends and with action as such. He or she does not enquire into the psychic processes, the content of valuations and goals, which give rise to action — and which do not affect the validity of his or her conclusions. This is the task of the psychologist (Mises, 1949/1966, pp. 11–12, 21, 1957/1981, pp. 271–272; Robbins, 1932/1984, pp. 83–90).

Mises' (1957/1981, pp. 264–271) statements on the respective roles of psychology and economics are perhaps the most comprehensive in the Austrian literature. He distinguishes between psychology and thymology, reserving the term *psychology* for "naturalistic psychology," that branch of psychology which proceeds with the methods of physiology and neuropathology. This is a natural science which has little bearing on the sciences of human action. Thymology, on the other hand, deals with human emotions, motivations, valuations, volitions, and so on. It derives from both introspection and historical experience.

Thymology has no particular bearing on praxeology, despite the fact that valuation is a thymological category. Mises makes his position quite clear: "[P]raxeology is not concerned with events which within a man's soul or brain produce a definite decision between an A or a B. It takes it for granted that the nature of the universe enjoins upon man choosing between incompatible ends. Its subject is not the content of these acts of choosing but what results from them: action." The belief that the marginal utility school is based on or connected with psychology therefore is mistaken, according to Mises (1949/1966, pp. 123–124). For Mises, the "class of wants' of Menger and Boehm-Bawerk is superfluous to modern thought. (Rothbard, 1976, p. 31, similarly argues that the law of diminishing marginal utility does not depend on psychological considerations.)

But Mises emphasizes that this should not be taken to imply that thymology is of no use to the economist. Thymology, as it derives from historical experience, is a branch of history. It can be used to catalogue human traits, and, on the basis of experience, to link different traits. As such it can contribute to the *understanding* of economic phenomena. But it does not qualify as a theoretical science (Mises, 1957/1981, pp. 272–274). Robbins (1932/1984, pp. 86–89) adopts a similar stance, arguing that while "it is not true that the propositions of analytical economics rest upon any particular psychology," they do involve elements of a psychological, or psychical, nature, which must be taken into account and without which the understanding of economic phenomena would be rendered impossible.

5. Hayek

Hayek has the unusual distinction amongst economists of having published a work on pure psychology: his (1952) book, *The Sensory Order*. A synoptic guide to this is presented in the appendix to this chapter to satisfy the curiosity of readers not familiar with it and, it is to be hoped, to stimulate some research on how it relates to psychological theories proposed by other subjectivist thinkers (such as the personal construct psychology of Kelly, 1963, discussed later in this chapter and elsewhere in this book). The reason for not addressing the content of Hayek's psychyological treatise in the body of this chapter is that it has little to do with economics. The views expressed in *The Counterrevolution of Science* (Hayek, 1952/1979) are quite clear on the place of psychology in the social sciences. Like Mises and Robbins, Hayek holds that economics is concerned with action rather than valuation — with conscious or reflected behavior in which individuals choose between alternatives open to them. The purposefulness of human action allows the social scientist to proceed from the thoughts and intentions of individuals. There is no need to inquire into the origins of these thoughts and intentions. (Nevertheless, Hayek, 1937, has raised questions about how individuals acquire knowledge.)

For Hayek, the major task of the theoretical social sciences is to trace origins of social phenomena which are not consciously designed. This is one step removed from the concerns of Mises and Robbins: Hayek is more interested in the consequences of action than with the logic of choice which proceeds it. He argues (1952/1979, p. 68) that the social scientist does not "*explain* conscious action. This, if it can be done at all, is a different task, the task of psychology. For the social sciences the types of conscious action are data and all they have to do with regard to these data is to arrange them in such an orderly fashion that they can be effectively used for their task."

Before moving on, it is worth noting that the statements of Hayek, Mises and Robbins on pure psychology in general only become truly hostile where they discuss behaviorism (Hayek, 1952/1979, pp. 78–79, 85; Mises, 1949/1966, pp. 40, 104, 121). This "queer cult" (Robbins, 1932/1984, p. 87) takes the view that human action can be studied purely from external, "objective" facts. As behaviorism excludes introspection (unless this can somehow be verified by observable events) and is quite contrary to the notion that individuals consciously choose and purposefully strive after ends, it comes as no surprise that it should jar with the Austrian scheme of things.

6. Praxeology and the Modern Austrians

The modern Austrians have different ideas about what economists should do. To trace the unintended consequences of human action does not require an extensive analysis of choice. As Hayek argues, the analyst takes the fact that individuals act as datum and proceeds from there. Lachmann (1986) and Rizzo and O'Driscoll (1985), however, indicate that the topic of "creative" decision-making is worth pursuing. But praxeology, as it is now commonly interpreted, promises to be little help in this endeavor. Moreover, recent discussions of these issues lean toward a psychology of choice.

For Mises, praxeology is a *logic* to spin out the implications of action. Recent commentators, however, seem inclined to view it as a *description of* action. For example, Latsis (1976, p. 24) characterizes Mises' conception of action as highly constrained reaction rather than genuine choice. Similar sentiments have been expressed from Austrian quarters: Lachmann (1982, p. 82) and Boehm (1982, p. 47), for example, accuse Mises of lapsing into behaviorism.

Given this view, many of the Shacklean criticisms of mainstream economics may be directed at praxeology with equal effect. Praxeology is a static explanatory scheme. Once ends and means are given to the praxeologist, who attempts to find if the means are consistently applied to achieve those ends, the problem is only one of computation. Praxeology differs from the situational determinism of neoclassical economics only with regard to its information assumptions (Langlois, 1982). Given the individual's knowledge of his circumstances, praxeology is also restricted to what Latsis (1976, p. 16) calls "single-exit" situations — where the individual's decision is uniquely determined by the situation in which he or she finds him/herself.

In single-exit situations the rationality postulate is sufficient to account for action. It is not inconceivable that individuals might apply an ends-means logic in simple and transparent situations; they may even behave like utility maximizers (Simon, 1959, p. 258). But in all other cases, the reasoning on which action is based is more likely to follow what Simon (1976, pp. 130–137) calls "procedural rationality." In Austrian terms, it is the question of *how the ends-means framework itself is selected* that assumes importance. Where outcomes are not situationally determined, the praxeologist is ill-equipped to trace the making of a decision by resorting to his or her own reason alone.

Simon's concern with procedural rationality arises out of an interest in complexity in decision making in general. The problems associated with time and uncertainty are a subset of this. Since the Austrians emphasize this particular theme, we will consider it here. With the introduction of time, uncertainty, and expectations we move on to a "dynamic subjectivism" (O'Driscoll and Rizzo, 1985, p. 39). This is the third stage in Lachmann's history of subjectivist thought: the subjectivism of "active minds" (Lachmann, 1982, p. 39). Here the scope of subjectivism extends beyond the given ends-means framework to include expectations and learning. This form of subjectivism was until quite recently pursued almost single-handedly by Shackle (1972), but since Lachmann's (1976) attempt to introduce Shackle to the Austrians, a literature of Austrian contributions to this view — sometimes referred to as "radical subjectivism" — has appeared (see O'Driscoll and Rizzo, 1985, for a summary and extension of this work).

Radical subjectivists stress that because human action takes place in historical time, uncertainty in decision-making, and hence expectations, are important. Specifically, while the past can be experienced, the future can only be imagined. Expectations may be colored by the past, but they are not bound to it. Since action is based on expectations, it follows that the future is also to some extent free from the past — it promises novelty and surprise. Knowledge of the future is thus precluded, as the consequences of any choice depend in part on the outcomes of the autonomous choices of others. Moreover, planning processes are themselves time-bound. Plans may change or fail as knowledge accumulates, either during the planning process or the course of action itself. Uncertainty is ineradicable in real time.

It may be argued that praxeology implicitly takes time and uncertainty into account. These factors are, according to this view, praxeological categories and are implied in action itself (Mises, 1949/1966, pp. 99, 105; Rothbard, 1976, p. 20). In his discussion of time, Mises admits that in an a prioristic deductive system "the notions of anteriority and consequence are metaphorical only." These refer not to the system, "but to our action in grasping it . . . As a system it is out of time. But change is one of its elements. The notions of sooner and later and of cause and effect are amongst its constituents. Anteriority and consequence are essential concepts of praxeological reasoning" (Mises, 1949/1966, p. 99).

But this, it is often pointed out, does not get us very far. As Lachmann reminds us, in a dynamic setting it is difficult to conceive of given ends; even the means can be problematic if they can only be obtained in the future. Praxeological theorems that incorporate some of the complexity of real world decision-making could no doubt be constructed. But this runs the risk of falling into the trap that mainstream theory has fallen into: introducing more "reality" by building ever more complex models. And it does not overcome the problem that time and uncertainty are not easily squeezed into a rationalistic scheme.

As a result, we find some modern Austrians departing from Mises, in their concern with what he would have relegated to thymology. Lachmann (1986), for example, aims "to trace the forces impelling market processes, whether convergent or divergent, to the springs of human action, i.e. our acts of will and imagination, as well as those of our acts which grasp experience and turn it into knowledge." This is something of a departure from his earlier views (Lachmann, 1977, pp. 155, 173). Here we may agree that "[a]s soon as our thoughts have assumed the firm outline of a plan and we have taken the decision to carry it out over a definite period of future time, we have reached a point outside the realm of psychology" (Lachmann, 1977, p. 155). But a dynamic subjectivism also extends to *how* our thoughts assume the outline of a plan and how changing thoughts may cause plans to change. This puts us back in that realm.

The return to thymological topics is also apparent in the writings of other Austrians. O'Driscoll and Rizzo (1985, pp. 17–18) focus on purposes, plans, valuations and expectations, all of which are prior to Misesian action. They also stress the need for a theory of learning. In an earlier paper, Kirzner (quoted in Littlechild, 1979, pp. 40–41) goes so far as to suggest that the whole Shacklean notion of the creative imagination belongs to psychology rather than economics.

Littlechild (1982; 1983, pp. 43–45) has borrowed ideas from psychology and argued that different conclusions regarding the nature of choice rest on different views of the fundamental nature of human action. For example, he associates the Mises-Hayek-Kirzner emphasis on purposefulness, learning, and problem-solving with the *Gestalt* view in psychology, and Shackle's emphasis on the imagination with the psychoanalytic view. He suggests that different conceptions of action might require a different emphasis in economic analysis (Littlechild, 1983, p. 45), and, while not going so far as to suggest that economists should immerse themselves in psychology, he does ask whether instinctive behavior should be ceded to other disciplines, should a preoccupation with purposeful behavior rule it out of the realm of economics.

The remainder of this chapter is devoted to a discussion of how some modern Austrians propose to deal with creative decision-making. We shall concentrate on two areas, beginning with the work of Kirzner (1978, 1979, 1982), who represents the more orthodox Austrian position. We then examine the radical subjectivist view represented by Lachmann (1986) and O'Driscoll and Rizzo (1985). Subjectivists of the Post Keynesian school (Earl, 1983a, 1983b, 1986a, 1986b; Loasby, 1983), as well as some consumer behavior theorists in marketing (Gutman, 1982; Gutman and Alden, 1985), make use of the personal construct psychology of Kelly (1955, 1963). In view of Lachmann's (1984b) comments regarding the possibility of a fruitful alliance between the Austrians and the Post Keynesians, we also take this opportunity to draw some parallels between Kelly's brand of subjectivism and that of the Austrians.

7. Kelly's Theory of Personal Constructs

Kelly proposes that the acting individual be viewed as a scientist attempting to predict and control his environment. Since the complexity of the world by far outstrips human comprehension, the individual is forced to take a partial view. This is done by creating imaginary constructs — "transparent patterns or templets" — which are fitted over "reality." While these constructs may not fit reality perfectly, they may help the individual to interpret his or her environment. Kelly's theory is an elaboration on this idea. It focuses on the subjective *processes* by which individuals anticipate the future, rather than on attempting to trace the physiological roots of psychological changes.

The erection of constructs ("construing," in Kelly's terminology) begins by identifying recurrent patterns in the flow of events. This complete, the individual may attempt to make predictions. Austrians are sometimes taken as holding that experience cannot provide a guide to the future. This is misleading. As Lachmann (1986) points out, information drawn from a large number of similar circumstances may, in favorable conditions, enable individuals to formulate general hypotheses which may be tested by later information.

While their origins may lie in experience, however, constructs are nevertheless very much the subjective *creations* of individuals. Consequently, while constructs are no less real than the objective reality they are fitted to, they need not correspond to it. The notion of the imagination acting as a knowledge-surrogate (Coddington, 1975, pp. 152–153) is familiar to Shackleans and Austrians: Kirzner (1982), Lachmann (1986) and O'Driscoll and Rizzo (1985) also view action as oriented toward an imagined future state of affairs. Anticipations differ, not only because individuals seek to anticipate different events but also because their constructions differ. As Lachmann — who does not refer to Kelly — puts it, information must be digested and interpreted before it can be transformed into expectations. "[E]ach mind provides a filter of different construction," involving an accentuation and abstraction of different elements of experience. Expectations may also differ where individuals have different stocks of knowledge (Lachmann, 1986).

Constructs are not only used as predictive devices but also to assess the accuracy of predictions after the event has occurred. The accuracy of predicted outcomes provides the basis for the revision of constructs. As the individual's constructs must be useful to him or her, they are vulnerable to contrary experience. They are thus unlikely to remain independent of the flow of events — that is, provide poor predictions — and survive. In Kelly's world there is a presumption that individuals' anticipations normally tend to improve over time.

8. Entrepreneurship and Creative Choice

While Kirzner cannot be described as a radical subjectivist (compare Kirzner, 1985, with Lachmann, 1985), he has made some interesting concessions to the Shacklean view (Kirzner, 1982). In earlier work, Kirzner (1978, 1979) shows how disequilibrium situations present profit opportunities to "alert" entrepreneurs. The exploitation of these opportunities leads to a dissemination of information and market coordination. The entrepreneur acts, in effect, as an arbitrageur. But this view ignores the dynamic, creative aspect of entrepreneurship (Littlechild, 1979; Shackle, 1983). Kirzner's (1982) solution is to extend his concept of alertness to the future, as well as to existing opportunities. Entrepreneurship, it is argued, is the force that identifies ends-means frameworks. It constitutes the active generation of imagined actions from which a selection is made.

Kirzner's (1982) paper has a distinctively Kellian flavor. Individuals, it is argued, act in the light of an envisaged future. While imagination, and hence choice, are free to diverge from what actually happens, choice is not "without moorings" with regard to the realized future (Kirzner, 1982, p. 149). The extent to which plans succeed depends on the degree to which the envisaged and realized future coincide. Experience indicates that plans do often succeed. This, Kirzner argues, is because individuals are motivated to envisage the future as accurately as possible. They are, in other words, induced to build useful constructs; those that predict poorly are abandoned. As there is little point in letting the imagination soar to unattainable heights, sudden and unpredictable shifts of behavior are constrained. Kirzner calls the motivated propensity to formulate an accurate picture of the future "alertness," the "extra-Robbinsian" entrepreneurial element of human action.

The lure of profits motivates Kirzner's agents to anticipate the future as accurately as possible. While this is not incompatible with Kelly's scheme, Kelly takes a wider view. His agents' choices reflect the desire to extend and define their construct systems. They choose, in other words, to enhance their anticipations. Some, by narrowing their fields of vision, might strive for a clearer definition of their constructs. Others, who might be more ready to face the uncertainty it entails, may choose to broaden their fields of vision and to increase the predictive range of their constructs (Kelly, 1955, p. 65).

In his earlier *Competition and Entrepreneurship* Kirzner (1978, p. 71) argues that to incorporate changing ends-means frameworks, "it is not necessary to explore the *psychology* of the learning process, which is the result of market experiences in which plans were found to be unworkable (or in which it has been found that alternative, preferable courses of action were in fact available)." This is left to the entrepreneurial element in human action. But Kirzner's (1982) dynamic "multi-period" view of entrepreneurship raises the possibility that the entrepreneur may, by his or her own creative actions, construct the future as he/she wishes it to be. He admits that in this case "[t]here can be no doubt that in the concrete fulfillment of the entrepreneurial function these psychological and personal qualities (vision, boldness, determination, creativity) are of paramount importance. It is in this sense that so many writers are undoubtedly correct in linking entrepreneurship with the courage and vision necessary to *create* the future in an uncertain world" (Kirzner, 1982, p. 155).

But Kirzner is quick to remind us that what really matters are the market coordinating properties of entrepreneurship. He warns against allowing undue attention on the psychology of entrepreneurship to draw attention away from this (Kirzner, 1982, p. 155). In *Competition and Entrepreneurship* he argues that it is necessary to build our theory on the "insight" that the entrepreneurial element provides the necessary learning process to ensure coordination (Kirzner, 1978, p. 72). For Kirzner, as for Hayek (1937), this is an empirical matter. The belief that entrepreneurship is market coordinating allows "entrepreneurship" to serve as a convenient blanket term for the psychological factors excluded in Robbinsian maximizing activity. At the same time it allows these factors to be bypassed. However, not everyone feels that such a belief is warranted: Lachmann (1979), for one, is far from convinced that we can rely on Hayekian "tendencies towards equilibrium."

9. The Radical Subjectivists

We have seen that Kirzner brings creative decision-making into his scheme by fusing it with his notion of entrepreneurial alertness. As far as he is concerned, this does not require the study of the psychological attributes of entrepreneurship. It is sufficient that entrepreneurship is a coordinating force in the market, and he suggests that we may assume that it is such a force. The radical subjectivists, a substream of Austrian thought represented by Lachmann (1977, 1986) and O'Driscoll and Rizzo (1985), however, are interested in pursuing the factors which precede action, as well as the outcome of action in the market process. Unlike Kirzner, they propose a more direct inquiry into the extra-Robbinsian element in human action, rather than relegating it to an entrepreneurial alertness.

The radical subjectivists wish to develop a dynamic subjectivism, where decision-making is not strictly determined by what went on before. The difference between static and dynamic decision-making is implicit in O'-Driscoll and Rizzo's (1985, pp. 29–32) distinction between single-valued and multi-valued expectations. From their preceding discussion it appears that the single-valued expectation (static decision-making) case corresponds to (single-exit) situational determinism. Here the individual expects only one possible outcome. Multi-valued expectations, on the other hand, are similar to Latsis' (1976, p. 16) multiple-exit situations, where the individual's choice is not strictly determined by situational considerations. In this case psychological characteristics assume importance in explaining decision-making.

Single-exit situations form part of the orderly world which is necessary for meaningful choice. We have already noted that these are reactions rather than choices in the Shacklean sense. O'Driscoll and Rizzo (1985, p. 29) view the empirical counterpart of single-valued expectations as "habituations." Kelly might regard these as past predictions that have consistently been validated. In general, the usefulness of constructs may be expected to improve over time, if the phenomena being predicted change more slowly than they are revised and if they are not applied in inappropriate situations. Expectations are then likely to converge and stabilize.

Matters are more complicated in multiple-exit situations. O'Driscoll and Rizzo (1985, pp. 30–31) suggest that multi-valued expectations require a "weighting" of the possible actions of others, as successful action depends on what others do. These weights are described as "logical constructs used to identify the constituents of a decision" and, like Kelly's constructs, are *attempts* to perceive objective propensities and to narrow the range of possible outcomes. It is stressed that they bear some relationship to objective reality; that they are "not merely self or social delusion." Behavior is thus "loosely determined." But O'Driscoll and Rizzo do not pursue the matter of decision weights at any great length. However, they emphasize that the empirical counterpart of static decision-making provides the necessary predictable foundation for dynamic decision-making (O'Driscoll and Rizzo, 1985, pp. 28–29). This idea may be extended along Kellian lines.

Choice is often described as the act of deciding between imagined rival future outcomes. Mainstream theorists might depict this in a probabilistic fashion, while subjectivists might resort to a "potential surprise" possibility calculus. But matters are not quite so simple. The difficulty is not merely that choice outcomes can only exist in the imagination at the moment the decision is made, but also that each outcome itself depends on a whole host of predictions of different aspects relevant to the situation, all of which are more or less uncertain. The ideas of Kelly are useful here. He describes a prediction, not as the whole view of an event, but as "simply the common intersect of a certain set of properties" (Kelly, 1963, p. 121). Prediction is also a construing process. But here the construct is one of "trend or movement perceived amid the context of elements. . . . The point of convergence of all relevant constructs — time, the movement construct, and the coordinate readings of the hypothetical event — constitute the prediction" (Kelly, 1963, pp. 122–123).

Moves from one ends-means context to another may thus be interpreted in terms of fresh combinations of existing constructs, or in terms of existing construct being applied in new situations. Novelty may lie in the manner in which elements of a decision are combined, rather in the elements themselves. Here creative choice may well be an alertness to the future, in the spirit of Kirzner (1982), if it consists of perceiving the possibilities implicit in combinations of different market trends. This underlines the the importance of complementary knowledge in decision-making. Loasby (1982, p. 118; 1983, pp. 106–107) has discussed this aspect in terms of the coordination of dispersed information *between* individuals within a firm. But the same idea is equally pertinent at the level of the individual.

Once a particular plan or course of action has been chosen, how much contrary evidence is required before it is revised? With regard to this question Lachmann approvingly cites Boland (1978), who proposes that responses to "out of date" or "false" knowledge be classified on the basis of how the individual believes knowledge is acquired. Boland therefore also compares the economic agent with the scientist: "A conventionalist about knowledge might find it possible to deflect such empirical criticism by some form of approximationism. . . . On the other hand an 'instrumentalist" . . . who knowingly accepts false assumptions may never change" (Boland, 1978, p. 256). But what Lachmann takes as Boland's main conclusion — that individuals who have the same information will revise their plans at different intervals — is by itself not very helpful. He suggests that information which is complementary to (relevant) knowledge is more valuable than isolated bits of information. This is likely to make such information more durable. The same applies to generalization — as opposed to knowledge of particular circumstances.

Kelly offers some useful ideas regarding this issue. Among his more obvious suggestions is that the more immediate the predicted events, the more open to revision constructs will be (Kelly, 1955, p. 13). And, the more useful they appear, the more vulnerable they will be to new evidence. But the variation in an individual's constructs is also affected by what Kelly (1955, p. 77) calls their *permeability*. A construct is permeable if it admits new elements which are not yet integrated within its framework, without having to be modified. Moreover, constructs are organized into hierarchical systems, in which subordinate constructs are determined by superordinate constructs. The more wide-ranging an individual's subordinate constructs are, the more is at stake in the event of a challenge to the construct that is superordinate to them. This may also lead to a reluctance or inability to change constructs.

The questions of how and when plans are arrived at, changed, and abandoned, require a dynamic theory of learning — one of how individuals "acquire, use, store and replace the knowledge daily required for successful action in the marketplace, workshop and household" (Lachmann, 1986). O'Driscoll and Rizzo argue that this theory must encompass more than mere computation. It must also allow for the setting up of the problem situation itself or the movement from one to another. They admit that, at present, we do not have such a theory (O'Driscoll and Rizzo, 1985, p. 37). But they do suggest that it must depict learning as lying somewhere between strict determinism and pure chance.

Quite how a dynamic theory of learning fits in with their proposed methodology of treating each decision-making unit (for example, the consumer or the entrepreneur) as a "mind construct" (O'Driscoll and Rizzo, 1985, pp. 20–21), however, is not clear. The mind construct is "a fictitious consciousness endowed with certain goals, constraints, knowledge and expectations," which engages in an activity that bears an "understandable" relation to the phenomena to be explained. Since it is only "loosely determined," it can depict the cut between an experienced past and the expected future — different decisions, for example, may be attributed to different decision weights. But as the mind construct is restricted to the outcomes of given knowledge, constraints, expectations and so on, it is incompatible with the *process* of learning. Kelly's approach, on the other hand, comprises a dynamic theory of learning. The individual's constructs vary as he successively interprets recurrent patterns in the flow of events — when something unexpected occurs he or she may be induced to change his/her hypotheses. Learning may be viewed as a Popperian process of erecting hypotheses which are continuously being put to the test.

10. Conclusion

In some respects the Austrian school has come full circle. Simon (1976) contends that the combination of substantive rationality with utility maximization rid neoclassical economics of psychology. This, some argue, did not apply to Menger, whose emphasis on time and uncertainty makes the application of psychology almost inevitable (Alter, 1982, p. 157). We have seen that Menger and his more immediate disciples do not advocate delving into pure psychology in quite the way that Simon does. But they certainly show no desire to banish psychology from a theoretical economics, as do Mises and Robbins. Mises and his contemporaries do not, of course, ignore time and uncertainty. But these factors lie outside the realm of a *logic* of choice.

Time and uncertainty have regained their earlier prominence in the writings of the modern Austrians. This has led to some concern with problems related to creative choice and the decision-making process. These problems have been approached in two ways. Kirzner indicates that the notion of the creative imagination is a matter of psychology rather than economics. He attempts to avoid the psychology of creative choice by subsuming it under his notion of entrepreneurial alertness. Nevertheless, Kirzner's arguments in support of the notion that entrepreneurship is a market-coordinating force rely on a number of broad psychological pre-suppositions. The radical subjectivists, on the other hand, seem intent on facing the problems of choice head on, and propose a direct inquiry into the realm of volition, expectations, and learning.

The modern Austrians are now at something of a crossroads. In the first place, there is the question of whether economists should be as preoccupied as they are with questions of choice: "If social phenomena showed no order except in so far as they were consciously designed, there would be no room for theoretical sciences of society and there would be, as it is often argued, only problems of psychology. It is only insofar as some sort of order arises as a result individual action but without being designed by any individual that a problem is raised which demands a theoretical explanation" (Hayek, 1952/1979, p. 69). If, on the other hand, choice continues to be a central issue, it must be accepted that the Robbinsian maximizing view is a narrow one. This raises the question whether the extra-Robbinsian element in human action should be relegated to an entrepreneurial alertness in dis-cussions of the market process, as Kirzner suggests. While this allows questions of psychology to be avoided to a large extent, it does lean toward a labeling of one's ignorance.

Tracing behavior to "the springs of action," on the other hand, as Lachmann seems intent on doing, is an invitation to psychology. It is true that Lachmann (1986) and O'Driscoll and Rizzo (1985, p. 32) also recognize the importance of institutions. But if institutions are seen as equilibrium phenomena, then quite how they fit in with an emphasis on time, uncer-tainty and the freedom of the imagination is problematic (Kirzner, 1976b). This suggests that it might be useful to distinguish between markets. The Shackle/Lachmann emphasis on the indeterminacy of divergent expecta-tions, for example, largely applies to stock markets, whose nature is such that they often exacerbate volatility and uncertainty. Any equilibria which obtain are precarious; the influence on the market process of decision-making are largely a question of psychology, as Keynes suggests. But this is less the case, for example, in ordinary retail outlets, institutions that offer relatively stable prices without the possibility of bargaining. Here expectations are likely to be more stable, rendering the psychology of choice less crucial to an understanding of the market process.

Appendix

Hayek's (1952) The Sensory Order

The Sensory Order addresses the problem of why the phenomenological order differs from the order represented by the physical sciences. Hayek suggests that the answer to this problem lies in the process by which physical impulses are classified by the nervous system. He argues that different mental phenomena — such as discrimination, abstraction, transfer, generalization, and conceptual thought — may all be treated as different forms of this process of classification.

Hayek represents the sensory order as a unitary system of relations. The different attributes by which the individual differentiates in response to different stimuli are not isolated "facts," but derive their meaning as part of the whole order. Therefore, to relate the sensory order to the physical order without moving in a circle (by explaining the sensory qualities in terms of each other), the whole network of relations which determine the sensory order must be explained. Hayek's solution is to show how external impulses may produce relations in the nervous system which correspond to the sensory order, by constructing a system of physical elements (the neural order) which is isomorphous (topologically, not spatially) with the system of sensory qualities. He concludes that the neural order and the phenomenal order are not only isomorphous but are one and the same thing.

Perception, for Hayek, is an act of classification. Classes are based on the response of the individual to different events. The effect of an impulse depends on the *position* in the structure of the nervous system of the fiber which carries that impulse, rather than on any attribute of either the event (the stimulus) or the impulse itself.

Classification is effected by a network of connections which transmit impulses from neuron to neuron in the nervous system. This network is built up when connections are established between fibers in which impulses occur at the same time. Impulses or groups of impulses which evoke the same "following" of secondary impulses are grouped together. (Impulses or groups of impulses may belong to a number of different classes at the same time.) Classes may themselves be classified at different levels in the nervous system. At lower levels impulses evoke specific responses. At higher levels impulses work to modify and control behavior in the light of the whole situation (represented by other impulses and a retained picture of the environment).

Hayek assumes that the structure of the central nervous system is complete before any connections between neurons are established. From birth, with every occurrence of combinations of stimuli, a network of connections is built up. Over time each neuron begins to acquire a more clearly defined place and function in the system of interconnections. At this (presensory) stage, qualitative distinctions are built up by "experience" of external stimuli, through the formation of "linkages."

Linkages between different impulses produce gradually changing "maps" of the individual's environment by reproducing regularities in the external stimuli. The mental order evolves through slowly improving approximations of the order of the external world. While the map provides a distorted picture of the environment, the maps produced by different individuals are nevertheless similar enough to allow for interpersonal relations. The map is static in that it represents the different kinds of stimuli which in the past have acquired significance for the individual. It provides a theory of how the world works but no new information regarding the individual's current environment.

Hayek refers to the pattern of impulses proceeding in the network of linkages (as a result of recent stimuli) as the "model" of the environment in which the individual currently finds him/herself. This is the dynamic element in Hayek's system, an apparatus of joint-classification which enables the individual to adapt to his/her current surroundings. The model extends the scope of successful adaptation by selecting relevant elements (on the basis of their persistence) for prediction from a complex environment, and by treating relevant information as instances of the same class of events.

The model is forward-looking. The representations of the possible outcomes of a situation are constantly compared to the newly arriving impulses which record the actual developments in the environment. The newly arriving impulses are in turn evaluated against the expectations set up by the previous pattern of impulses. The model will persist if it responds appropriately to beneficial or harmful influences and if it has the capacity of retaining a "memory" of the factors that precede these influences, thereby being able to anticipate them. Should the model encounter an anomalous experience, new classes are formed to accommodate that experience.

Hayek (1952, p. 143) sums up his account in a statement he acknowledges to Popper: "all we know about the world is of the nature of theories and all 'experience' can do is change these theories." Particular classifications made by the nervous system may turn out to have been incorrect. Reclassification is part of the learning process. Although the sensory order is in part a product of past experience, knowledge is not restricted to the past alone. As sensory experience conforms to certain general principles, the mind is equipped to deal with new experiences. Knowledge of these principles constitutes our knowledge of the external world.

Acknowledgment

I am grateful to Mark Addleson, Joseph Labia, Ludwig Lachmann, Karl Mittermaier, Duncan Reekie, Peter Rosendorff, and Chris Torr for their kind help. However, this should not be taken to imply that they would endorse everything I say in this chapter; the usual disclaimer applies.

8 SUBJECTIVISM, PSYCHOLOGY, AND THE MODERN AUSTRIANS: A COMMENT

A. M. Endres

Joseph Schumpeter once maintained that the pure "theory of economic equilibrium," except for some minor phraseological influence, had no dependence on what he called "professional psychology." He insisted that equilibrium economics did not inquire into the facts that shaped choices; it had no brief to investigate the psychological bases of valuation, for example, it accepted scales of demand price as ultimate facts (1954, pp. 27–28, 796–798, 1057–1059). In Menger's (1871/1976) *Grundsätze*, where the concept of general economic equilibrium is absent, we find that Menger asked how and why people with less than full relevant knowledge come to choose as they do. He answered by constructing a theory of the lexicographic ordering of wants, based on certain psychical observations about individuals as well as on observations of their physiological and social nature (Georgescu-Roegen, 1968, pp. 250–252; see also section 3 in the next chapter). In the context of Menger's growing or "progressing" economy, the notion of an individual's stable and consistent preference ordering is frequently violated — as is pointed out in further discussion of Alter (1982) in Endres (1984) (cf. the incorrect assertion by Lachmann, 1978, p. 58, that Menger allowed "little scope for changes of taste or fashion"). In being assimilated by the Jevonian tradition, which stressed a marginalist, static subjectivism, Boehm-Bawerk and Wieser abandoned these salient features of Menger's theory (Streissler, 1972). The subjective character of Menger's theory had the makings of a dynamic "process analysis' (Hayek, 1973, p. 10) and, although rudimentary in this respect, Menger's contribution provided some impetus for further work by Austrian psychologists/ philosophers Franz Brentano, Meinong, and Ehrenfels (see Eaton, 1930, pp. 92–93, 113ff; Johnston, 1972, p. 80). In fact, this group of Austrian psychologists were thoroughly to dispute Wieser's claim that his "psychological method" remained separate from pure psychology.

It is not very helpful, historically speaking, for Runde to say that Menger and other first generation Austrian economists did "not advocate an overlap between economics and psychology." This is not merely because of the dangers of using labels artificially compartmentalizing branches of social science but also because of the fact that, in attempting to explain why people behave in one way or another, the Austrians drew as much, if not more, on economic sociology which had a psychological orientation. Here we only need think of Dilthey and Weber who attempted to develop the method of *Verstehen*, which subsumed establishing premises by introspection, at the forefront of social science explanation. (Menger's own use of the term *observation*, for instance, implied *Verstehen* — see Hayek, 1973, p. 8.) It is thus no coincidence of intellectual history that vestigial elements of this tradition, developed in the work of, among others, Husserl, Schutz and Luckmann, have now found favor with modern radical subjectivists. In particular, the treatise by O'Driscoll and Rizzo (1985) looks to investigate knowledge dynamics with the assistance of Schutz' "phenomenological psychology" (as Schutz once termed it).

From this perspective, the Mises/Rothbard doctrine of given ends and means looks a particularly long way from Menger's theory of wants. Runde is correct to label Misesian praxeology a "static explanatory scheme," even though Mises himself may not have construed it that way. The praxeological specification of the rationality postulate in terms of a logic of choice is a cul-de-sac where not only are concerns for knowledge dynamics downplayed, their further development with the assistance of psychology or any other social science is denied.

Runde's discussion is without doubt useful in drawing parallels between Kelly's personal construct psychology, as employed by behavioral/Post Keynesian subjectivists, and work by modern Austrian subjectivists. However, future work by scholars in the Austrian tradition should not forget that Schutz (and Luckmann) are the actual mentors for the radical subjectivism of O'Driscoll and Rizzo. Full realization of the promise of their research program may therefore necessitate not merely the incorporation of Kellian themes but also, following Schutz, the phenomenology and sociology of knowledge. Hence, considered *within* the Austrian tradition, a sketch of the relationship between the O'Driscoll and Rizzo adaptation of Schutz' ideal type, "mind constructs," and the psychology underlying Schutz' work, would be even more constructive. This seems especially so, given Caldwell's (1986, p. 1186) suggestion that it "may provide a solution to a number of persistent and troubling problems surrounding the issue of how best to characterize the rationality assumption."

Schutz' work had vital inputs from William James's (1890) *Principles of Psychology* and was also an admixture of philosophy and sociology of knowledge (see Zaner, in Schutz, 1970, pp. xiv–xv). That Schutz' approach to modeling decision-makers was much more broad-minded than that of conventional economics is particularly evident in the following passage from his (1967, p. 244) work:

> There is no limitation whatsoever regarding the ways of construction of ideal types. . . . Both "empirical" [in the sense of the sum and substance of experiences of the outside world] and "eidetic" [derived from speculative insights into the essence of things (in Wessensschau erfasst)] ideal types can be formed; though taken as invariant, the ideal type may be obtained by whatever method of generalization, abstraction, formalization, idealization, or imagination, provided only that the principle of meaning adequacy is observed.

That Schutz should, in this passage, allow a variety of methods for constructing "ideal types" and yet write as if, once constructed, they should be "taken as invariant" is something that might lead one at first to concur with Runde when he argues that the "mind construct" approach developed by O'Driscoll and Rizzo is rather opaque when it comes to providing a dynamic theory of learning, and that it is "incompatible with the process of learning." However, it seems doubtful that Runde's claim that mind constructs rest on the outcome of *given* knowledge, constraints, expectations, and so on, can be sustained as a part of picture of how O'Driscoll and Rizzo believe economists might usefully proceed. For example, it should be noted that, in discussing the uniqueness and open-endedness of market processes, O'Driscoll and Rizzo (1985, p. 78) argue that "from the experience of any given event [individuals] derive certain interpretatively relevant conceptual structures that modify any subsequent experience." They suggest that it would be methodologically possible to incorporate learning in a mind construct via attempts to show how moves from one mental framework to another may be seen to be intelligible. Indeed, this is something they must advocate to remain true to their Schutzian foundations as they seek to explain knowledge dynamics, investigate what knowledge is (as perceived by decision-makers), and how it is acquired and used both to construct and revise plans. For Schutz, the constructs used by social scientists are constructs of common-sense constructs employed by individuals (reflexive thinking is a hallmark of Schutz' work, as it is of Kelly's). These, to paraphrase Schutz, do not merely concern the texture of interlocking activities of individuals on the social scene — that is, a world which individuals (among whom are numbered social scientists) *share* with other individuals living and acting within it in common activities. *In addition,* "the particular experiential form in which common-sense thinking takes cognizance of the social cultural world . . . *is a result of a process of learning and acculturation*" (Schutz, 1971, p. 56, emphasis added). If subjectivists follow this latter theme, they will be able to avoid the complaint that Boland and Newman (1979) leveled at Lachmann (and Shackle), namely, that they had attributed a *single,* unsatisfactory, theory of knowledge to all economic agents. As Runde suggests, this problem may be circumvented by Kelly's concept of "permeability," but O'Driscoll and Rizzo (1985, pp. 41–42) at least deserve credit for broaching (if not solving) it using the mind constructs of Alfred Schutz.

Schutz' emphasis on the social side of the construction of every individual's knowledge is entirely compatible with the inclusion of Kellian psychology in work that tries to follow the pathways outlined by O'Driscoll and Rizzo; for personal construct theory stresses, in a manner not fully enunciated by Runde, that choices are made in a social context and have a social function (see Earl, 1983b). However, readers of Runde's chapter would do well to note that O'Driscoll and Rizzo themselves seem to have no intention of implicitly following the Kellian maxim that would merge their subjectivism with the behavioral approach to economics, namely, "If you want to find out how somebody sees a situation, ask him." They state (p. 36) that their "approach differs from individual psychology insofar as there is no real-world individual-by-individual investigation of perceptions. Instead, there is only a conjecturing of the perceptions of an ideal-typical individual or mind construct." Kellian theory might thus be welcomed by them as a way of explaining how a particular kind of mind construct might come to change through time, but Kellian research methods, as means of constructing a particular ideal type, are things we might be surprised to see them incorporate into their research program. In short, the radical subjectivist philosophy appears, in Schutz' terminology, eidetic, rather than empirical.

9 INTERVENING VARIABLES IN ECONOMICS: AN EXPLANATION OF WAGE BEHAVIOR

John L. Baxter

1. Introduction

Wage behavior lies at the heart of two of the most pressing problems facing economists at the present time: inflation and unemployment. It is now clear that the control of inflation cannot be viewed simply as a matter of controlling the money supply. Ultimately, we must grapple with the fundamental forces at work in societies, and many of these, as we should expect when dealing with human beings, are of a psychological nature. This chapter argues that intervening variables must be accorded a more central role in economics. In this chapter it is demonstrated how they may help improve our understanding of the forces generating inflation. Similarly, using this broader approach to economics we can hope to gain valuable insights into the reasons for wage "stickiness," and therefore into the reasons why the labor market may not clear, even in the long run. Keynes (see Trevithick, 1976), Tobin (1972), Solow (1979), and numerous others have stressed the importance of pay comparisons in explaining the downward stickiness of wages, but their views have still failed to gain general acceptance. The problem, it seems, is the lack of convincing microfoundations for these ideas. This chapter advances some proposals for filling this gap.

2. Intervening Variables

Although economists generally try to confine their analysis to "economic" matters, they are obliged to incorporate certain crucial assumptions in their theoretical models of the way people behave, in order to make their models manageable and enable conclusions to be derived from them. It is frequently assumed, for example, that individuals act "rationally," and that they are utility maximizers when spending their incomes, and profit maximizers when running businesses. Such assumptions about human behavior are more in the nature of psychological laws than economic laws, yet they are keystones of the whole edifice of orthodox economic theory (cf. Rutherford's discussion of psychologism in section 2 of chapter 3). The crucial role of expectations in economics has long been recognized, and their importance is probably greater now than ever before. Yet expectations are subjective in nature and can hardly be regarded in any sense as a purely economic variable. In essence, since economics deals with the activities of human beings, it cannot hope to escape entirely into a world in which only economic variables count.

Expectations in economics provide us with a good example of what is often referred to as an "intervening variable." To take the consumption function as an example: we normally say that an increase in income will, other things equal, tend to result in some increase in comsumer expenditure. However, as Katona (1960, 1975) frequently pointed out, among the things that may alter are consumer expectations. If, for example, consumers fear that during a period of growing unemployment they may lose their jobs, they may feel it only prudent to save most of any increase in income rather than spend it. Changed expectations, in other words, may alter the normal link between income and consumption (see section 2 of chapter 13 and Earl, 1986b, p. 103, for details of pertinent empirical work). Expectations, however, are only one of a range of potentially important intervening variables which are, for the most part, ignored in standard economic theory. Many of these intervening variables may be grouped under the broad headings of "motivation" and "attitudes."

Among social scientists, motivation and attitudes have mainly been the preoccupations of psychologists, though there is a long tradition of marketing science being interested in the psychologists' output in these areas. Let us consider motivation first: the term is usually applied in psychology to those factors that *energize* behavior and give it *direction*. An outline of the development of the concept of motivation and the various forms it has assumed is given by Atkinson and associates (1983), who trace its beginnings to the early ideas of *rationalism*, which assumed that people were rational beings with intellects, who freely chose goals and decided on courses of action, making the right choice if it were known — much in the manner, it seems, of that mythical figure Economic Man.

In the seventeenth and eighteenth centuries, the *mechanistic* view developed that personal actions arose from internal (to the human being) and external forces over which people had no control. One form taken by this approach was to attribute the underlying causes of all behavior to the tendencies to seek pleasure and avoid pain. This hedonistic doctrine, as we know, also influenced early economists such as Bentham and Jevons. The extreme form of the mechanistic view — a viewpoint diametrically opposed to the rationalistic view of human beings — was that human behavior was the consequence of inherited *instincts*. Psychoanalytic theory, based on the work of Freud and others, exerted a powerful influence in this field.

Dissatisfaction with instinct theory as a means of explaining *all* human behavior led to the development during the 1920s of *drive theory* — a drive being defined as "an aroused state that results from some biological need such as the need for food, water, sex, or avoidance of pain" (Atkinson et al., 1983). The concept of drive also stressed the importance of goals, and made it possible to test predictions about likely goals. The drive approach sees individuals being *pushed* into activity by internal forces, and therefore still left room for the development during the 1950s of yet another approach to motivation based on *incentives* — external stimuli tending to *pull* individuals to act in particular ways.

Finally, the cognitive approach to psychology also provides useful insights into motivation, stressing that the beliefs, expectations, and anticipations individuals have about future events also play a major part in determining their behavior. Human behavior is thus seen as purposeful, goal-directed, and based on conscious intentions (Steers and Porter, 1979).

Attitudes are also linked to personal behavior. Likes and dislikes, affinities for, and aversions to, objects, person, groups, etc., are examples of attitudes. Under this broad heading Katona (1960, 1975) also included expectations, bringing in the temporal aspect. We should not, however, be overconcerned with the niceties of classification. All that really matters for the economist is that a prima facie case can be made out for taking particular influences into account, and that these should subsequently be shown by empirical evidence to have the predicted effects. We should also expect that the relative importance of particular motivational factors and attitudes will vary, depending on the context. In the present study we are especially concerned with individual and group behavior in the work situation. We shall also be concentrating principally on the motivational aspects, since these appear to be the most useful in filling a number of important gaps in economic analysis.

When we turn to the question of motivation at work, we find in fact that there is a large degree of consensus about the key motives, based on research work in the field. Any listing of theories about work motivation would be likely, it seems, to include needs theories, equity theories, goal setting theory, and expectancy theory. We do not have the space to detail the various theories, but the following analysis attempts to integrate certain of the theories with conventional economic analysis in an effort to throw new light on old problems. In particular, we shall be looking at the way in which in which the motivational variables, especially those based on needs satisfaction and equity, serve to emphasize the importance of *relative* pay, and in so doing help to explain wage behavior. Finally we should note that the various theories of motivation are complementary rather than competing, and that a comprehensive theory of motivation would undoubtedly incorporate elements of each.

3. Needs, Wants, and Consumer Utility

In order to understand better why pay, and in particular *relative* pay, is important to the individual, it is necessary to retrace our steps to an early stage in the development of consumer theory. As Georgescu-Roegen (1968) has pointed out, the early economists analyzed consumer behavior in terms of *needs* or *wants*, and indeed it was the early theorizing about needs and wants, as in the work of Menger (1871/1976), that constituted the major source of inspiration for those who laid the foundations of utility theory. The crucial importance of needs and wants is well summed up by Georgescu-Roegen (1966) when he says, "The reality that determines the individual's behavior is not formed by utility, or ophelimity, or any other single element, but by his wants or his needs."

The tendency of economists in more recent years to reduce all needs and wants to a common yardstick, such as "utility" or "satisfaction," and to construct their analysis on this common base, has in fact resulted in the neglect of much that is important. In particular, it has drawn attention away from needs and wants, and thus from the *manner* in which utility is actually derived from their satisfaction. Attempts to change the focus of consumer theory back in the direction Menger had tried to take and away from the common yardstick philosophy, such as the work of Lancaster (1966, 1971) and Lutz and Lux (1979), have so far failed to bring about any fundamental change in the approach of the typical modern theorist. It is one of the principal contentions of this chapter that, in order to understand the basic forces influencing wage behavior, we must examine needs and wants more closely.

What precisely are these needs and wants which are so important? In contrast to most modern theorists, Marshall (1890, Book III) devoted a good deal of attention to their analysis in his *Principles*. He claimed that there was a hierarchy of wants, and that wants altered over time, with new ones developing as old ones were satisfied. An analysis of Marshall's work has led Haines (1982) to classify Marshall's hierarchy of wants as: biological needs (mainly food, clothing, and shelter, with a concern not just for quantity but also for variety and choice); health, education, and security; friendship, affection, belonging, conformity with social customs; distinction; activities and excellence; morality.

As we saw earlier in our discussion of motivation, needs figure prominently in psychological explanations of human behavior. Maslow's (1954) work still exerts a powerful influence on theorizing about needs (see Lutz and Lux, 1979, for example) and Haines makes the interesting observation that Marshall's hierarchy has many similarities with that developed later by Maslow, working from the perspective of a psychologist. Maslow identified five main categories of what he described as needs: physiological; safety and security; love and belongingness; esteem (a desire for reputation, prestige, competence, etc.); and self-actualization (the need of an individual to fulfill his or her potential). Subsequent research has suggested that there are probably only two principal categories of needs, with lower order needs (such as physiological and security) and higher order needs (such as esteem and self-actualization) clustering independently. Works by Herzberg and associates (1959), McLelland (1961), and Alderfer (1972), for example, have tended to stress fewer categories of needs: for an outline of their work see Judith R. Gordon (1983).

It appears, therefore, that needs and wants have a good deal in common, whether looked at from the perspective of an economist or a psychologist, but there do seem to be strong grounds for distinguishing between the two. It is the needs which give rise to the wants. Lutz and Lux (1979) express the connection as follows: "Wants, as the economist understands the term, can . . . be technically defined as the various preferences within a *common* category or level of need." Categories of needs and wants bear a strong resemblance because they are closely interlinked: but they are not identical. A need for food may be expressed by a variety of wants, depending, for example, upon a person's nationality, geographical location, etc., and these wants may well exceed needs — food being a very good example of such excess. It is the wants which are directly translatable into the demands for particular goods and services.

For present purposes, a study of needs and wants enables us to draw a number of significant conclusions. First, it is in the process of meeting wants that the consumer derives utility, or satisfaction. The satisfying of many needs and wants, such as those for love and belonging, and for esteem, imply social intercourse, and indeed the process of satisfying most needs and wants must surely be viewed within a social context, in which social comparisons will frequently be made.

Second, in modern society the ability to satisfy needs and wants is in great measure dependent on income, and this is true not only of physiological needs, such as food, heat, and shelter, but also of, for example, the need to belong (which might entail a desire to join clubs or societies), the need for esteem (requiring perhaps the purchase of fashionable clothes like those worn by one's peers) and the need for fulfillment (possibly requiring expenditure on educational facilities). In the light of the above, certain major weaknesses of the standard utility analysis in economics become more apparent. The standard utility function relates utility to the quantities of commodities purchased by an individual or sometimes a family. Inherent in this approach is the independence of utility, which is gained or lost by the individual as he/she varies his/her expenditure, wholly in isolation from the rest of society. Clearly, in the light of our discussion above, such an approach cannot hope to capture all the benefits a person derives from spending his/her income, nor fully explain *why* changes in the pattern yield particular benefits or disbenefits.

Take expenditure on clothing as an example: the purchase of a new brand of jeans may yield high utility, perhaps even greater utility than previous equivalent purchases of jeans, if the new ones are especially fashionable and provide the wearer with a certain prestige and status. Conversely, if in order to pay for the jeans the purchaser had to give up expenditure on hats, no loss of utility whatsoever might be entailed if hats had gone out of fashion. The point is, as Leibenstein[1] (1976), Boulding (1972), Thurow (1983), Duesenberry (1949), and others have stressed, that purchases of commodities by an individual, and the benefits derived from them, are not wholly independent of the purchases of others. It follows therefore that the utility derived by a person from spending his/her income is derived not just from his/her absolute level of income, but from his/her income relative to that of other consumers, since it is the latter which largely determines the extent to which the individual consumer is able, if he/she so wishes, to imitate the purchases of others.

We can take the analysis a stage further. Consider first the standard textbook example in which the consumer has to allocate his expenditure between two commodities, say apples and pears. The commodities yield a pleasant but different taste, and they may also satisfy hunger, so they meet personal needs. Being relatively cheap, they can be purchased by most consumers, who therefore have a choice of how much of each to consume in relation to their total budget and the satisfaction obtained. However, when it comes to the consumption of expensive items, such as clothes and the better cuts of meat, these face the poorer consumer with more serious problems of choice. Some low income families may even find that they do not have the option of buying meat every day or of buying better quality clothes. When we move on to consider yet more expensive items of consumption, such as yachts or holidays in distant, exotic locations, the proportion of the population to which such a choice is available becomes smaller still. In effect, the budget constraint imposed by a person's absolute income not only limits the *quantities* of different commodities which may be consumed, it also limits the *choice* of commodities available.

In the circumstances just described, marginal changes in income become very important. This is especially so for those on lower, and also for many on middle, incomes, since after meeting the cost of basic household requirements, such as accommodation, heating, lighting and food, a relatively small proportion of income remains uncommitted. It is this "uncommitted income" and changes in it which are the most important in determining the range of consumer choice available. Even if their real purchasing power is steadily rising, consumers are by no means guaranteed to feel they are succeeding in escaping from the chronic anxiety (cf. Kelly, 1955, p. 495) of being involved in a struggle to satisfy their basic household requirements: what are regarded as basic household requirements in an affluent society will be very different from what people regard as essentials in poorer societies. Consumers will tend to look at each other to judge how well they are coping with life. Thus, for example, if most people a consumer knows can afford to "get away from it all" on a foreign holiday or with the aid of escapist home videos, the consumer may well feel a sense of failure if unable to to choose likewise. It is therefore perfectly understandable if a consumer is very conscious of, and attaches considerable importance to, differences in absolute incomes, especially to the difference between the size of his/her income and the incomes of those with whom he/she normally compares him/herself.

This line of argument looks especially powerful if, like Lutz and Lux (1979), one views want-hierarchies in the manner suggested by Georgescu-Roegen (1954) and others, who note that consumers may not in practice be prepared to trade highly valued goods for others — at *any* cost. For example, consumers might only consider buying goods that enable them to meet their self-actualization needs *if* they judge they can do so without compromising their goals in respect of Maslow's four other needs categories; if their incomes do not permit this, they will feel boxed in, frustrated with the possibilities seemingly open to them. The higher the standards their external points of reference lead them to set for their goals, the more frustration they are likely to feel if their underlying psychologies are such that they choose in a strictly hierarchical manner, for the more income they will need before they can get on with meeting their self-actualization needs. (Once their four other needs are being met, consumers may only expand their expenditures on goods that pertain to them insofar as such actions constitute efficient routes to meeting their self-actualization needs.)[2] The importance of such a "lexicographic" mode of consumer behavior is a matter for empirical investigation. Lutz and Lux quite probably overplay the conclusions they draw from integrating the ideas of Maslow and Georgescu-Roegen: at one extreme, it may be that only goods required for mere survival would not be traded, and that the hierarchy therefore only had a limited influence on consumer decisions; however, it is not hard to find instances in which some consumers do not appear prepared to trade goods which could scarcely be said to minister essentially to physiological survival needs (see Earl, 1986b, chapter 9). Indeed, it is far from unknown to see workers prepared to fight for wages relativities "at all costs."

The importance of relative income to the consumer can be demonstrated in a still more forceful fashion by reference to what Hirsch (1977) has called "positional goods." These are goods which, because of their nature, must always be in short supply. In countries with large populations relative to land area, for example, or in densely populated urban areas, not all are likely to be able to afford a home with a reasonably sized garden. Access to certain desirable leisure facilities, such as golf clubs or country clubs, may also be available only to those on relatively high incomes. Even if the level of all absolute incomes were to be increased tenfold overnight, it would not help all those on relatively low incomes to gain access to the desirable facilities, since their cost would rise accordingly. These are obvious cases in which it is the *relative* income which yields the satisfaction, not simply the absolute level of income.

Until now, our discussion has centered on the individual within a narrow context, in which he/she has been making direct purchases of commodities for his/her own consumption. We turn now to examine the position of the individual within the context of society as a whole. In today's society, the needs of the individual are generally met not only by direct purchases but indirectly by government expenditure, which most individuals help finance through the taxes they pay. In a progressive tax system, some of the income inequalities we referred to earlier are offset. For example, those on very low incomes may have their purchases of food augmented, or a contribution made toward payment of their rent. Even many of those on somewhat higher incomes will still be net beneficiaries of government expenditure on such services as education and health. Such indirect assistance, and changes in it, must influence the individual's decisions on how he allocates his/her own after-tax income, and ought therefore to figure in the individual's utility function, in addition to the interpersonal influences on consumption noted earlier. Even so, one still should not downplay the significance of social inequalities rooted in income inequalities — for example, the neighborhood in which a person lives often has a bearing on the quality of local schools, and possibly also the quality of local health and social services provision. In other words, despite the progressive nature of most tax systems, a person's whole lifestyle, and the utility derived from it, can in large measure be traced back to his/her income, not just absolute income, but also his/her relative income in society.

4. Reference Groups and the Form of the Utility Function

Our preceding discussion has emphasized the importance of economic and social comparisons in determining the benefits derived by an individual from consumption of commodities. Empirical work in the field of psychology and sociology suggests that such comparisons are not simply haphazard or whimsical. Investigations by Runciman (1966) and others have found, for example, that individuals tend to compare themselves with particular "reference groups." Various forms of reference groups have been distinguished, not all of them relevant to our present discussion, but two seem of special importance. First there are "comparative reference groups," generally defined as groups whose situation or attributes a person contrasts with his/her own. Second there are "normative reference groups" — groups from which a person takes his/her standards. These reference groups, and some of their implications for economics, are discussed at greater length in Baxter (1973); they have also received attention in models of consumer behavior proposed in marketing (for example, see Fishbein and Ajzen, 1975).

The work of Runciman and others suggests that reference groups with the strongest influence tend to be those with whom individuals come into closest contact, perhaps at work, or in other aspects of their lives. Comparisons with such groups may, however, operate at different levels of aggregation, ranging from a single individual to large groups containing many people. With respect to the consumption of an individual, his or her particular reference group will be especially important in determining the extent of utility derived from a given pattern of consumption associated with interpersonal comparisons. We should note, too, that reference groups may alter over time, with consequent implications for the utility derived from a given pattern of consumption expenditure. In other words, one of the reasons for the changes in tastes which frequently feature in economic discussions, as of the consumption function, may be a change in reference groups.

For the reasons outlined above, pay comparisons will be among the most important comparisons made by an individual between his or her own situation and that of his or her reference group(s). With this in mind, we are now in a position to propose a more precise form for the utility function of the individual. It is as follows:

$$U_i = u \left(W_i, \ \frac{W_i}{\overline{W}_{r_1}}, \ \frac{W_i}{\overline{W}_{r_2}}, \ \text{---} \ \frac{W_i}{\overline{W}_{r_n}}, \ G_c, P \right) \tag{9.1}$$

where: U_i is the total utility obtained from consumption by individual i; W_i is the money wage of i, representing the income at the disposal of the individual, and therefore the budget constraint imposed on his or her consumption of commodities; $W_i/\overline{W}_{r_1}$ represents the money wage of i relative to the average wage of individuals in reference group r_i, denoted by, $\overline{W}_{r_i}$ (similarly for reference groups r_2 to r_n, should there be groups other than r_i); G_c is that part of government expenditure having an influence on the utility derived by i from his/her own consumption; P is the general level of prices which affect the real purchasing power of wages.

In equation (9.1), which is expressed in the form of an indirect utility function, it is the relative wage variables and the government expenditure variable which catch the important effects on consumer utility omitted from the standard treatment. We are not in any way suggesting here that there are no other relevant variables — Morgan (1978), for example, has suggested others, including uncertainty and ignorance of facts — but we are trying to fill one glaring gap. Note, finally, that we have not addressed the question of whether it would be possible to add the utility functions of individuals, as expressed in equation (9.1), to obtain an equation for a group of people. To the extent, however, that individuals act as a coherent group in matters of pay, it would not seem unreasonable to express a group function in the same form as equation (9.1), with W_i becoming the wage rate of the group.

5. The Downward Inflexibility of Wages

We now introduce a second motivational variable, namely equity, to our discussion of wage behavior. In Baxter (1980) it was argued that the individual will judge fair pay by reference to at least two principal criteria: first, pay in the job situation, where the main consideration will be equitable pay in relation to the job performed; second, at the more general level of society as a whole, where the general principles which govern, or ought to govern, economic and social inequalities are more important. In both contexts, notions of equity appear to exert a powerful influence on individuals' behavior in relation to their pay.

With regard to equitable pay at work, one of the most convincing approaches is that of Adams (1965), who has argued that there exist normative expectations of what constitute fair correlations between inputs and outputs (or, in Adams' terminology, *outcomes*). Included in inputs are effort, skill, education, experience, etc., while outcomes comprise pay, fringe benefits, status, etc. Equity exists for an individual when:

$$\frac{\Sigma O_p}{\Sigma I_p} = \frac{\Sigma O_r}{\Sigma I_r} \qquad (9.2)$$

where: O and I are the weighted sums of outcomes and inputs, respectively, and p and r are subscripts denoting Person (the individual making the comparison) and Other (any individual with whom Person is in an exchange relationship, or with whom he/she compares him/herself). We should note that the inputs and outcomes are those *perceived* by Person, and may not wholly accord with objective criteria or the perceptions of others.

In the light of his/her perceptions of the various inputs and outcomes, Person will form his view of the equitable wage (W_e), which may differ from the actual wage (W_p). In circumstances in which Person perceives $\Sigma O_p/\Sigma I_p < \Sigma O_r/\Sigma I_r$, he/she will be motivated to try to rectify the situation, either by increasing O_p or reducing I_p, or a combination of the two. If on the other hand, to take another example, the conditions for equity expressed in equation (9.2) held, and in addition $W_e = W_p$, then any attempt to reduce the actual wage would give rise to a situations of inequity and we would once again expect a reaction from Person.

At the broader level of society as a whole, we have already noted the importance of inequalities. Few people, if any, argue in favor of complete equality as a goal for society. Most are prepared to accept certain inequalities, but beyond some point inequalities may be such as to give rise to resentment. It would be helpful if generally acceptable criteria were available by which inequalities could be judged. None yet exist,[3] but given the importance of pay in meeting personal needs, and in determining human well-being, it is not surprising that relative pay is widely seen as one of the principal criteria by which equity, not only in the job situation but equity overall, is judged.

It will be apparent from the above that notions of fairness entail an important element of social comparisons — we saw earlier that this was also true of the satisfaction of needs and wants. These intervening variables are in turn closely linked to an individual's goals and expectations. The utility function expressed in equation (9.1) suggests that the minimum goals for an individual will be to maintain both the absolute level of W_i (assuming that $W_i = W_e$ and that P remains unchanged) and the relative position of W_i in comparison with wages in reference groups. Failure to do so would result in a drop in total utility. However, for most people a notable feature of the changing environment has for many years now been a tendency for money wage increases to outstrip the rise in prices, thereby enabling the quantities of commodities purchased and total utility to be increased. It seems highly likely that this has in turn influenced the goals and expectations of individuals, at least of those in work. Many employees have now been led to expect a continued rise in their money wages at a faster pace than inflation — if not every year, then at least on average, and in the short as well as the long term — and this must seem a realistic goal in wage bargaining. We assume such a goal in our subsequent analysis.

We turn, finally, to the response of individuals to changes in the objective environment and the influence of intervening variables. The end result is that the individual formulates a perception of the level of pay to which he/she feels entitled, and realistically expects to achieve from his/her employment, taking into account all the factors noted above — that is, the individual sets an aspiration level, a personal target defining what he/she will see as a satisfactory wage (cf. Simon, 1959, 1979). The important question then is, does the perceived entitlement match the pay he/she actually receives? Should the perceived entitlement fall short of the actual, the individual will experience a sense of what, following Runciman (1966) we call "relative deprivation" (RD). Runciman defined RD as follows:

> A is relatively deprived of X when (1) he does not have X, and (2) he sees some other person or persons, which may include himself at some previous or expected time, as having X (whether or not this is or will be in fact the case), (3) he wants X, and (4) he sees it feasible that he should have X.

We can see from this definition that the concept of RD fits closely with the idea of reference groups. An extensive discussion of RD and its economic implications is contained in Baxter (1973, 1980), and we shall return to this topic further below.

6. Surplus Labor and the Downward Inflexibility of Wages

Numerous reasons have been advanced for the failure of prices to vary sufficiently downwards to ensure that markets always clear. Gordon (1981) has reviewed the ways in which firms' price-setting decisions in product markets may contribute to price inflexibility. Wage and employment decisions also influence price movements, of course, and it is these labor market aspects with which we are primarily concerned. Here, too, a variety of theories are already on offer to explain why wages are sticky, and in a review of the theories (some of which have ancient pedigrees) Solow (1980) makes a point which many economists often seem reluctant to accept — perhaps because it adds greatly to the complexity of analysis — namely, that all may have something to contribute to a full explanation of labor market failure. It is is this spirit that we attempt below to provide stronger microfoundations for the "wage comparisons approach" to wage stickiness, without which there would be a glaring gap between the theories and the institutional workings of the labor market.

To understand why money wages are inflexible downwards in conditions of surplus labor, we have to examine the different interests of the parties involved. Most of the unemployed seeking work will probably already have been in employment, but their utility functions will now be different. They will now be living on some form of social security benefit which is less than their previous wage, and their consumption of commodities, and the range of commodities available to them, will have been reduced. Their reference groups may also have changed. The most likely point of comparison now is the wage previously earned. Comparisons with the wages of other groups may be maintained, but perhaps less strongly, or they may assume a more general nature, in which the position of the unemployed as a group is compared with all those in employment. The utility function of an unemployed person might therefore be represented as follows:

$$U_j = u(B_j, \frac{B_j}{W_j}, \frac{B_j}{\overline{W}}, G_c, P) \qquad (9.3)$$

where: B_j is the unemployment or other social security benefit received by j when unemployed; W_j is the wage received by j when in employment; $\overline{W}$ is the average wage of those in employment, the assumption being that individual reference groups used previously have been abandoned.

Unless the unemployed person blames him/herself, or no one else, for his/her plight, he/she is now likely to feel a sense of grievance, or more precisely of relative deprivation, when comparing his/her situation with what it was previously. Since the way to overcome this is by obtaining employment at a wage comparable with the previous wage (not necessarily in the same line of work) the unemployed will generally seek work. Should it prove impossible to obtain employment at the previous wage, there will still be an incentive to take work at a lesser wage, and some may even be prepared to offer to undertake their previous work at a reduced wage. A sense of RD could nevertheless be expected to persist.

In the case of a person in employment, there are a number of reasons why he/she could be expected to resist strongly any attempt to reduce his/her money wage, even in the face of a widespread labor surplus. First, it would reduce his/her total consumption of commodities, assuming no compensating fall in prices. Equally important, however, it would, in the absence of a proportionate reduction in the money wages of those in his/her reference groups, reduce his/her consumption relative to these groups. He/she would therefore suffer an even greater loss of utility, probably no longer being able to afford as many of those commodities which they enjoyed in common, perhaps even having to forego some altogether. The reduction in utility could in fact be quite disproportionate to the reduction in income, because at the margin certain goods yielding a high utility for a given financial outlay only become available above a certain level of income, and might be lost if income fell.

There is also the question of equity. If we assume that at the outset equity existed, and the employee was being paid the equity wage W_e then any reduction in his/her money wage would be judged unfair and would be resisted. To the extent that the reduction in pay subjected the individual to greater inequalities in society at large, the resistance would be greater still. Feelings of relative deprivation would have been created, with inevitable consequences for the third party involved, the employer. However, before we turn to consider the employer's position it is appropriate to note that in the above analysis the general price level is assumed to remain unchanged. Keynes rightly saw that a reduction in purchasing power would be less strongly resisted if it occurred through the medium of a general rise in prices, with relative money incomes being unaffected — the loss of utility would then derive only from the fall in absolute real income. But while this might be far easier to engineer (for example, by an injection of purchasing power) than a simultaneous proportionate money wage reduction for everybody (which would not necessarily do anything to remove a deficiency of effective demand), problems of inequity could still arise due to the non-indexation of financial assets and liabilities. One should also note that feelings of relative deprivation could arise if wage earners as a whole observed that profit incomes were rising in real terms while wages and salaries were falling in their purchasing power.

As far as the employer's position is concerned, Baxter (1973) noted that one consequence of a feeling of RD would be to alter the employees' attitudes toward their employer(s). It could be expected to make employees less cooperative, perhaps accompanied by a reduction in effort at work, obstruction, and resistance to change. There might even be a work to rule, or strikes, with consequent loss of output and productivity. We can illustrate these effects by specifying the short-run production function of the firm in the following form (a form closely resembling that used by Annable, 1977, although arrived at by a rather different route):

$$Q_A = q\left(L, \frac{W_i}{W_e}\right) \tag{9.4}$$

where: Q_A is the volume of output of firm A; L is the labor input; W_i is the money paid by firm A to individual i; W_e is the equitable wage as perceived by individual i.

The implication of our analysis is that Q_A will be maximized when $W_i \geqslant W_e$. When $W_i = W_e$, output of firm A will depend in effect simply on the input of labor, and will be no different from a conventional production function. When, however, $W_i < W_e$, the normal functional relationship between Q_A and L will alter, with the value of the coefficient of L falling as output per unit is reduced by the actions of the aggrieved employee. This will in turn have implications for the profit maximizing output of the firm.

In a situation in which $W_i = W_e$, and the employer is offered alternative, or additional, labor at a wage rate less than W_i, an employer will, in purely financial terms, have to weigh the effect of the reduction in labor costs on profits against the possible reduction in output or revenue caused by the sense of RD created among existing employees. (RD, as we saw earlier, might also exist even among the new employees, if recruited from unemployed who were previously employed at higher rates of pay.) The quality of labor offered may also be inferior to that of existing labor (cf. Dow and Earl, 1982, pp. 205–206).

Where $W_i > W_e$, it should be possible to reduce W_i without causing a sense of RD, although if it has for long been customary for an employer to pay above the fair wage, then it is possible that employees will have come to consider W_i as the appropriate yardstick and still fell aggrieved if they are paid at a lower rate. The reference group in effect becomes the individual in his/her previous, more highly paid, state.

In a firm already paying less than W_e, RD will already exist, and reducing W_i still lower could be expected to add to the sense of RD. (Whether proportionately to the reduction in W_i, or not, is a matter that can only be resolved empirically.) We must mention, finally, that the decision of an employer not to accept labor offered at a lower wage rate may not, of course, be taken wholly on financial grounds. The idea of the implicit contract suggests that an employer may feel he/she has a moral commitment to, among other things, maintaining certain differentials vis-a-vis reference groups or to paying the equitable wage. (If one dimension of the employer's self-image is that of a fair person rather than a ruthless capitalist, then he/she may only be willing to contradict this aspect of his self-image if this is the only way he/she can see of avoiding even greater damage, such as to his/her view of him/herself as a solvent businessperson). Habit and inertia may also play their part.

We should note, too, that public sector employment is now very important in many countries. If anything, pay comparisons seem even more important to public sector employees (in, for example, the public utilities). Financial considerations, too, may be less tight in the public sector, and greater importance may be attached to social considerations (as they relate to employees). The balance of forces, then, in both the private and public sectors, seems to be heavily weighted against the use of reductions in money wages as a means of fostering employment, certainly where the reductions apply only to some, not all, workers. Since many policy makers seem not to have picked up Keynes' (1936, chapter 19) message that money wage cuts may fail to promote increased employment, the use of the present analysis could be said to lie in its power to deter policy-makers from unknowingly embarking on a potentially futile strategy by making such a strategy seem unworkable in the first place, owing the the role of pay comparisons in labor market behavior.

7. Pay Comparisons and Inflation

In his presidential address to the American Economic Association, Tobin (1972) drew attention to a myth of macroeconomics, ". . . that relations among aggregates are enlarged analogues of relations among corresponding variables for individual households firms, industries and markets." He went on to outline how an economy in which wages in different sectors were linked through a system of comparability could be in perpetual sectoral disequilibrium even when it had settled into a stochastic macroequilibrium. Such a system might also exhibit marked trends over time and appreciable fluctuations around these trends. We explore this type of system in this section of the paper, and its implications for inflation.

The links between wage settlements in different sectors of the economy have been described as a "wage spillover" process. (Surveys of the literature in this area are given in Burton and Addison, 1977; Mitchell, 1980; and Addison and Burton, 1984). A number of specific forms of the spillover process have been suggested. Among these have been: wage contours (Dunlop, 1957); the union politics hypothesis (Ross, 1948); wage leadership (Ross, 1957; Eckstein and Wilson, 1962; Turner and Jackson, 1970; Edgren, Faxen and Odhner, 1973); and wage rounds (examples include Levinson, 1960; Knowles and Robinson, 1962; Eckstein and Wilson, 1962; and McCarthy et al., 1975).

The extent to which particular forms of wage spillover exist, or perhaps have existed, is a matter for empirical research. Given the large number of bargaining units involved, and the complications caused by numerous variables, such as changes in hours, holidays and fringe benefits, trying to find conclusive evidence of linkage poses many problems. There is a growing body of evidence, nevertheless, to indicate that linkage does exist. Some of the evidence is contained in the studies referred to above. Other examples include Sargan (1971), Addison (1974), Brown and Sisson (1975), Mehra (1976), and Foster et al. (1984).

A weakness of spillover studies, noted by Wood (1978), is that the microeconomic behavioral underpinnings of the models are generally not spelled out to any great extent, and the characteristics of the processes described are not properly expressed. Wood's study makes a considerable contribution to filling some of the gaps, but it does not really get to grips with many of the behavioral issues raised, such as the underlying reasons for the constant upward pressure on wages, the reasons why relativities are so important to employees, and the basis of employees' notions of fairness. We now go on to offer an explanation of some of the fundamental forces underlying the spillover process, using the analytical framework outlined earlier. One major attraction of this approach is that it is not tied to any particular pattern of spillover, but is rather in the nature of a general explanation of the process.

We considered earlier how any move to reduce money wages could give rise to a sense of RD. Similar feelings may also arise even in circumstances in which money wages are rising. The response to the objective environment, and to the influence of intervening variables is a perceived wage entitlement, which is compared with the actual wage received. Our earlier analysis suggests that the perceived entitlement will be based on the expectation of achieving an increase in money wages which will not only outstrip the rise in prices but also insure that the individual (or group) is able to maintain his/her relative wage in relation to reference groups. A sense of RD would be created if either of these conditions ceased to hold and the perceived entitlement fell short of the actual wage. We can see that in these circumstances expectations assume a more crucial role, both expectations of the likely rise in prices and the likely rise in reference group wages during the period covered by the wage bargain.

Should the actual wage fail to match the perceived entitlement, we could expect pressure from employees to increase their actual wage until equality was restored. Various ways in which employees could take steps to increase their bargaining power in order to try to achieve this objective, independently of the state of demand pressures in the labor market, were outlined in Baxter (1980). Employees might, for example, come together in a bargaining group, such as a trade union, or increase the proportion of the labor force already joined in such a group; make improvements in organization, perhaps by strengthening links between group representatives and members of the group; or find ways of drawing upon outside sources of power, perhaps in the form of financial arrangements.

Operating within the context of our analytical framework, the wage spillover process can explain both short-term variations in the rate of increase in money wages and the continuous upward pressure underlying the longer term upward trend in wages. It can also explain differences in wage behavior between countries. Marked fluctuations in the rate of growth of money wages would be caused by *any* relatively large wage settlement(s), whatever the reason. An increase in labor demand pressures is one obvious source of such an increase, but it could equally well be the knock-on effect on prices and wages of a shock increase in import prices, a new technological development leading to high productivity and profits in one sector of the economy, or it could be a large public sector wage settlement. The effects of such increase would be once-and-for-all unless they set off other, even larger, increases — gradually petering out as other wage-linked groups of workers insisted on corresponding wages increases. Such a process maybe at work even when the labor market is far from buoyant.

In any economy in which the labor market is characterized by numerous independent bargaining groups, and there is therefore the likelihood of one or more groups obtaining wage increases substantially above the prevailing norm at any given time, the spillover effect will tend to provide a continuing upward impetus to wages, even during periods of prolonged high unemployment. Only if wage settlements occurred simultaneously could it be avoided — even then there would be spillover from one bargaining period to the next. Moreover, our analysis in the previous sections suggests that there are strong reasons for employees to press continually for higher incomes, since this is the main route to greater utility. Our analysis is therefore entirely consistent with the target growth of real wages hypothesis, for which some economists (for example, Foster et al., 1984) have claimed empirical support. There is always the possibility, too, of even greater gains if a person can increase his/her money wage relative to that of other workers, even if in the process prices are pushed up faster. Even if the community as a whole loses, there may be benefits to the individual from any *relative* improvement in wages he is able to obtain.

In the light of the above, our wage equation for the individual employee (and a similar format will also apply to a group of employees) takes the following form:

$$\dot{W}_i = f\left(T, \frac{\dot{W}_i}{\dot{W}_{r_1}}, \frac{\dot{W}_i}{\dot{W}_{r_2}}, \dot{G}_c^e, \dot{P}^e, x_1\text{-------}x_n\right) \tag{15}$$

where: T is the target growth of money wage rate, which will take account of the expected rate of change of prices ($\dot{P}^e$); $\dot{W}_i\dot{W}_{r_1}$ represents the rate of growth of the person's money wage relative to the expected growth of money wages in reference group r_1 (and similarly for reference group r_2); $\dot{G}_c^e$ is the expected rate of growth of government expenditure as it affects the individual's spending decisions and utility; $x_1\text{-------}x_n$ is a vector of other variables having an influence on $\dot{W}_i$.

At the level of the economy as a whole, the aggregate rate of growth of money wages ($\dot{W}$) is influenced by the sum of individuals' satisfaction or dissatisfaction with their pay — how they perceive their pay entitlements in relation to the pay actually received. In effect we are dealing with the sum of RD, and our wage equation would take the form:

$$\dot{W}_t = f\left(T_t, \dot{R}D_t, \dot{G}_{ct}^e, \dot{P}_t^e\text{-------}x_{nt}\right). \tag{9.6}$$

Since RD is a subjective variable and not directly measurable, a suitable proxy would have to be devised. The development of the technique of-subjective measurement scales, now widely used in market research sample surveys, suggests that this problem could be overcome, even at the aggregate level of the total economy as set out in equation (9.6). Experience would determine the usefulness of the particular measures adopted.

We turn, finally, to the international aspects. In any economy, but probably especially in those growing and developing rapidly, the influences of the intervening variables could be expected to vary over time. With the advent of new industries, reference groups will change, for some at least. The growing influence of the media must also, it seems, contribute to changing perceptions; so too will changes in government policy. Many goals and expectations have doubtless had to be revised in the light of the changes in economic circumstances since the early 1970s. Moreover, given the wide social, economic, and political divergences between countries, there is no reason why the suggested analytical framework should produce the same results when applied in different countries. The objective environments, reference groups, notions of fairness, goals, and expectations are all likely to differ in some degree, and so too might the responses. The framework is nonetheless of general application, and it would be surprising if some common tendencies did not emerge.

8. Conclusions

This chapter has attempted to demonstrate that the study of intervening variables can improve our understanding of economic problems and help in suggesting solutions to them. Motivation theory seems especially useful, drawing our attention to the importance of needs and wants, notions of equity, and other key intervening variables. We have tried to show how these ideas might be incorporated in economic analysis.

Our study indicates that an analysis of needs and wants is essential to a full understanding of the influences that determine consumer purchases of goods and services; yet, in recent years especially, these influences have been neglected by most economists. Instead, economists have concentrated on analyzing such general constructs as utility, or satisfaction, or the response of consumers to price and income changes. The latter approaches may reveal a good deal about consumer behavior, but they hide even more since they operate at too aggregated a level. A further consequence of this approach, it seems, has been a continuing tendency to ignore the significance of interdependent preferences among consumers, who, after all, are social beings. In a world in which consumers are now more than ever aware of the consumption behavior of others, it is simply no longer possible to go on ignoring the interdependence of personal decision making if economists wish their views to be taken seriously.

Once the rightful role of interdependent preferences is accepted, it becomes possible, with the help of ideas developed in some of the other social sciences, to advance a more convincing theory of money wages. In particular, it becomes clear why individuals and groups of employees put up staunch resistance to attempts to reduce their money wages. They have a great deal more to lose than the conventional utility analysis would lead us to believe; and so too, indirectly, do employers. The conclusion, inevitably, is that attempting to solve a serious unemployment problem by reductions in the money wages of employees does not seem a practical proposition, especially if it is done selectively — a general reduction in real wages through a rise in the price level may be another matter.

The omission of interdependent preferences from the standard utility function probably also helps explain the failure to accord pay comparisons their rightful role in explaining inflationary pressures. At the very least, the wage spillover process must feature in any comprehensive analysis of how wage and other increases are transmitted into higher prices. But our analysis suggests we ought to go much further. Wage spillover may be the fundamental source of a price increase, with employers and even governments having to accommodate the social, economic, and political pressures that build up. If we wish to get to grips with the ultimate causes of inflation, analysis cannot be restricted solely to monetary variables, important though these may be, since they tell us only part of the story. Tackling the problem of wage spillover. however, is no easy matter. It would seem to require either the development of a national consensus in each country about appropriate relativities and wage increases, such as seems to exist in only a few countries (for example, Austria) or the development of more formal incomes policies which address the central problem of relativities.

The analysis in the present chapter has been concerned with particular aspects of wage behavior, but it will be clear that the analytical framework could be applied to other wage problems, such as equitable pay for women and nonunion/union wage differentials. Unfortunately, limitations of space have made it impossible to pursue such matters in the present chapter.

One final conclusion seems worth drawing from our analysis, namely, that much conventional analysis in economics is prone to oversimplification. This may sound strange in an era of large-scale macroeconomic models and economic journals filled with often complex mathematics, but the basic theoretical structures underlying these are often unduly simplified. In particular, they make insufficient allowance for the complexity of human responses to economic events. This weakness is especially apparent in situations in which people do not conform to their normal pattern of behavior. If we are to make real progress in understanding how humans respond in certain situations, economists must inevitably forge stronger links with other social sciences.

Acknowledgments

The author is grateful to J.L. Ford, B.J. McCormick, and the editor for helpful comments and suggestions, but accepts sole responsibility for the chapter in its final form.

Notes

1. Leibenstein demonstrates that such ideas have a very long lineage indeed.

2. In this latter case, hierarchical wants would not have to imply an absence of substitution between goods as relative prices changed — see Earl (1983a, chapter 6).

3. The attempt by Rawls (1971) to devise acceptable criteria has been widely discussed without, however, any consensus emerging. An outline of his approach is given in Baxter (1973).

4. In equation (9.1) we dealt with reference groups used by a consumer, whereas equation (9.5) includes reference groups used by a wage earner. There is, however, likely to be a strong link between the two (with different working groups living in the same community, for example), and to emphasize this link we retain the same notation.

10 THE PSYCHOLOGICAL ECONOMICS OF CONSPICUOUS CONSUMPTION

Roger S. Mason

1. Introduction

Those interested in the demand for status goods will find it difficult to identify a recognizable and significant body of literature on the phenomenon of conspicuous consumption. Indeed, the subject has been generally seen as a side issue well away from mainstream economic and social thought and having little or no relevance to present day preoccupations.

Motivated by a desire to impress others with the ability to pay high prices for prestige goods, conspicuous consumers are inspired not by the economic or physiological utility of goods and services but by social and psychological considerations. The "pure" conspicuous consumer is in fact persuaded to buy only if the price of a commodity is high enough to allow for the ostentatious display of purchasing power and the actual utility of the good in question — that is, the utility of the product in use — is of no real interest. Consumer satisfaction is achieved through gaining the admiration of a target audience for the amount spent — more simply, wealth display is all. Under such circumstances, product price becomes the only factor of any importance to the buyer.

As a phenomenon, conspicuous consumption has always been with us.

The existence and consequences of such behavior had been recognized long before the publication of Thorstein Veblen's (1899) *Theory of the Leisure Class.* At the time of the Roman Empire, the authorities became so concerned about the spread of status-spending that sumptuary laws were introduced to suppress it; other societies have shown equal concern for excesses which they considered were undermining the stability and security of the state. Today, such extravagances can still be found in many parts of the world and even in those countries where it is less obvious in its pure form, status display is very much in evidence. Snob and bandwagon effects, themselves derivatives of conspicuous consumption, are commonplace and have a significant effect on spending patterns.

2. The Motivation to Consume Conspicuously

Within any community, the propensity to consume conspicuously is determined by dominant cultural traditions and values and by the social and economic environment. Social structure and the means by which social mobility is achieved also heavily influence such behavior. At the individual level, demand for status goods is affected also by those subcultures to which a person belongs (or to which he/she has been exposed) and which have the strongest influence on his or her social aspirations. Social class and reference group influences also have a marked effect on individual consumer behavior and can themselves encourage ostentatious economic display (see Mason, 1981, chapter 2).

These influences shape social character and produce conditions in which conspicuous consumption either prospers or is rejected. However, a sympathetic environment is a necessary but not sufficient motivator, for the need to consume conspicuously requires the individual to have not only a social character that has been made sympathetic to such behavior but also a positive wish or drive to consume conspicuously for him/herself. The second element of motivation therefore requires the individual to have a high propensity to achieve, a high propensity to "role play" and a high sensitivity to social relationships at all levels (Mason, 1981, pp. 26–27). While these three characteristics are generally conceded to be determined in part by social and cultural conditioning, they are also partly determined by innate personality traits which are independent of environmental influences. It is this independent random variable which explains why all individuals who are exposed to identical or near identical environments do not all choose to be conspicuous consumers.

3. The Economics of Conspicuous Consumption

The economics of conspicuous consumption are equally complicated. An individual's ability to indulge in ostentatious economic display is primarily determined by the discretionary wealth he/she is able to command. However, it is not only absolute but relative wealth which is important, in that conspicuous consumption is directed toward achieving status gains through the admiration of a target audience for the wealth which has been displayed in making any given purchase. It is therefore income and wealth relativities and not absolute levels of wealth which can be expected to be the determining factor in encouraging conspicuous consumption.

The conspicuous consumer can have two objectives in mind when undertaking any particular act of display. First, he or she may be hoping to make status gains from others within an existing membership group. On the other hand, it is possible that the consumer is intending to impress a higher group in order to be "elevated" in terms of social position and prestige. In the former case, if the price paid for any particular product would normally appear to be beyond the buying power of the group's members, then the status value of consumption will be seen as significant. However, the consumption decision is complicated by the difficulties the consumer has in knowing whether or not a particular choice will provoke countermeasures by those whose status positions it would call into question. The discretionary income and wealth of other group members is clearly difficult to assess. There may be those within the group who for one reason or another have mortgaged a particularly high level of their funds, while others, earning approximately the same amount, enjoy far greater discretionary income. Clearly the reaction of these two groups to any observed expenditure on status goods will be markedly different.

When conspicuous consumption is motivated by the desire to gain recognition from higher socioeconomic groups, then the income of the status-seeker becomes a far greater constraint on his/her ability to indulge in ostentatious economic display. Purchase for display to a richer audience requires the individual to cross the economic divide between the two groups, but there is now substantial evidence to show that so great is the desire for status that many consumers are prepared to contract substantial debts in order to produce the required audience reaction and to benefit in terms of upward social mobility.

At the macro level, therefore, the propensity to consume conspicuously varies according to economic and social factors. In economic terms, levels of absolute and relative wealth distribution are prime determinants although it must be remembered that what constitutes an economic surplus is very much a social phenomenon which may itself be a product of past acts of ostentatious consumption (many of today's "essential" items being the status goods of a less affluent era). Overall, however, the more unequal the distribution then the fewer the number of people who will have a substantial economic surplus to invest in ostentatious display and economic waste. These few people are able to indulge in particularly high levels of conspicuous consumption. In contrast, those societies in which income and wealth are more broadly distributed give far more people the opportunity to seek status through purchasing display but do not allow individuals the opportunity to indulge themselves to excess.

General economic theories of consumer demand are not capable of dealing adequately with status spending and conspicuous economic display although they work well in describing market behavior with respect to more normal purchases. First, conventional theories assume that people demand and choose products for reasons which are rational in economic terms. This rationality then means that as the price of a good increases so demand will, other things being equal, fall. Conspicuous consumers, however, are rational not in economic but in social-psychological terms, and an increase in the price of a product can be attractive rather than unwelcome to the potential buyer. Secondly, and more fundamentally, status spending conflicts with the entire reductionist philosophy of neoclassical economics and points toward structuralism and the need to study social networks in order to understand patterns of demand. Neoclassical theories, centered on the concept of market equilibrium rather than on market segmentation, are not able to respond to such a challenge.

4. Conspicuous Consumption and the Literature of Economics up to 1960

As an exceptional form of consumer expenditure, conspicuous consumption lies outside marginal utility theory and in that sense does not challenge general economic theory. What is worrying, however, is that many economists have tended to dismiss the phenomenon of status consumption as being so esoteric a matter that it does not warrant consideration. As we shall see, studies of the intricacies of individual preference formation have been seen as serving no useful purpose. Consequently, work has continued to focus on aggregate data rather than on the heterogeneity of mass markets at a time when others are paying attention to explaining the preferences and behavior of market minorities, including the demand for status goods and the related need for ostentatious economic display.

Since Veblen, therefore, economists' studies of conspicuous consumption have been remarkable more by their absence than by their quantity. Alfred Marshall's (1920, p. 16) view that "the economist studies mental states rather through their manifestations than in themselves" still finds general acceptance, although over the years there has been some significant dissent from this view. Keynes, for example, was not prepared to dismiss the importance of mental processes and the way they shape patterns of demand, arguing that the needs of human beings "fall into two classes — those needs which are absolute in the sense that we feel them whatever the situation may be and those which are relative only in that their satisfaction lifts us above, makes us feel superior to, our fellow" (Keynes, 1931, pp. 365–366). he refers also in his (1936) *General Theory* to the role of ostentation and extravagance as influences on the individual's propensity to consume and implies again that such effects cannot sensibly be left out of any comprehensive theory of demand. However, the warnings of Keynes and other had very little success in generating any greater increase in the study of what could be termed the psychology of demand.

After Keynes, the first paper to look at the conspicuous consumer in any detail was published in the 1945 *Review of Economic Studies*. Here Tibor Scitovsky argued that status conscious consumers were likely to see the prices of certain "snob" purchases as product features which served to enhance the desirability of the goods and services in question. Price, therefore, could be seen as a product attribute by such consumers, rather than as a purely negative cost. (Scitovsky was, in fact, looking at products and at their attributes in ways which became wellknown following their development many years later by Lancaster, 1966.)

Scitovsky's views on such perverse demand went unchallenged because they did no more than acknowledge a type of behavior which could easily be observed in the market place and whose existence could not sensibly be questioned. The paper did not explore the implications of status-directed expenditure for demand theory, but in the next few years the importance of interpersonal utility functions in determining demand for certain goods came more to the fore. Conspicuous consumption per se was not discussed but new approaches to price/demand theory were being explored. Duesenberry (1949) presented his theory of the "demonstration effect" — a work which gave added impetus to exploration of the psychology of individual preferences — and several other economists began to recognize the importance of socially determined consumer behavior to a far greater extent: Reder (1947, p. 64) for example warned that "There is another kind of external repercussion which is rarely, if ever, recognized in discussion of welfare economics. It occurs where the utility function of one individual contains, as variables, the quantities of goods consumed by other persons."

In 1950, Leibenstein presented a paper that addressed the subject of conspicuous consumption directly and which still remains one of the most important studies of price-dependent preferences available in the economic literature. Leibenstein (1950) made no reference to Scitovsky's earlier work but argued, like Duesenberry, that no better understanding of the nature of such preferences would be possible unless economists were prepared to remove the basic assumption of classical demand theory that each individual's consumption is entirely independent of the behavior of other consumers. Once this assumption is removed, Leibenstein argued, then the role of social psychology and the importance of individual and group aspirations in shaping patterns of demand could be taken into account. In essence he was pressing for a redefinition of what is "rational" behavior in economics.

Leibenstein attempted a partial explanation of those forms of demand which are motivated more by external than by internal affects and offered an economic analysis of the so-called "Veblen Effect." However, the analysis did not move from effect to cause because while Leibenstein was prepared to relax a basic tenet of economic theory in order to further his analysis, he also sided with Marshall in arguing that while psychology could have an influence on demand, it was not part of the economist's job to become expert in the psychological reasons for such behavior. In essence, Leibenstein argued that the psychology of nonfunctional behavior, as he termed it, would have to be explained by others. However, what was important was his admission that it was not possible to explain Veblenian consumption in purely economic terms: the limits to "economics without psychology" had been conceded.

Leibenstein's paper could have been expected to generate a far greater level of interest in interdependent preferences and in the psychology of demand, but in the event there was very little response — indeed, the whole area of non-economic consumer behavior was largely ignored throughout the 1950s. Although the meaning of utility was still occasionally questioned, attention was directed towards the problem of subordinate choices and their relationship to first-order indifference — an area which had been the subject of research many years previously (see Little, 1949, pp. 90–99).

5. Marketing's Attitude to Conspicuous Consumption

Away from economics, however, the existence and importance of many "irrational" consumer motives and preferences had long been recognized, particularly by those more directly concerned with the marketing of consumer goods. New motivation research theories, borrowing heavily from the behavioral sciences, argued that individuals could regard their consumption preferences as entirely rational even though their purchase intentions might appear totally irrational to others.

By 1960, the importance of social group influences on consumption behavior had been well documented (see Bourne, 1963, and Katz, 1957). "Ego-bolstering" needs had been identified, which motivated people to gain in prestige and which consequently shaped a large part of their consumption behavior (Bayton, 1958). The symbolism of products was also seen to be a powerful stimulus to purchasing, as was the fact that the goods people buy make social statements about their position and aspirations as well as offering utility in purely economic terms. Products, in short, say something about the social world of the people who consume them (Levy, 1959).

By 1960, Woods was able to bring together growing evidence of the importance of social and psychological influences on consumer decision-making. Among other things, Woods (1960) concluded that the markets for most consumer goods can be broken down quite clearly into two basic buyer groups — one rational, the other seemingly irrational and influenced by emotion, symbolism and images. On the supply side, irrational groups are then offered both prestige and status goods for their symbolic and social value.

At the heart of Woods' paper was the message that not only do these irrational consumers constitute a significant part of many markets but that certain products are manufactured and promoted to cater to their specific needs. Conspicuous consumption, therefore, has to be seen not as the pursuit of a few very rich people but as a far more widespread activity which cuts across all product and income groups.

Woods was in fact acknowledging that by the mid-1950s business organizations had come to realize that the potential demand for status goods offered a great potential for profits. As a group, conspicuous consumers are not deterred by high prices — as the cost of a product increases so does its social utility — and the supplier of status goods is provided with a clear opportunity to take substantial profits over manufacturing costs.

The markets for status-related goods were being exploited in two ways. One group of manufacturers — not volume dependent — came to specialize in supplying a limited range of custom products, taking their profit on high unit markups. Volume manufacturers, on the other hand, unable to meet the requirements of the "pure" conspicuous consumer, began feeding the status sensitivity of many social groups and undertook major marketing and advertising campaigns in order to emphasize the real or imagined social status of their products. When successful, they achieved volume sales and at the same time could maintain prices at levels which were highly profitable.

The industrialized societies were particularly well suited to the creation and exploitation of the demand for status goods. Mass communication provided the mechanism through which ideas, opinions, social values, and trends (whether real or "manufactured") could be transmitted. The advertising industry was able to promote products in such a way that their social attributes were heightened and emphasized. Finally, modern retail distribution systems had arrived and could deliver status goods in the most socially effective ways.

The visual impact of television was (and is) such that products would be placed in a social context appropriate to status-sensitive markets. Producers were quick to see the advantages of locating their products within the right social environment and or making high-priced socially visible products for potential conspicuous consumers. Producers were also not satisfied with demand for status-linked goods which was not capable of generating sales at a repurchase rate sufficient to justify and maintain volume production. But technology and advertising, working together, could produce acceptable levels of repeat business by shortening the conspicuous "life" of socially visible products. Many goods bought for status purposes have a built-in "social obsolescence" which is achieved by insuring that they are rapidly outdated by later, more sophisticated versions. The obsolescence, however, is not primarily functional or material but social in the sense that the goods are made quickly unfashionable.

Having recognized a considerable potential demand for status goods, producers faced the additional problem of overcoming the difficulties met by consumers in finding the money to purchase for ostentatious display out of their limited earnings. However, the significant expansion of credit facilities (including the in-house finance company subsidiaries of the manufacturers themselves) allowed potential buyers to meet the costs of consuming for status display. By 1960, the growth of credit-linked consumption was under way. In effectively increasing present income by allowing individuals to discount future earnings the market for conspicuous status goods was being significantly expanded and the promise of future credit support was encouraging individuals to believe that the risks associated with current overspending were being substantially reduced.

Companies, therefore, were gearing up in the late 1950s to supplying status goods and selling much of their output on a credit basis. To do this they needed — and obtained — the support of two important allies.

First, the development of credit business was backed by financial institutions who were not averse to seeing their assets underpinning sales of manufactured goods and services at highly profitable interest rates. The growth in credit usage bears witness to the success of policies which persuaded customers that the conspicuous symbols of social and economic success were available for immediate consumption. So successful were these policies that the use and "display" of credit cards itself came by the 1970s to represent a form of conspicuous consumption, the method of payment for goods and services having become a status symbol in its own right.

The second major stimulus to sales of status-linked products came from the growth and expansion of retail distribution that occurred after 1955. By financing sales through charge accounts and through installment credit, retailers soon realized the business they could achieve by catering to the conspicuous consumer. Customers were persuaded to modify *perceptions* of their buying power and downgrade the importance of current income as a constraint on status spending: it might thus be misleading to follow the economist's conventional practice of treating budget constraints as well-defined "objective" phenomena.

Woods' (1960) paper, therefore, served to highlight the fact that conspicuous consumers were now to be found in all economic and social groups and that, in either pure or modified form, conspicuous consumption was indulged in by many millions of people. Earlier treatment of such consumption as exceptional behavior indulged in only by the very rich could no longer be defended: status-linked products were now openly promoted and supplied by business organizations to all income groups. The era of mass conspicuous consumption had in fact arrived.

While these new market developments were now self-evident, the inability of economists to cope with the era of the "status-seekers" was equally obvious. Classical utility theory, quite simply, was incapable of explaining behavior which was classified as irrational in conventional terms. Economists were put on the defensive — a major part of consumer spending lacked any explanation in Marshallian terms.

6. Work on Conspicuous Consumption by Economists Since 1960

In 1961, Houthakker, surveying the current state of consumption theory, recognized the importance of noneconomic preference formation and in

particular the role of social interactions in shaping the content of preferences. Given that there was still no satisfactory theoretical explanation of
such irrational behavior in economics, he conceded that

> The formation of preferences is to some extent a social process, in which imi-
> tation and differentiation are important elements. The formation of preferences
> itself is usually held to be outside the realm of economic theory but some of
> the consequences of social interaction are nevertheless of economic interest
> (Houthakker, 1961, p. 733).

Houthakker was still unhappy at the prospect that large parts of consumer behavior could find no rational choice explanation. Looking at the
work of Duesenberry (1949) and his theory of the demonstration effect,
he argued that the consequences of social interaction could well be found
to be "rational" if and when an individual's budget constraints were taken
into account (Houthakker, 1961, p. 734). However, he conceded that economists had not done any significant work in this area and acknowledged
the need for more research into non-economic preference formation, add-
ing (p. 734) that

> There is much to be said for regarding the explanation of the content of pref-
> erences (that is, the question of why an individual prefers one bundle of goods
> to another) as outside the economist's competence. Nevertheless, there is also
> a danger in such delimitations of responsibility, namely that the problems thus
> excluded may not be studied at all. It is easy to say they belong to psychology
> but this does not mean that psychology will find them sufficiently interesting to
> look into them. Indeed, the whole concept of preference as used by economists
> may be hard to fit into the psychologist's framework.

Houthakker's appeal did not generate any response from other leading
economists, but he need not have worried that psychologists would also
find the subject of little interest. Woods' work on the role of products as
symbols was taken further in the early 1960s by many other behavioral
scientists who saw this as a potentially rewarding area of study (see Lazer,
1964; Sommers, 1964). The model proposed by Grubb and Grathwohl
(1967) was significant in that, allowing for some modification, it was able
to accommodate the phenomenon of conspicuous consumption as a special
form of symbolic purchasing behavior. But, again, the model was social
and psychological and needed to be complemented by an economic perspective.

The response was, to say the least, limited. Kalman (1968) presented a
paper that focused on those elements of demand formation which seemed
irrational to economists and looked at the consequences for demand which
can arise when prices enter the individual's utility function. Kalman argued

that high price could be an attractive proposition for certain buyers. But, like Scitovsky before him, he did not distinguish between two very different types of consumer — one who uses price as an indicator of quality and who is prepared to pay more for what he/she perceives as a superior good in conventional utility terms, the other the Veblenian conspicuous consumer for whom price *is* quality and the only significant indicator of social value.

Two years later, Alcaly and Klevorick (1970) did in fact draw attention to the distinction made by consumers between the physical and social utility of products and further developed the theme, in a Lancaster-type model, that price can be viewed as either a negative or positive characteristic. After 1970, however, interest in non-functional demand preferences tended to shift away from the complications of price determined utility and toward another aspect of so-called irrational consumer behavior, namely the possibility that an individual's interdependent preferences were founded more on relative consumption levels than on price-based status-seeking. Schall (1972) and others argued that there was ample evidence to show that an individual's consumption was often made "irrational" not by attempts to secure status through price display in respect of individual purchases but through attempts to match the rate of consumption of others — behavior which is equally conspicuous and status-driven in that it is intended to display to others what one can afford to spend on goods and services in general.

Exploring interdependent utilities further, Scott (1972) pointed to two significant yet conflicting aspects of consumer behavior. Consumption, he argued, can certainly display elements of avarice when individuals seek happiness through being able to buy and consume more than others (Schall's point on relative rates of consumption), but can also be motivated by considerations of altruism when consumers are concerned to see others receiving their fair share of goods and services. Scott's work does bear indirectly on conspicuous consumption theory in that a price-motivated status-seeker would be seen as wholly avaricious not in terms of the quantity of goods bought but in terms of the perceived cost (that is, the level of wealth display) associated with any given level of purchase. Scott contended rightly, however, that wholly avaricious consumption is often not sustainable in the long term as society imposes its own sanctions against such antisocial behavior. (The hostility to the "Gilded Age" conspicuous consumption in the United States illustrates the point — see Mason, 1981, chapter 5.)

In 1977, Pollak contributed to the discussion on price-quality relationships but, like Kalman, quality was once again taken to be tangible and utilitarian rather than social and psychological. Two years earlier, however, Miller had written a paper on the relationship between status goods and luxury taxes which made a greater contribution to the still very limited literature on conspicuous consumption. Looking at the effect of taxes on luxury goods Miller (1975) first of all acknowledged that status goods were not purchased in order to gain from some tangible utility but to communicate with a target audience. he argued that the purchase of status goods generates gains for those who are able to impress others with the products they buy but that, in so doing, those who are unable to match such purchases suffer psychological losses. Other losers from the process are those who may already possess the product in question but who find its status value reduced by the fact that another individual has acquired the good in question.

Miller's paper also examined the extent to which conspicuous consumption can be explained in terms of conventional indifference analysis. The difficulty with neoclassical theory is that it assumes that utility functions are interdependent and charts preferences between money (income) and goods. However, with regard to ostentatious economic display, because of the interdependence of wealth and status goods — that is, the higher the product price the more attractive the purchase — Miller showed that indifference analysis was not possible. When the price of a product is a part of its (positive) utility then not only are utility functions interdependent but the perceived quality and nature of a good changes as price changes. In this way, "new" products are frequently created, and it is not possible to construct sets of indifference curves which implicitly and explicitly seek to deal with a single unchanging product relative to its rivals.

Miller's conclusion that neoclassical analysis was incapable of explaining the psychology and economics of demand for status goods was unremarkable. However, his paper merited respect in that, unlike many economists before him, he argued that this inability to cope was not a valid reason for avoiding the problem by dismissing such market behavior as trivial and unimportant.

Taken overall, economists' contributions to the better understanding of conspicuous consumption in the 1970s were meager, and by 1980 behavioral scientists had moved well ahead in researching status-directed consumption. As early as 1965, marketing analysts had been discussing and working with buyer-behavior models which did not derive in any respect from marginal utility theories of demand (see Kotler, 1965). By 1973, Schewe had described the component parts of a Veblenian social psychological model of consumer behavior. Parallel with these developments and throughout the 1970s, the noneconomic literature continued to develop new insights into status-seeking and its expression through the purchase of goods and services. Building on the work of Kassarjian and others, a substantial body of research into the psychology of ostentatious economic display was being developed (Kassarjian et al., 1965).

Since 1980 the trend has continued. Interest in status symbolism remains high among those psychologists more concerned with consumer behavior and market research than with economic theory. Hirschman and Holbrook (1981) have brought together recent research work into symbolic consumer behavior and moved on (Hirschman and Holbrook, 1982) to explore the wider field of "hedonic consumption" where empirical research dates only from the late 1970s. The first comprehensive study of conspicuous consumption, tracing its origins and history within different social and economic environments, has appeared (Mason, 1981). At the same time, economists have continued a tradition of showing no interest in the subject with the result that, while the psychology of status-inspired consumption is now well understood, the economic perspective is absent. In short, we still lack a substantive economic theory of conspicuous consumption.

7. Tensions and Prospects

Any review of research into conspicuous economic display succeeds most of all in showing that the subject has still not been seriously addressed by economists. This lack of interest, however, has been repeatedly commented upon by the few writers who have examined the subject. In his 1945 paper, Scitovsky conceded that "economists are wont to minimize the importance of this factor [that is, price-dependent preferences] fearing the havoc it may wreak with the whole theory of choice" (p. 100). Chipman (1960, p. 222) admitted that it was certainly the view of many other economists that discussion about interdependent and price-dependent utilities was "hair-splitting" and of little practical difference. And Pollak (1977, p. 65) conceded that the literature on price-dependent preferences remained sparse, with little time having been spent on the topic since Scitovsky's paper first appeared.

The greatest barrier to more work being carried out into the economics of status-directed consumption is the refusal of economists to abandon theoretical constructs which assume that individuals behave rationally in economic terms. The limitations such inflexibility imposes on economic theory were pointed out as early as 1953 by George Katona, who recognized the impotence of economics in trying to explain consumer behavior that appeared psychological and irrational rather than utilitarian and rational.

Any behavior which does not fit with the theorem derived from neoclassical utility theory — that is, behavior that generates so-called irrational purchases — still needs to be rationalized, however. Quoting Stigler (1948, p. 603), Katona (1953, p. 313) argued that this poses no problem, in that such consumption "can always be attributed to a change of tastes (a catch-all 'free variable' in the economic theories of consumer demand) rather than to an error in the postulates or logic of the theory."

Adherence to economic theory founded on rational behavior has meant that economists have successfully ducked the issue of whether they need to be involved in examining and accommodating the psychology of demand in their work. It has also meant that consumer behavior has been explained in aggregate (market) terms rather than at the level of the individual consumer. Leibenstein's analysis of conspicuous economic display, for example, was weakened by the fact that he was determined to provide a market explanation of the consequences of conspicuous consumption — and implicitly assumed that all conspicuous consumers had identical motives and identical price perceptions. Leibenstein himself saw it as no part of his job to look behind market demand curves and to take economic analysis down to the level of individual consumers. While it is theoretically possible to derive a market demand schedule for conspicuous consumers as a whole (best achieved by segmenting the population into near-enough similar groupings and then aggregating approximately from these different categories), the cumulative error factor would be unacceptably high, particularly when it is recognized that conspicuous consumers must not reveal the extent of their status-driven consumption to others. In reality, research can focus at no higher than group level, and even here significant differences between individuals must be expected.

Economic analysis, therefore, needs to allow for research and explanation at the level of the individual or small group. More importantly, it has to come to terms with consumer psychology and to escape from classical theories of utility and value. This last requirement poses no problem, for models of buyer behavior which owe nothing to marginal utility theories of demand have been available for many years. More specifically, behavioral scientists have worked with Veblenian social psychological models since the early 1960s, models in which man is seen as primarily "a social animal conforming to the general forms and norms of his larger culture and to the more specific standards of the subcultures and face-to-face groupings to which his life is bound. His wants and behavior are largely molded by his present group memberships and his aspired group memberships" (Kotler, 1965, p. 42). In 1973 Schewe identified the four basic cues or drives which, separately or together, supply the motive force underpinning conspicuous consumption behavior. These drives — achievement motivation, role playing, dissonance reduction, and social character formation — explain the status linked market preferences which have been so often observed and described since the mid-1950s and which the business community has worked to encourage.

Social psychologists have, in short, elevated the economist's catch-all "tastes and preferences" to the center of their models of buyer behavior. They have, however, been unable to integrate economic theory into their work. In particular, there is a need for work on price and income effects to be incorporated into models of status-driven conspicuous consumption and for research to be carried out into the judgmental heuristics employed by conspicuous consumers in sizing up how much they need, and can afford, to spend to achieve particular results. It is here that a substantial contribution can be made by economists.

The framework for analysis is not difficult to construct. In essence, there are today two types of conspicuous consumer — those for whom money is no object and who seek not only "social visibility" in their purchases but also exceptionally high prices, limited product availability, and exclusive product distribution; and those (far more numerous) who have to recognize that financial constraints must modify their conspicuous behavior and direct attention toward status products which they judge they can reasonably afford to purchase. Such consumers also look for social visibility in products but are clearly unable to emulate the richer conspicuous consumer who is well able to pay inordinately high prices for goods and services. For the income-constrained buyer, the market needs to supply products which are affordable but which have status conferred upon them by appropriate advertising and publicity.

The absolute and relative wealth of individual consumers can also be expected to influence attitudes to product utility. The very rich are able to care little or nothing for the conventional utility of the goods they buy and may make deliberate decisions to select products for consumption which are conspicuously wasteful (thereby showing they have no worries about money relative to their needs). In contrast, the income-limited status seeker will be more inclined to look for some significant utility from his/her purchase — although his/her interest in such "rational" product attributes will be more covert than overt.

In seeking a more comprehensive examination of conspicuous consumption, therefore, research needs to center on the relationship between prices and status-conference at different income levels. It is price which decides the social status of a particular product while price relativities determine which products are relatively more attractive in status terms.

At the same time price and status perceptions will be shaped by the individual's wealth and income measured in both absolute and relative terms.

When economists are able to tell us more about price and income effects on conspicuous consumers' budgeting decisions, it will be possible to marry social psychological models of such behavior with the economics of status driven demand and supply. Research into the subject will never be easy, for conspicuous consumption is a form of behavior to which individuals will not admit (by acknowledging that a purchase was made to impress others the consumer effectively loses any status gains which may have resulted). At the same time, such purchase and consumption must by definition be conspicuous, and this allows researchers to match such behavior with the economic conditions under which it occurs. The need for a more positive research effort into the phenomenon of conspicuous consumption is becoming increasingly urgent, not least because the demand for and supply of status goods represents a significant and growing area of economic activity in modern societies. Status-seeking consumption which was once thought to be the preserve only of the very rich now extends across all social and economic groups, and a better understanding of the underlying motivations, strategies, and dynamics of such behavior is long overdue.

11 INDIVIDUALIST ECONOMICS WITHOUT PSYCHOLOGY

Lawrence A. Boland

1. Introduction

Neoclassical economics is often thought to need an infusion of social psychology. There are two reasons for this. One is that economics should be able to recognize the social interaction between individual decision-makers; the other is that economics should recognize that the nature of an individual's utility function is essentially psychological. Both of these criteria involve the methodological requirements of an individualism that is at the foundations of neoclassical economics. In this short chapter I would like to explain why the requirements of methodological individualism do not necessitate an infusion of social psychology.

It is always important to avoid confusing methodological individualism with psychologism. Methodological individualism is the view that all social events must be explained as the consequences of choices made by individuals — things do not choose, only individuals do. Psychologism is the view that in any explanation (individualist or otherwise) the only exogenous givens other than natural constraints allowed in any explanation are those representing psychological states of either individuals or groups. Methodological individualism as a view or doctrine about how social events and situations are to be explained does not require us to base individualism on psychology (see further, Boland, 1982, chapter 2). Before I discuss the social and psychological aspects of an individual's choice situation, I need to present the explanatory problem confronting any methodological individualist.

2. Individualism and the Legacy of Eighteenth Century Rationalism

There is no more to methodological individualism than an explicit commitment to individualist explanations. Since the eighteenth century, for any explanation to be acceptable it must be "rational" and thus it must be universal. By rational, we mean that the explanation forms a logically valid argument such that if the premises of the argument are all true then the conclusions logically derived will also be true. By universal, we mean that *anyone* who accepts the truth of the premises of a logically valid argument will also accept the truth of its conclusions. The tradition of compounding rationality with individualism is problematic in two ways which together represent the classic intellectual dilemma between unity and diversity (see Agassi, 1969). On the one hand, the universality of rationality undermines individualism by making all individuals identical in a significant way. On the other hand, the nineteenth century tendency to view rationality as a psychological process also undermines individualism by making individuality exogenous and thus beyond explanation.

To illustrate these methodological problems, consider the following hypothetical situation. Our closest friend has been caught robbing a bank. Demanding an explanation, we ask, "Why did you rob the bank?" Before we allow our friend to answer we must recall that to be an acceptable explanation the explanation given either by us or by our friend must be rational and methodological individualist. Individualism only precludes choices being made by things. Rationality is established by examining the logic of the situation facing our friend, the bank robber. By asking our friend for an explanation we are asking him to give a description of the logic of his situation. Specifically, we ask him to give his reasons which represent (1) his aims and (2) the constraints that restrict the achievement of his aims. If he can describe the logic of his situation so that we would agree that anyone who faced that exact situation (aims and constraints) would also rob the bank, then we would say that we understand why he robbed the bank. For example, he may tell us that his child needs a very expensive operation and he wants his child to have that operation but there is no legal way he could afford it before it would be too late. Robbing the bank was the only way to achieve his aim. If his description of the situation is true (that is, there really is no other way possible), then given his aim (to save his child) it would be rational for him to rob the bank — in fact, it might be considered rational for anyone with that aim and those constraints.

The logical requirements of an explanation of individual behavior are the same whether we are discussing our friend the bank robber or the individual consumer choosing to spend his or her money on tomatoes and cucumbers. In the case of the individual consumer, the aim is supposedly the maximization of utility obtained from consuming what one has purchased while facing the constraints of given prices, given purchasing power (one's budget or income), and a given utility function. Such utility-maximizing behavior is rational in the sense that any two individuals with the same utility function and same income facing the same prices will choose to consume the same quantities of goods so long as each individual aims to maximize his or her utility.

Rationality assures such universality and uniqueness of choice. The idea that rationality assures universality is characteristic of eighteenth century rationalism and thus is fundamental to the origins of ordinary economics. The identification of rationality with utility maximization is a late nineteenth century perspective and the foundation of neoclassical economics. In terms of modern economics, the quantities the individual consumes are considered endogenous variables. Only the utility function is unambiguously exogenous. Income and prices are treated as constraints to the individual but not to the economy as a whole, so whether they are endogenous or exogenous depends on the situation we choose to model. In neoclassical economics our task is to explain individual choices in order to explain how prices affect demand so that we can explain how demand influences prices in the market; in other words, prices and incomes (which depend on factor prices) are endogenous.

From a logical point of view (and contrary to the impression given by Mason in chapter 10 of this book), a single individual's choice is easier to explain than a market demand curve. This is because in consumer theory we can treat the prices and income facing the individual as exogenous variables leaving only the consumer's choice as the endogenous variable to explain. Any explanation of a market's demand curve requires us to explain all consumers' choices as well as all the other market prices that these consumers face. Of course, we would also have to explain the supply curve in every market in question.

3. Unity Versus Diversity in Methodological Individualism

Neoclassical economics, nonetheless, claims to explain all prices and the allocation of all fixed resources. How is it possible for one theory to explain so much? The particular value of prices (or state of resource allocation) depends, of course, on the nature of each individual's utility function. In this context methodological individualism allows both diversity and unity. Diversity is promoted by recognizing that some people will spend more of their incomes on tomatoes than other people do. Unity is promoted by the claim that all individuals are maximizers. This means that all people face falling marginal utility curves (a necessary calculus condition for maximization). Does this mean all people are identical and thus deny individuality? No: as long as everyone faces downward sloping marginal utility curves, the absolute position of that curve (relative to other goods) need not be the same for all individuals. For the same amounts of tomatoes and cucumbers, some may get more satisfaction from tomatoes, others get more from cucumbers. Also, some people may have steeper marginal utility curves than other people do. We see that on the one hand individuality is preserved, since even facing the same prices and incomes, two maximizing individuals may choose different quantities if their exogenously given utility functions are different. On the other hand, universality is provided by the common nature of utility functions if it can be shown that as a matter of human nature all utility functions exhibit diminishing marginal utility.

This is the methodological dilemma of individualist-cum-rationalist economics. If the (equilibrium) values of prices depend only on the different utility functions which are exogenously given, then prices are actually determined outside economics. Whatever determines the nature of the given utility functions ultimately determines prices. Does this mean that economics must surrender to psychology as has often been suggested (for example, by Scitovsky, 1976)?

Identifying the individual with his or her psychologically given utility function is a rather sophisticated and subtle type of psychologism. A more blunt and obvious use of psychology would be for us (or our friend the robber) to explain the event by claiming that our friend has a "criminal mentality." But such a crude psychologism would seem to be our only recourse if we are to avoid the moral dilemmas involved in the explanation based on the logic of the situation. If the robber's choice to rob the bank was a rational one, how can we object?

Crude psychologism also avoids an intellectual dilemma. When our friend (as a bank robber or a consumer) provides an "acceptable" explanation, one which says that anyone facing that position would choose to do the same thing, the individuality of the situation is revealed to be empty. If any individual would do the same, then there is nothing individualistic about the choice made. Crude psychologism (that is, the view that behavior is predetermined by given mentalities) as an explanation of individual choices may seem to be a way to promote psychology. It is not; it only begs more questions. What determines who gets which mentality? How many different mentalities are there? In the extreme, crude psychologism may even lead us to discard psychology in favor of sociobiology.

If we therefore reject crude psychologism, we are then left with our two dilemmas. The moral dilemma (the rationality of one's choice to commit a crime) is not easy to overcome and in the end is more a question of philosophy than of psychology. The intellectual dilemma is the foundation of attempts to promote psychology in the development of economic explanations of individual behavior. If we allow ourselves to assume that psychologically all individuals are given different exogenous utility functions, then individuality will seem to be preserved in our explanations of rational choice. However, whenever psychologism is adopted as a means of promoting individualism, it is a defeatist methodological stance.

Individualism is in trouble here only because neoclassical economics misleadingly identifies the individual's aims with the individual's psychologically given utility function. Two individuals facing the same prices and with the same income will usually choose different consumption bundles if they have different utility functions. If our problem as economists is to explain a wide diversity of choice made by people in the same income class, then the psychological reasons for why people have different given utility functions would certainly seem to be a promising line of inquiry. But it is not a necessary line of inquiry, since one may just as easily presume that the individual's utility function is socially determined.

The traditional emphasis on individualism seems to force an excessive concern for diversity to the point that economists (as opposed to sociologists) tend to overlook obvious social circumstances where diversity is more conspicuous by its absence. Specifically, the problem that should be of concern to individualist economists is to explain the widespread conformity whenever considering consumption patterns. In most cultures, each social role is closely associated with a specific consumption pattern. Accountants or lawyers in similar income brackets will usually have consumption patterns much like their colleagues. Nonconforming individualism is more the exception than the rule in organized society. For example, corporate lawyers tend to dress alike, belong to the same social clubs, acquire the same ostentatious goods such as expensive automobiles, houses, etc. Moreover, their conspicuous consumption is not a psychological phenomenon (cf. the preceeding chapter) but rather it shows how profoundly one's preference ordering is dependent on social structure. In short, one's consumption may be determined more by one's social position than one's personal tastes (see Newman, 1972; Hayakawa and Venieris, 1977).

4. Unnecessary Psychologism

I do not want anyone to think that by my recognizing that utility functions (or more generally, personal aims) are matters of sociological inquiry that I am thereby rejecting individualism. Such is not the case. Social situations and institutions are the consequences of individual choices (see also Boland, 1979). All that I am arguing here is that there is no necessity to see deviations from narrowminded neoclassical economics as expressions of irrationality and hence a demonstration of a need to study the individual. Irrationality is easily interpreted as merely an expression of the incompleteness of the description of the logic of the situation facing the individual (Becker and Stigler, 1977). Perhaps a more complete description might involve psychology, but psychology is not a necessity here. An individual whose utility function is completely determined by social conventions is no less capable of making a rational decision than the individual whose utility function is psychologically given. In summary, a successful methodological individualist explanation of the behavior of a rational decision-maker is a matter of establishing the logical completeness of the decision-maker's objective situation. It is not necessarily a matter requiring the recognition of a possible role for the decision-maker's psychological predisposition.

12 TOWARD A BEHAVIORAL ANALYSIS OF PUBLIC ECONOMICS

Michael A. Brooks

1. Introduction

During the last 30 years a large and wide-ranging literature has emerged on the economic analysis of politics or, as it is more commonly called, public choice. Mainstream public economics has to some extent taken heed of some of this development. Most public finance books now have an obligatory chapter on public choice. Public choice, however, has not subsumed the entire field of public economics; the lessons tend to be kept to one side. Yet at the very least the central propositions now receive some recognition. This has not been the case with the theoretical developments which have occurred in behavioral economics. One would search the public economics textbooks in vain for any reference to Simon's Nobel Prize-winning work on behavioral economics. It is not altogether clear that neoclassical economists should be solely blamed for ignoring these developments. Little has been written on the intersection between behavioral economics and public economics. Aside from a few papers on the intersection between welfare economics and behavioral economics (Rosser, 1977; Steedman and Krause, 1986) and an appendix in Little's (1957) critical book on welfare economics — in which he analyzes the Edgeworth box from the kind of standpoint that has found favor among behavioral economists — there is very little on which to work. Even simple questions such as whether the concept of market failure is meaningful within the confines of behavioral economics or whether the Pareto criterion is relevant when individuals are modeled as boundedly rational satisficers have received short shrift. All in all, behavioral economists seem to have been more concerned with developing a descriptively more accurate analysis of choice than exploring the policy applications of their alternative paradigm. This chapter has the simple objective of attempting to set out some of the implications of behavioral economics for public economics. It should be noted at the outset that no attempt is made here to examine all of the themes in public economics from the standpoint of behavioral economics. Nor is any attempt made to examine exhaustively even the small number of topics raised here. The themes have been chosen to focus on two basic questions: (1) In what ways are the basic tenets of public economics affected if behavioral precepts are used as basic building blocks? (2) Can public economics broadly conceived be enriched at all by taking on-board some of the central elements of behavioral economics?

2. Human Behavior and Behavioral Economics

Public economists, particularly those who have adopted the fundamental insights of public choice, model behavior in the public sector using precisely the same approach to that employed in analyses of market behavior. Bureaucrats, politicians, and voters are analyzed as if they are self-interested utility maximizers. Indeed, public choice is to a considerable extent the application of neoclassical economics — with subjectivist Austrian overtones here and there — to public sector issues. The wholesale reliance by some public economists on the neoclassical framework clearly stands in direct contrast to the methodology advanced in behavioral economics. Behavioral economics, as mentioned, has attempted to provide a descriptively more accurate analysis of choice. In doing so it emphasizes the information problems that individuals face and the resulting bounded rationality. Individuals are assumed to satisfice rather than maximize. This raises a fundamental question: is the message of behavioral economics in any way consistent with the broad methodology employed in public economics?

Recent research on the methodological principles of public economics (Brennan and Buchanan, 1981) stresses the fact that if the objective at hand is to carry out a comparison of the effect of the market and that of the public sector on welfare, then the same maximand must be assumed for the economic agent in both institutional settings. If this fundamental principle of comparative institutional analysis is not followed, then it is difficult to discern whether it is the structural or the behavioral assumptions which are leading to the differences in the performance of the two institutions. Although this is a valid defense of the self-centered utility maximizing postulate it does not in any way imply that public economists are correct in analyzing institutions only from the standpoint of neoclassical economics. The comparative institutional methodology merely maintains that the same maximand ought to be used in analyzing both institutions, not that the appropriate behavioral assumption is utility maximization. If the market is analyzed from the perspective of behavioral economics in which consumers and producers are treated as boundedly rational satisficers, then the methodological principle calls for the use of the same behavioral precept in analyzing the alternative institution. Seen from this standpoint, public economics and public choice in particular need not just be the application of neoclassical economics to public sector issues; the application of the behavioral precepts of bounded rationality and satisficing are not inconsistent with the broad methodological principles employed elsewhere in public economics, and their use should not cause the methodological purist any concern.

3. Pareto Optimality and Priority-Based Choice

In view of this it is interesting to re-examine some of the basic issues in public economics from the behavioral economics perspective. Specifically, is the concept of market failure meaningful within the confines of behavioral economics? What is the relevance of the Pareto criterion to behavioral economics?

Before these matters can be dealt with it is important to recognize that there are a number of different approaches in behavioral economics to modeling choice, just as there are a number in neoclassical economics. The issues at hand are analyzed from the standpoint of behavioral lexicographic choice (see Earl, 1986b, chapter 7, and cf. section 3 of chapter 9 of this book). In this approach individuals are assumed to have wants no different from those found in neoclassical models. But to each want is assigned an aspiration level: to satisfy a particular want, the individual aspires to have so many units of a particular commodity (or of a particular characteristic that some commodities can produce). These targets are in turn ranked in terms of their degree of importance — the individual has a set of priorities.

It is assumed here that if an individual cannot reach his/her target on a particular priority, then he or she will select the goods combination that comes closest to meeting this target.

In order to go some way in examining the intersection between behavioral lexicographic choice and market failure take the case of an external effect.[1] The discussion is presented in terms of two-dimensional diagrammatics which depict the choice sets of individuals K and J. Individual K owns a radio and likes to listen to loud music. In fact, if the radio is turned up to any level beyond P_K^2, then his noise target is satisfied. Alternatively, if he has to turn his radio down below the level indicated by P_K^2, then he fails to achieve his target. Individuals K and J are neighbors and J hears the music blaring through an adjoining wall. For expositional simplicity it is assumed the wall is so thin that K and J consume identical units of radio music. This means that individual J's origin can be located in the top lefthand corner of the Edgeworth box in figure 12–1. The initial set of endowments is described by point E.

In order to apply the Pareto criterion to the various allocations it is first necessary to specify whether it makes sense to speak of an improvement in the individual's well-being in a priority-based approach to choice. If it does not, then it will not be possible to apply the Pareto criterion. The criterion requires that alternative states and reallocations can be judged by the individual as representing an improvement or a reduction in well-being. This issue is examined within the simple framework set out above. In terms of their priority structure it is initially assumed that the achieve-

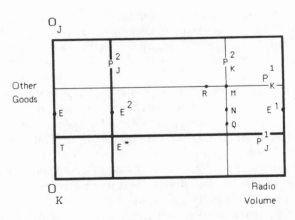

FIGURE 12–1. Edgeworth box and priority-based choice.

ment of the goods target for each individual is more important than the attainment of the noise target, that is, P^1 represents a more important target than P^2. The priority approach specifies an improvement in the individual's satisfaction with reference to the number of targets which the individual can satisfy in order of their importance. Individual K would like to consume a goods combination which will place him in the region above and to the right of the intersection of P_K^1 and P_K^2 — the area in which both targets are met. For individual J the satisfactory region lies below and to the left of the intersection of P_J^1 and P_J^2. He does not like to listen to music which is too loud and regards P_J^2 as representing a satisfactory level.

Note that the individual is not concerned with satisfying the greatest number of targets if this means that he or she fails to achieve some of his/her higher order priorities; the behavioral lexicographic approach does not involve the trading of priorities at the margin. The individual's objective is to search instead for the goods combination which will satisfy his foremost priority. He then searches among the goods combination which satisfies the first target for the goods combination that will meet his second most important target.

It is important to bear in mind that the target lines which depict the individual's set of priorities should not be interpreted as indifference curves. The target lines are not indifference curves; the lines merely indicate what is an acceptable level of the commodity. The individual's level of well-being is not the same for all points along the line. Individual K, for example, is better off at M than N in the sense that he would satisfy both priorities. Alternatively, he is better off at M than at R because he comes closer to meeting his second priority and does not sacrifice his performance on the first priority. The individual is better off the more he has of a commodity as long as the "additional" units do not lead to a sacrifice in the achievement of a higher order priority. It should be noted that an individual would be willing to sacrifice a lower order priority if he can by doing so come closer to satisfying a higher order priority. Individual K would be better off at R than at N because he would be able to meet his foremost target. In addition, note that the target lines need not represent a point of satiation. It can simply represent the minimum level of the commodity which is acceptable. In view of all this it is possible to conclude that despite the absence of indifference curves it is possible to specify the goods combinations which represent an improvement in the individual's well-being.

As it makes sense to talk of individual improvement in the priority framework, it is at least in principle possible to rank movements from one state to another by means of the Pareto criterion. One state is socially preferred to another if it goes further toward meeting an individual's set of priorities in order of their importance without reducing the achievement of priorities by any other individual. Reconsider the endowment point E. The movement from E to E^2 represents a Pareto desirable movement. Individual J now meets his target on radio volume because he likes to listen to some background music while he is working. Individual K is also better off because he comes closer to meeting his second priority. It would be possible to carry out this sort of procedure for a number of different reallocations. However, this would not alter the essential point that although the approach of priority-based choice is fundamentally different from that of orthodox choice theory, the notion of Pareto desirability and with it Pareto optimality equally apply. This of course raises the question of whether there is anything to be learned from the behavioral framework. Is the framework merely just another way of viewing the standard theorems? In order to explore this issue it is useful to consider the case of the Coase theorem from the standpoint of the radio noise example.[2]

The Coase theorem maintains that as long as transaction costs are zero and property rights are well-defined and enforced, social efficiency will be achieved irrespective of the initial assignment of the property rights. If K is assigned the property right over the radio, then he will listen to it at a level indicated by E^1. Although he fails to achieve his first priority he clearly satisfies his volume target. Since the radio blares through the adjoining wall individual J consumes more noise than he regards as acceptable. Despite the fact that J suffers at K's hand, it so happens that this allocation is Pareto optimal. It is not possible to find a movement which will make one individual better off without making the other person worse off. It might be thought, for example, that J could compensate K for reducing the volume on his radio. But recall that individual K would be only willing to sacrifice some of his performance on his second priority if he could come closer to achieving his foremost target. To do so J would have to give K some portion of his endowment. The trouble with this is that it would move J further away from the achievement of his first priority. Individual J would not be prepared, therefore, to make any compensation to K. By a similar process of logic it is easy to demonstrate that there is no possible Pareto desirable movement from E^1.

If the property right were assigned instead to J, then allocative efficiency would also be secured. The initial assignment of property rights results in point E — in which the radio is not turned on at all. This state is not however, Pareto optimal. Individual J could indicate to K that he does not mind if the radio is played to the volume level indicated by P_J^2, and as a result of this both individuals could be made better off. Individual J would reach his second priority and K would come closer to meeting his second priority. Notice, though, that K would not be willing to give up any of his goods in the form of compensation to J as this would move K further away from obtaining his first priority. Pareto optimality could only be achieved here by J's unilaterally relinquishing some of his property right over radio volume. Judged from the standpoint of orthodox public economics this is not a wholly unconventional result. In the case of jointness in consumption a Pareto desirable movement is often brought about at least theoretically by a unilateral process.

It is easy to accommodate within the general framework employed here the familiar proposition that the externality can be corrected by a process of negotiation. Suppose individual K's target for other goods is coincident with J's target line. Accordingly, at the initial endowment K has more commodities than the minimum he regards as acceptable. In this setting K will pay up to ET units of commodities to J in order to have the right to play the radio to the volume indicated by P_j^2.

Up to this point the behavioral framework does not appear to offer any additional insights to the problem of external effects. Despite the somewhat unusual analytics the basic premise that voluntary exchange can correct external problems appears to apply equally in the behavioral lexicographic framework. And much the same impediments to Pareto desirable exchange can be examined within this framework as found in the neoclassical analysis. Individual J, for example may act strategically and refuse to allow the radio to be played at all. In terms of figure 12–1, suppose J mistakenly believes K's target for commodities is coincident with his own P_j^1 and reasons he ought to be able to achieve outcome E^* rather than the point achieved under unilateral exchange, E^2. He believes K is acting strategically when K says that his target for commodities is not satisfied and is not prepared to compensate him for any part of the radio volume property right. Individual K thinks that J is unreasonable. He had told J that he was not prepared to forfeit his already unsatisfactory achievement of his goods target and reasons that they could both be better off if only J would let him at least turn on the radio. However, it would be wrong to conclude from all of this that the behavioral framework has nothing to offer to the analysis of market failure other than a recantation of familiar themes in a different guise. Certainly, this is not insignificant in itself; it is worth demonstrating that cases exist where there is no intrinsic conflict between behavioral economics and conventional normative issues. At least this reduces the potential conflict between behavioral and neoclassical economists. But I believe that behavioral economics will only be taken heed of by orthodox public economists if it offers insights which are not part and parcel of the conventional wisdom.

In order to explore some of the difference between the two schools of thought, consider a slightly different version of the information depicted in Figure 12–1. Suppose J's target on radio noise is coincident with the vertical axis, that is, he is not willing to tolerate any level of radio noise. Further, imagine J is given the initial assignment of property rights over the radio. This means the initial endowment point is E. If K's target for commodities lies below E, then it is clear that he will be willing to pay some commodities to J in order to come closer to his target on radio listening. Individual J would be willing to give up silence because the compensation moves him closer to his foremost priority on goods. Once again, there is no substantial difference here behavioral and neoclassical economics.

The situation changes dramatically if J's priorities are reversed — that is, the radio volume target is considered to be the more important priority. In this case J will not be prepared to give up any of his property right over radio volume irrespective of how much K is willing to offer him in the form of compensation. To do so would involve him in forgoing his foremost priority for the sake of more lower order priorities — a situation he would regard as less satisfactory than his initial endowment. The lesson to be drawn from this is that, in contrast to the neoclassical approach, not every individual has his/her price. Whatever the price, the individual is not willing to give up his/her property right. This is an important insight. Neoclassical economists seem to me to stretch credibility when they maintain that everything has a price. The couple who refuse to sell their home to a government authority that wants the land for a building program would be cited as an example of individuals who are merely engaged in strategic behavior. If the authority is only willing to pay enough to the old couple, then it will get the property without recourse to the law of eminent domain. Neoclassical economics conveys the message that it is all just a matter of haggling over the price. Behavioral economics does not rule out the possibility that such individuals are behaving strategically. But it goes on to admit, as in the discussion of figure 12–1, that no such compensation may be possible. If the individuals feel that living in a particular house is their foremost priority, then they will refuse to leave the house not for strategic reasons but simply because this would involve them in sacrificing their top priority for the sake of being able to afford more lower order priorities. This is something they would regard as totally unsatisfactory.

To be sure, the policy implications to be drawn from this are far from clear. Should a government which is bound to applying the Pareto criterion refuse to alter a situation if it appears that this will violate some individual's foremost priority? In order to illustrate some of the inherent problems, take the case of an event which actually happened recently in Tasmania. The state government wanted to flood an area in order to build a dam for an irrigation project. For three years a farmer who resided in the area in question refused to leave his 164 year-old family home. At one stage a proposal was even put forward to build a dyke around his home. To all appearances it seemed that he did not wish to give up his residence in his home for the sake of acquiring less important priorities. The state government in the end moved him out of the house and built him a new home, complete with new-found conveniences — at least as far as the farmer was concerned — such as an electric stove and a shower. It is, of course, entirely possible that the farmer's long fight with the government was simply designed to elicit the largest compensation possible. Equally feasible, he could have felt that the departure from the family home would involve the sacrifice of one of his top-order priorities. We cannot know for certain which thoughts guided his actions. One thing that is certain is that the farmer has indicated that he finds living in the new house more acceptable than the old colonial home. It appears to be the case, judging from his most recent comments, that his aspiration for living in the family home has waned after the experience of residing in his new home, and that his consumption of the new conveniences has taken on more importance than he thought was conceivable.

The example illustrates the general point that an individual's aspirations can change as the result of new experiences. This is problematic for the analyst because he has to decide whether the individual's ex ante or ex post aspirations ought to be used in policy evaluations. Neoclassical economists are, of course, aware of the problem. The issue has troubled public finance economists who have wrestled with the question of merit goods and constitutional design. But to a considerable extent the public finance economists have been able to relegate the whole issue of endogeneity of tastes to one side, worth no more mention than a footnote here or there. The behavioral economist interested in policy issues is not going to be able similarly to push the issue aside. New-found experiences will alter the individual's perception of some of his/her priorities and how he/she can best meet basic deep-seated priorities. Indeed, the possibility that an individual's aspirations will be altered in light of changing circumstances seems to be a central feature of the behavioral framework (Simon, 1959). Accordingly, behavioral economists will not be able to relegate the issue of endogenous preferences to some backwater, and progress in normative behavioral economics requires that a good deal of further work on the policy implications of endogeneous preferences should be undertaken.

4. Public Goods and Behavioral Economics

The priority-based approach to choice has some potentially interesting implications for public goods theory. It turns out that the "optimality" condition for the provision of a pure public good differs substantially from the Samuelsonian condition in which the sum of the individuals' marginal rates of substitution is equated to the marginal rate of transformation. The behavioral approach also has some interesting implications for collective action.

In order to analyze the matter of optimality (with reference to the Pareto criterion, not utility maximization) in the simplest context consider figures 12–2(i) and (ii), which are behavioral based variants of Samuelson's geometric derivation of the requirements for optimal provision of public goods.[3] In figure 12–2(i), the production possibility locus between the private good X and the public good G is given by xg. The priority structure of individuals A and B is depicted by the lines marked P^i_j where j represents the individual and i the individual's ranking of the good. For example, P^1_B signifies that individual B ranks fulfillment of the private goods target as more important than the public goods target, P^2_B. Initially, suppose the private goods target is considered by both individuals as more important than the public goods target.

Pareto optimality, of course, requires that a state be reached in which it is impossible to improve the well-being of one individual without making someone else worse off. To find such a point individual A is set to consume the bundle represented by E; the individual obtains a satisfactory outcome on both priorities. If, for example, the level of public goods supply is reduced below G^0 and private consumption is expanded, then A will be worse off in the sense that he would fail to satisfy his minimum requirement on public goods consumption. In the orthodox analysis an indifference curve would be passed through point E in order to depict the goods combinations which would keep A on the same level of satisfaction. The vertical difference between this indifference curve and the production possibility frontier would be mapped in the figure below in order to determine the maximum increase in welfare which can be sustained by B given A's level of welfare. But under the behavioral lexicographic approach to choice there are no other points in figure 12–2(i) which correspond to the same level of well-being as bundle E. The concepts of an indifference curve and utility level are completely alien to the behavioral approach. The behavioral approach, therefore, calls for an amended treatment.

The idea is to determine to what extent B's priorities can be satisfied given that the other individual's achievement on priorities is not reduced.

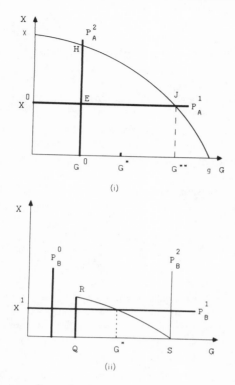

FIGURE 12–2. Priority-based choice and
optimal public goods provision.

It follows that the combinations of X and G which can be made available to B and yet holds A at least to the level of well-being given by point E are given by the region between EJ and the portion of the production possibility curve lying vertically above it (the area EJH). The resulting opportunities[4] available to B are depicted as the consumption possibility set, QRS in figure 12–2(ii). Given B's priority structure, P_B^1 and P_B^2, individual B would decide to consume G^* units of the public good. The amount of the private good which will satisfy his first priority is X^1 leaving G^0G^* of the available consumption possibilities to go toward his second priority. As G is a public good, B consumes the amount provided to A and thereby consumes in total G^* (equals G^0 plus G^0G^*). The level of public goods provision which is consistent with the Pareto criterion is, therefore, G^*.

It is apparent from all of this that the condition for optimal provision of a public good in behavioral economics differs from the familiar condition as specified by Samuelson. This much is obvious from the simple fact that the behavioral approach does not employ the concept of a marginal rate of substitution between commodities. What, then, is the behaviorally equivalent condition for Pareto optimal provision of a public good? What general principle, if any, characterizes the determination of optimal output as set above? The principle is stated first and then explained in terms of the simple two-person two-goods geometrical model. The Pareto optimal provision of a public good, at least as far the priority-based choice framework is concerned, is a level of production at least consistent with the largest instrumental aspiration held by any individual in the population for the public good. The term *instrumental* is used to denote the lowest order priority which can, subject to feasibility considerations, be either partially or totally satisfied through the provision of the public good without the attainments of higher order priorities being compromised.[5] After satisfying his primary target — the private goods aspiration — individual B asks himself what is the lowest order priority which can still be either partially or totally satisfied. In the simple setting here, it was his public goods target. The priority P_B^2 is therefore individual B's instrumental aspiration. In the case of the other individual, he satisfies his target for X by consuming x^0 and then asks which priority he can still satisfy given his endowment. Here G^0 units of the public good will meet his second-order priority and constitutes his instrumental aspiration. Recall that the optimal level of public goods provision is defined as coinciding, subject to feasibility considerations, with the larger instrumental aspiration of the two individuals; here P_B^2 exceeds P_A^2. Suppose the level of public goods provision is expanded from G^0 in order to attempt to satisfy B's instrumental aspiration. Individual B is made better off because the expanded production will go further toward satisfying B's public goods priority. Individual A is also made better off by this expansion. He now obtains better than a merely satisfactory performance on his public goods target.

In order to illustrate further the nature of the optimality condition proposed here, consider the case in which B's aspiration for public goods, P_B^2, now represents a higher-order priority than his aspiration for private goods, depicted again as P_B^1. Note that P_B^2 is B's instrumental aspiration. The amount of resources avaliable to satisfy B priorities is only sufficient to satisfy B's target for public goods.[6] Due to this change in priorities the level of public provision should be expanded from G^* to G^{**}. Individual B is better off in that he at least satisfies his first priority and A is also better off in the sense that he has better than a satisfactory performance on his public good priority. The difference between this case and the one previously analyzed is that there are only sufficient resources upon satisfying A's priorities to meet B's foremost priority.

As a final example consider the case in which individual B's second order priority for public goods is given as P_B^0. Points along the frontier RS but above B's target on private goods all fall within the set of points denoting a better than satisfactory performance on both priorities for individual B. If B had more than two targets, then he would attempt to satisfy still lower order priorities which implies that P_B^0 would not constitute his instrumental aspiration. In this two-person collectivity the larger instrumental aspiration over public goods would be that of individual A, P_A^2 is greater than P_B^0. The optimal level of public goods would be G^0. In the absence of any other priorities, it is clear that both individuals can obtain better than a satisfactory performance on at least one of their priorities. In order to determine the optimal level of public goods provision, the individuals would have to employ some form of tie-breaking rule: it is not possible on the basis of their aspirations to narrow down the optimal degree of public provision to a single point; the range G^0 to G^* is consistent with the application of the Pareto criterion.

All in all, the behavioral framework leads to a fundamentally different condition for the optimal provision of a pure public good. Under the neoclassical approach the idea is, of course, to find the level of public goods provision at which the collectivity's marginal rate of substitution is equal to the marginal rate of transformation. At lower levels of output the summation of the individuals' marginal rates of substitution exceeds the marginal rate of transformation, indicating that there should be an expansion in output. The collectivity derives a social surplus from these additional units measured as the difference between what it was willing to give up and had to give up. The idea is, of course, to allocate resources in such a way that this social surplus is maximized. This is, of course, familiar fare to all neoclassical economists. The behavioral approach, at least as interpreted here, sets out to satisfy an individual's foremost priority[7] and then attempts to fulfill, in descending order, his lower-order priorities subject to resource availability and the requirement that no other individual receives a less satisfactory performance on his priorities. Maximization of social surplus is not the objective of the analysis. There is no comparison of the social surplus gained by expanding public goods provision with the social surplus lost by reducing the output of private goods. The goal instead is to reach a satisfactory outcome on as many targets as is feasible. It is important with all of this geometry not to lose sight of the point that the individual's target with respect to public goods will be shaped by social experience. Consider the neoclassical explanation for the lack of collective action. It would be couched for the most part in terms of the effect of contributory and free-riding behavior on the individual's budget set. The issue of the individual's preferences would receive short shrift. To be sure there are sound arguments for attempting to explain economic behavior without resorting to questions of taste.[8] The problem with employing this methodology in a wholesale manner is that some potential aspects of public choice involving preference formation are overlooked.

Consider a setting in which a large number of individuals are apparently affected by some externality. The neoclassical economist as indicated will explain the inability of the group to come to some collective action on the basis of transaction costs and relative price effects.[9] The possibility that the collective inaction may have more to do with the fact that the affected individuals themselves do not consider that the situation warrants any corrective action is never raised. Specifically, if the pollution as measured by technical instruments is widespread, then each individual may not perceive that the situation is unacceptable and therefore one which demands collective action. Individuals who are boundedly rational may use the lot of others around them in order to form a view of what they should expect to be able to achieve on some particular activity (for an excellent discussion of reference standards, see Loasby, 1976, chapter 6). Alternatively put, the ubiquitous nature of the pollution raises the possibility that each individual may not perceive that there is a problem to correct: they have set their standards in the light of what seems possible, and as long as the pollution does not worsen and they do not happen to visit other areas that could form superior reference standards, they are meeting their aspirations in this area, blissfully ignorant of scope for improvements. Economists armed with readings of the pollution count over a city may point to the "fact" that the affected individuals do not engage in collective action for reasons of self-interest. The behavioral argument raised here points to the possibility that the "affected" individuals may merely look around themselves and wonder what all the fuss is about: they are used to the situation as it is and find it quite manageable; narrow self-interest may have nothing at all to do with the lack of collective action. This leads to the hypothesis that we would expect to see collective action to internalize externalities more often in those cases involving small numbers. For here the individual can plainly see that he/she has been made worse off relative to the surrounding group. Two neighbors, for example, observe that their water pressure is lower than that experienced by their friends down the road and put the blame down to a towering poplar which is near their homes. They hire a plumber in order to gather information for a potential legal action — to check whether there are roots clogging their pipes. If so, then some collective attempt may be made to correct the externality. Notice that behavioral economics does not replace the neoclassical theory of collective action. Once the individuals have perceived that there is a problem, the orthodox theory can come into its own in explaining whether the individuals will do anything about the externality. Viewed in this light behavioral economics opens up the possibility of a far richer theory of collective action; it provides a discussion of the elements of choice which neoclassical economics normally takes as given.

Interestingly, the general logic here points to the same prediction about collective action as that employed in more orthodox circles. Public economics suggests that collective action is more likely in small group situations because there the free-rider problem is less severe. In large number situations the public economist predicts that voluntary collective action will in general fail. I do not believe that behavioral economists would be wholly unhappy with the general logic advanced by the neoclassicals: in small number situations peer pressure can be important in motivating an individual and thereby promoting collective action. The behavioral economist might, however, point to the additional possibility that collective action in similar settings may occur for the markedly different reason raised above. In the case of widespread pollution, which would, of course, be a large-number issue, the individuals may not perceive that there is any "market failure" to correct. In situations where the externality is localized — which will coincide with a small number situation — the individual is more likely to notice that there is a problem to correct and that collective action may be warranted. I fully admit that it is not at all clear to me how information can be collected on such matters. One thing, though, that *is* clear is that the spate of experimental tests on collective action are not going to tell us much about this potential aspect of choice. Experiments performed in which the participants have to resolve a predetermined issue within the limits of the class period tell us little about how an individual's aspiration changes over the course of time. More importantly, these studies do not tell us much about how an individual's target is conditioned by societal factors, for the individuals in the experiment are told at the beginning what is the particular damage function that they will hold for the game.

5. Public Choice and Behavioral Economics

The principle in behavioral lexicographic choice that individuals may undertake activities to achieve priorities in a noncompensatory manner has some potentially important implications for research in public choice. Although the points made here are general in nature, the following analysis focuses on one particular argument: the recent charge that voter choice will lead to socially bad outcomes owing to expressive voting.

Over the last couple of years the most damaging criticism of public choice, at least in its fiscal exchange guise, has come from public choice specialists themselves. Brennan, Buchanan, and Lomasky, in a series of independently and jointly written papers, have questioned the very basis of much that has been written on the intersection between public choice and democratic politics (Brennan and Buchanan, 1984; Brennan and Lomasky, 1984, 1985). Their argument is that citizens when they vote do not in general express their economic interests. Citizens express rather their feelings and whims about political issues in much the same way as they cheer the local football team. Since they do not believe that their vote or support will alter the final outcome, what looms large in their calculus is not the expected material benefits from the outcome but rather the benefits from supporting or voting itself. A person's vote or support is not shaped by a careful evaluation of the projects canvassed by the political parties. It is the psychological benefits he/she expects to accrue from the act of voting itself, rather than the material payoffs he/she stands to gain from the outcome, which determine how he/she votes. Accordingly policy outcomes are generated from the act of expressive voting; questions of resource allocation and foreign policy decisions reflect the whims rather than a careful evaluation by the collectivity. Once this line of argument is accepted the attempts by public choice economists to match marginal tax prices with "demand" loses much of its normative significance: why should we devote a large amount of resources catering to mere whims?

Before examining some of the tenets of this argument from behavioral precepts it will be useful to set out more fully some of the details of the public choice argument. In large number electorates the probability an individual will be the median voter is so low that each individual will reckon when he votes for A that he is merely forgoing a vote for B rather than forgoing the outcome B. Individuals will, therefore, maximize their expected benefits on the basis of how they fill in the ballot paper itself. The distinct possibility emerges that individuals may vote for outcomes which in a sense they do not really prefer. To see this consider the payoff matrix of voter k, shown in figure 12-3. The voter is assumed to get the various payoffs from voting for A or B depending on how the majority votes. Note that the voter gets $5 of benefits[10] from expressing a vote for A irrespective of how the other citizens vote. As long as each voter is risk-neutral and concludes that the probability he will be decisive is less than 0.05, the individual will focus on the first two columns of the payoff matrix 1. Since

Majority Votes for

		A	B	Tie
Individual votes for	A	$5	$105	$5
	B	$0	$100	$100

FIGURE 12–3. Payoff matrix.

a vote for A is row dominant the individual will cast his vote in favor of A. However, it is clear from an examination of the payoffs that all such voters would prefer to have outcome B — that is, $100 is preferred to $5. To the extent that all voters base their decisions in this fashion, the distinct possibility emerges that political decisions will be made on the basis of inconsequential feelings; decisions in the public sector will not be guided by the maximization of the collectivity's benefits. Does behavioral economics have any insights to offer to this criticism of the fiscal exchange process?

Perhaps the first point to make about all of this is that the whole tone of their argument is normative. Like the neoclassical treatment of consumer choice, the treatment here of voter choice seems more concerned with laying down the items which should form the center of the individual's interest rather than modeling the factors they do in fact take into account. The argument seems to be more of a prescription of the factors a rational voter ought to take into account when casting his vote — a prescription that a rational utility maximizer should largely ignore the potential benefits of the outcome and take into account the expected payoffs from expressive voting. Indeed, Brennan, Buchanan, and Lomasky do not offer any clear evidence that individuals do in fact vote on the basis of the benefits they get from expressing their feelings. What support they call on is largely couched in terms of examples which they feel orthodox public choice is hard-pressed to explain. For example, support for their thesis comes from the finding that individuals appear habitually to vote for one party rather than the other when the orthodox argument suggests that the individuals should be assessing each election on its merit and voting for the outcome which maximizes their economic interests. There is a need, however, to take on board the behavioral economist's predilection to dirty his hands by surveying individuals on how they actually make their political decisions. The fiscal exchange framework should not be judged and cast aside solely on the weight of purely theoretical analysis.

The strength of the public choice attack rests on the assumption that the benefits the voter expects to get from expressive voting for issue A are less than the potential benefits from outcome B. It is this assumption which drives the result that individuals may end up with an inferior outcome, $5 rather than $100 in figure 12–3. But clearly there is no reason to believe that expressions ought to count for so little in an individual's overall ranking. The priority-based framework suggests the distinct possibility that the individual feels, as did Sir Thomas Moore, that it is more important to express a preference for one issue over another than it is to obtain the benefits from the outcome. The fact that he/she could not alter the outcome may count for little in the case of an individual who feels that he/she must be true to him/herself. This form of priority structure implies that the psychological return from the act of expressing a vote for A over B could, in prospect, swamp the payoff derived from the outcome B. For example, if issue B goes through the individual may stand to gain a large pecuniary payoff from the logging company which is interested in leasing his land. He may nevertheless vote for A — against woodchipping, say — because he feels that a vote recorded for conservation is more important to him than dollars in the bank. In the setting in which the individual places more importance on the principle than the outcome, nonevaluative or expressive voting would result in the socially preferred outcome. It is important to bear in mind that in the behavioral framework the benefits from voting for a principle may not be comparable to the benefits from the expected outcome. For this reason it may not be possible to illustrate the point at hand with reference to a payoff matrix as this implies that all activities can be brought down to a common denominator. This does not imply that it is impossible to recognize that one issue is preferred to the other. All that is required is that the individual can, as in the case of the analysis of public goods provision, rank one aspiration as more important than the other.

The neoclassical economist might respond that he could change the payoffs in a way which would generate the identical conclusion that expressive voting may not be a social bad. This can be easily illustrated to be so if the payoffs in row 1 are each increased by at least $96 to reflect the higher ranking accorded to the principle embodied in a vote for issue A.

Despite the fact that the two approaches appear to permit an identical conclusion, I believe that behavioral economics has contributed to the debate. The possibility that principles can be of considerable importance to an individual has not been a feature at all of the neoclassical analysis.

This is not surprising. Since principles themselves are not reflected in the marketplace the neoclassical economist, taking heed of the elementary lesson that only effective wants are of interest to economics, naturally accords little importance to expressions of principles. On the other hand, the behavioral framework with its emphasis on underlying priorities, in addition to market outcomes, is conducive to a model in which expressions are weighted more significantly that outcomes. This raises a central advantage of employing the behavioral framework; by asking the same question in a fundamentally different framework our understanding of choice processes is enriched. Instead of treating all expressive voting as reflecting mere whims and thereby something largely to be ignored — which is the direction the neoclassical public choice economists appear to have adopted — the behavioral analysis has raised the worthwhile point, at least to me, that expressions of principles can be more important than outcomes. Evidently expressive voting may be an evil or a grace as far as the individual is concerned depending on the importance he/she attaches to beliefs as opposed to outcomes.

6. Conclusions

Normative behavioral economics is consistent with the broad methodology employed elsewhere in public economics. The Pareto criterion, the notion of market failure, and the idea of gains from trade can be employed in the behavioral framework. Normative behavioral economics differs in that the objective is not to maximize social surplus but rather to achieve a satisfactory outcome on resource allocation. This led to some technical differences between the neoclassical and behavioral conditions for "optimal" provision of a public good. It is also clear that public economics based on behavioral principles is more than a recantation of the conventional wisdom using unusual tools of analysis. By employing the priority-based framework, some useful insights, I believe, have been raised on the reluctance of individuals to trade, the lack of collective action in large number situations and the potential importance of principles.

Acknowledgment

I am deeply indebted to my colleague Peter Earl who has devoted many hours to discussing the ideas set out in this paper. He should not be held responsible though for my bounded rationality.

Notes

1. The analysis of exchange and behavioral precepts in terms of an Edgeworth-Bowley-Pareto box is not new. For an early exposition see Little (1957), Appendix 3.

2. See, Gjerdingen (1983) for a psychological explanation of why one might reject the implications of the Coase theorem.

3. See Samuelson (1955) for a geometric interpretation of the optimality condition for a pure public good.

4. If it is decided that A should not be made better off, then the consumption possibilities available to B is given by EH.

5. In Ironmonger's (1972, p. 23) priority-based treatment of choice, which is couched within the utility maximizing framework, this aspiration is referred to as the "marginal want." Since the framework here deals with satisficing, the term *instrumental aspiration* seems preferable in order to avoid potential confusion.

6. This case implies that B can live by public goods alone. This assumption can be relaxed, however, without affecting the substance of the argument.

7. In practical terms the individuals themselves would indicate whether they were made better off or worse off. No mind-reading is implied in the following discussion.

8. See Stigler and Becker (1977) for some discussion of this methodological point.

9. See Olson (1965) and Chamberlin (1976) for an example of the type of methodology employed.

10. Presumably the payoffs are net of the cost of voting. This payoff matrix is the same as used by Brennan and Lomasky (1984, p. 156).

13 SOME METHODS IN PSYCHOLOGICAL ECONOMICS

Alan Lewis

1. Introduction

Since the first volume of the *Journal of Economic Psychology* was published in 1981 many researchers interested in the engagement of economics and psychology have used the pages of the new journal to present empirical results from experiments, interviews, and questionnaire studies. These researchers share an interest in the human aspect of economic affairs; this can take many forms. A useful distinction made for this area (but not necessarily by the *Journal of Economic Psychology*) is between "psychological economics" and "economic psychology": the former refers to the "psychologizing" of economics and the latter to the extension of the study of human behavior to include economic behavior (for example, Furnham and Lewis, 1986). Thus psychological economics (or behavioral economics) is concerned with forwarding what the converted see as a more comprehensive economic discipline where economic predictions may be improved. This follows the tradition set by George Katona and his work on psychological economics. On the other hand, economic psychology makes no such claim; the main thrust is the idea that studying the economic realm can increase our understanding of human behavior, and that such an endeavor is sufficient justification (and a big enough challenge) as it stands. This chapter is generally concerned with psychological economics and the tools that researchers use in going about their business.

Psychological economics sets the agenda for a behavioral research program. Consequently it is concerned with how people make choices and decisions. The methodology employed is inductive rather than deductive: the emphasis is placed less on explaining, for example, aggregate consumer demand by changes in incomes and prices, and what a rational consumer would do given these changes, and more on *how* choosers choose. Demand is interpreted from this perspective by the variables consumers themselves consider important in their decisions and these variables are the ones utilized in the explanation.

This kind of inductive research requires some further comment as, like the common axiomatic and deductive approach in economics, it makes a number of assumptions, albeit of a radically different type. The major assumption is that people have a pretty good idea why they do things, and an inquiry into these reasons is worthwhile. This need not be the exclusive frame of reference, as the ensuing pages will reveal, in that the explanations are partly determined by the researcher in the alternatives provided in experimental designs or the questions posed in interviews and incorporated in questionnaires. It is, of course, possible for people to act or make preferences for reasons other than those they are aware of or would be prepared to admit to: people's intentions may not necessarily reveal themselves in the way the actor had hoped and the actions (and the intentions) may be misinterpreted by others. Consequently the value of a purely subjectivist approach (for those interested mainly in prediction) is in part dependent on the accuracy and cogency of a person's self-knowledge and awareness. The view taken in modern social psychology is that action comprises intentions, preferences, attitudes, values, and so on in one package, structural and environmental constraints in a second, and postrationalizations as a consequence of action in a third. Rarely have these three broad conceptual packages been examined together. The second package has in common the notion of constraints to maximization used in economics; the third package is often scathingly referred to by economists as evidence of the comparative worthlessness of subjective data (an exception is the use of "dissonance theory" by Akerlof and Dickens, 1982). The present chapter is generally concerned with the first package, namely perceptions, preferences, attitudes, values, and subjective expectations, but, for the reasons stated above, this is only a portion of the process.

Researchers in this inductivist tradition have no magic wand to wave giving them access to consumers' mental states. And it may be a disappointment to many to learn that precious few empirical studies have observed economic behavior in situ. Researchers rely instead on a series of indirect methods for the examination of these processes. To social psychologists and marketers the most obvious way to proceed is to ask consumers about their tastes and preferences and use these answers in predicting economic behavior. This is done via interviews, and, more commonly, with the use of questionnaires. This approach is usually carried out in the field where people might be asked, for example, about their future expenditure plans on consumer durables such as cars, and whether it is, in their opinion, a good or a bad time for buying things of this sort (for example, Katona, 1975, 1977; Ward and Pickering, 1981; Williams and Defries, 1981). An alternative strategy involves experimental simulations. In these cases consumers are asked to make (often hypothetical) choices between goods which possess varying combinations of attributes. Analysis of this sort has reached a high level of sophistication where, at first sight, weird and wonderful techniques such as the Kelly Repertory Grid, Conjoint Analysis, and Factorial Analysis abound. These will be described using examples from the contemporary literature. But first let us return to the use of questionnaires.

2. Field Questionnaires and Interviews

Questionnaires and interviews are frequently employed in conjunction with representative sampling. There is a substantial literature on the do's and don't's of surveys and sampling: readers are directed to Moser and Kalton (1971) and Kish (1965) for a comprehensive review of the techniques involved. All methods of sampling require the selection of individuals from a population that is carefully defined. For the sample to be representative, the selection process has to be random — that is, each individual has an equal, known, and nonzero chance of selection. The precision of the sample is dependent on the variance and sample size: where individual respondents provide a wide range of different replies, this increases the variance and necessitates a larger sample size where replies are less heterogeneous. Surveys, too, can be biased. All surveys are biased to some extent; the task is to identify biases and to minimize them. Common biases involve a listing of names and addresses which is in itself not representative of the population the researcher has in mind — for example, if the population consists of inhabitants of a particular city or zone, selection from a list of telephone numbers is biased as telephone ownership is not evenly distributed, in that poorer people are less likely to have one. Questionnaires themselves can be biased because of the phrasing of questions or the way answers are recorded. Questionnaires are also often filled in with the help of interviewers and respondents may be influenced in their replies by those interviewers. A major bias involves nonresponse; not everyone is happy to complete questionnaires: this can be crucial in, for example, a survey on tax evasion where a disproportionate number of nonrespondents are self-employed, a group with more opportunities to evade taxes illegally. Finally it has to be decided whether respondents are telling the truth and whether their replies are superficial or well informed, uninterested, or salient.

Ways of increasing precision and reducing bias are well documented. High quality survey research requires teamwork, piloting, and careful management. Consequently some survey research is naturally better than others and a proper appraisal of its quality requires careful scrutiny by the scholar reading such pieces. This is made easier by a comprehensive recording of the details, often found in appendices by the reporting researcher.

2.1. The Work of Katona

A good example of the use of surveys and questionnaire techniques is illustrated by the work of the late George Katona and his colleagues at the Survey Research Center, Ann Arbor, Michigan (see Katona, 1975, 1977; Juster, 1981). These surveys were based on representative samples in the United States conducted quarterly. The major methodological tool was the speciously simple *Index of Consumer Sentiment* (ICS). The ICS measures the subjective expectations of consumers and involves five interview questions. These questions cover: (1) whether respondents considered themselves financially better or worse off than a year ago; (2) whether they think they will be better or worse off in a year from now; (3) whether it is a good time for buying things; (4) whether the next 12 months and (5) the next five years will be better for the economy as a whole. The index was principally used to predict upswings and down-turns in the purchasing of consumer durables, particularly cars. Katona's central argument was that a major part of the economy is dependent on what consumers do and, furthermore, that consumer decisions are based on the subjective perceptions of consumers, their attitudes and expectations. This empirically based view of expectations is very different from the "rational expectations" models used by modern economists. Juster (1981) has written that rational expectations are more appropriate in their application for professional speculative activity and where such activity is the dominant force. When looking at "ordinary" consumers, Katona argues that we cannot assume that their implicit theories are the same as those held by professional economists, or what professional economists expect them to be.

In a review of the comparative success of the ICS, Katona (1967) points to some impressive results for the years 1952–1966 derived from regression studies of time-series data, where the index, combined with the income level, explained 91 percent of the variance in consumer expenditure on durables. (Expectations alone explained 46 percent.) This said, it has also been indicated that variations in the ICS can be explained by objectively measured economic antecedents. In addition, the contribution of ICS is very modest when compared with economic indicators of a more objective nature (for example, consumer price and stock exchange indices) in regression relationships (see, for example, Shapiro, 1972; Hymans, 1970; Vanden Abeele, 1983). There have been many improvements in scaling methods used in consumer surveys in recent years (see Pickering, 1977), and both Williams and Defries (1981) and Ward and Pickering (1981) present a more optimistic view of the use of perceptual and subjective data generally. Ward and Pickering (1981) have reported on the explanatory power of surveys conducted by the Commission of the European Communities between 1975 and 1979 for the British context. The questions asked in this survey included attitudes toward the general economic situation, prices, unemployment, the households' financial circumstances, saving, and durable purchasing expectations. "Expectations" variables were predictively superior over this period to measures of personal income and, perhaps surprisingly, were broadly independent of real personal disposable income, seasonally adjusted.

Williams and Defries (1981) used survey data collected by the Melbourne Institute of Applied Economic and Social Research in Australia. The authors estimated equations for expenditure on motor cars, and household durable and nondurable goods. The equations compared subjective and "objective" measures of inflation and unemployment as well as the familiar "consumer sentiment" measures in traditional models of the allocation of consumers' income. The study therefore included not only measures of consumer sentiment and expectations of future price increases but also perceptual data on the seriousness of inflation and unemployment rates. For nondurable goods, influencing factors are diverse but relate particularly to how consumers perceive their present and future economic well-being. Objective inflation levels were much better than subjective measures of inflation as predictors of motor vehicle expenditure. This said, for other kinds of consumption both objective measures of unemployment and inflation were superior to their subjective counterparts.

2.2. The Public Sector

There is a growing literature using surveys which investigate attitudes toward taxation and preferences for public expenditure (Citrin, 1979; Coughlin, 1980; Lewis, 1982; McCrohan, 1982). These survey results can be used as an indication of the demand for public goods, the comparative visibility of particular taxes and services, and the willingness to pay for public services. They also provide an opportunity to appraise the accuracy of economic incidence analysis in predicting preferences (see Fisher, 1985; Cullis and Lewis, 1985; Lewis and Cullis, 1987). Surveys have even been used, in the form of telephone interviews, to assess attitudes toward tax crimes and the propensity to evade (Warneryd and Walerud, 1982).

The wording of questions asked of survey respondents is crucial. People, as witnessed by results in many Western capitalist countries, show a great deal of support for favored aspects of public expenditure — especially provisions for the elderly, education, and health care. Alternatively there is equally consistent disfavor with taxes of almost every kind (although so-called "indirect taxes" on goods and services are less visible to the public and favored more if revenue needed to be increased — see Cullis and Lewis, 1985). Both sets of results, for public expenditure and taxation, are tempered when the "fiscal connection," between taxes paid and benefits received, is made explicit in the question posed to survey respondents. When it is made plain that extra provisions for the elderly will require an increase in revenue to pay for them, the enthusiasm for such an extension of public welfare is reduced: mention that the taxes you pay finance education and needed health care, and antipathy toward taxation is reduced. Many of the surveys conducted in this area fail to make the so-called fiscal connection and could be viewed as misrepresenting preferences. The question becomes: to what extent is one interested in the naive preferences of consumers of public goods as compared to preferences expressed where information is supplied which may not otherwise have been pertinent? (This problem reappears when considering experimental studies of the decision-making process in the consumption of private goods.) For Fisher (1985), the relative failure of economic incidence analysis to predict preferences as expressed in surveys (compared with voting patterns and ideological allegiance) arises as respondents are unable to make accurate calculations of how they should value proposed fiscal programs in terms of their own self interest. When questions are more precise and informative, the replies engendered become more "informed" and more rational in the sense that they more closely resemble what many economists would consider was in the respondents' best interests. The alternative "naive" and subjectivist approach states that a central point of interest is the perceptions and "misinformation" of respondents, since on these, their "true" preferences are based (see Cullis and Lewis, 1985). There is good evidence, too, that economic preferences and politicoeconomic socialization are closely linked (Lewis and Cullis, 1987). The destination to which the naive path eventually leads is not necessarily toward the continual use of survey questionnaires since these elicit responses that people may not otherwise have stated unless asked — the preferences are not observed when expressed in situ.

The use to which surveys are put also includes the examination of tax evasion. There has been growing concern in recent years that the amount of tax illegally withheld is growing, yet the true extent of tax evasion is notoriously difficult to assess (O'Higgins, 1981).

Surveys have generally assumed that behavior is more common if it is approved of and less common if it is disapproved. It therefore follows that if the general public's attitudes toward evasion are complacent or ambivalent and that this lack of censure is becoming more apparent, then tax evasion behavior is likely to be growing. Quite a number of behavioral tax models have now been put forward, and a contemporary review prepared for the American Bar Association is presented in Kinsey (1985). Economic models stress the importance of size of fines, the probability of detection, and the models of decisions made under uncertainty (for example, see Allingham and Sandmo, 1972). The behavioral models recognize the importance of these effects but stress the perceptual element — the perception of the probability of detection and so on. In addition, these behavioral models attempt to assess the motivation to evade, rather than taking this as self-evident, by examining personal attitudes toward tax evasion, perceptions of its incidence and whether it is practiced by people known to the respondents, the appropriate punishments for tax evasion (if any), and the social approval or disapproval of important others (friends, colleagues, etc.).[1]

Problems in testing these models have always concerned the quality of the measurement of tax evasion itself, the dependent variable. Ingenious devices have been developed in response to this problem for use in questionnaire surveys, including the "locked box" and "randomized response" techniques.[1] In the locked box technique, respondents complete self-administered questionnaires and then place them in a box similar to a ballot box so as to reassure respondents about confidentiality. Aitken and Bonneville (1980) have reported how this technique was used in a survey of 4888 individuals conducted for the Internal Revenue Service (IRS) in the United States. The results showed that 13 percent said they sometimes underreported income on their tax returns; 4 percent said they listed more tax deductions than they were entitled to; and 3 percent made illegal claims for dependents. The IRS study also employed the randomized response technique. Here respondents answered questions about tax cheating (A) or other questions (B) at random. Which questions were answered were not known directly by the researchers but replies to the cheating questions could be assessed by taking a subset of people who were required to answer B questions only and comparing the results.[2] The technique proved particularly successful. Those admitting underreporting rose to an estimated 21 percent of the sample; 11 percent said they misled the tax authorities about deductions; and 16 percent rendered inappropriate dependents.

3. Experiments and Experimental Simulations

Experimental studies differ from social surveys in several important respects. First of all, participants in experiments are rarely drawn randomly from the population, nor are they representative of any population. Second, while social surveys are often used to investigate macroeconomic issues, experimental studies are generally employed to investigate individual decision making at the microanalytic level. Experiments are set up to test differences between groups and conditions in a restricted environment rather than to investigate population parameters. Most of the pertinent literature appears in marketing and management journals and uses specialist techniques such as repertory grid analysis, conjoint measurement and factorial analysis.

Each of the above-mentioned techniques will be described in turn with examples.

3.1. Kelly's Repertory Grid Technique

Examples of the use of repertory grids (pioneered by Kelly, 1955) appear in articles by Olson and Reynolds (1983), Reynolds and Gutman (1984), and Reynolds and Jamieson (1985). All of these papers are concerned with how people make choices, for example between retail stores or motor cars with varying combinations of characteristics. The theory, or more properly, the model underlying these investigations is called chain analysis and is represented below (following Gutman, 1982; Reynolds and Gutman, 1983):

Con-crete Attri-butes →	Ab-stract Attri-butes →	Func-tional Conse-quences →	Psycho-logical Conse-quences →	Instru-mental Values→	Ter-minal Values

Concrete atrributes are what Lancaster (1971) would term *characteristics* — that is, objective and measurable features. In an example of choice between airlines, these concrete attributes might include the fare, facilities for advanced seat reservations, and punctuality records. This is where the economist Lancaster would wish to stop (and most mainstream consumer demand theorists do not even consider this stage); to quote Lancaster, the market for goods "is readily available to rational analysis in terms of straightforward physical characteristics . . . without using such imponderables as 'style' or any sex at all" (Lancaster, 1971, p. 174). As one moves along Gutman's and Reynolds' chain, things become increasingly "sexy" (and for critics, increasingly imponderable). In the earlier airline example, abstract attributes include such things as comfort and whether or not the airline cabin and departure lounge generate a relaxing environment. The functional consequences of these attributes might be that one is able to read or sleep on the plane, feel at ease, and able to plan a trip with confidence. The psychosocial consequences might be that one feels in control and reassured that one is being treated as a worthy customer and not just a piece of baggage; the instrumental values may be of accomplishment and safety; and finally the terminal values of self-esteem and security come into play (cf. Baxter's discussion of Maslow's work, in section 3 of chapter 9 above).

The authors who have followed this chain analysis recognize that not all decisions need continue along its full length, but inherent in the model is the idea that so-called "imponderables" are of considerable importance and form the major bases, so to speak, of advertising campaigns. Furthermore, because the appraisal is subjective, it is for the consumers to decide which characteristics differentiate airlines, and, even with physical characteristics, these may not always be the ones one might suppose them to be without posing the question to the consumers themselves. The next question becomes: how are these characteristics, and especially the more abstract characteristics, to be generated?

The first step is to take part in "triadic sorts." People are given three brands of, for example, toothpaste and are asked: "Tell me how two of these are alike and different from a third." The procedure continues until an appropriate number of attributes are generated by respondents.

The next stage of the technique involves "laddering." Laddering "forces" the consumer along the chain (or "up the ladder") from concrete attributes toward abstractions, ultimately, of instrumental and terminal values. This is done by asking participants to explain why the attributes they choose, for discrimination purposes, are important to them. The question is repeated following the answer to the previous inquiry, and so on, until explanation is exhausted and the answer comes back, "I don't know" or an exasperated "Just because!"

Studies of this kind require only between 40 and 50 subjects: Olsen and Reynolds report that in larger studies involving up to 250 respondents few additional concepts were generated in the laddering exercise. How many steps do people usually make up the ladder? This of course depends on the people and the goods in question. As a guide, one can note that in the Reynolds and Gutman (1984) study of 26 respondents 113 ladders of varying lengths were provided: 41 percent had two steps, 38 percent had 3 steps and 21 percent had 5 steps. More steps are generally associated with more abstraction.

The data derived from the application of the repertory grid technique can be analyzed in myriad ways; one of the simplest is described by Reynolds and Gutman (1983). In this case all the attributes are amassed and an aggregated cognitive map developed. Clearly, not everyone brings the same attributes to mind, nor do they make the same connections between them. The purpose of the mapping procedure is to identify common at-

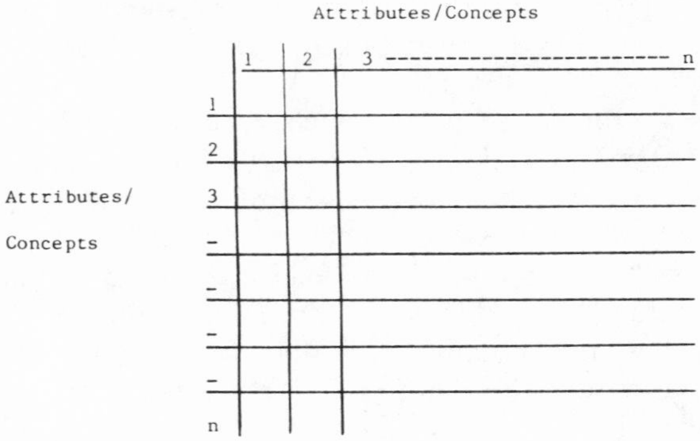

FIGURE 13–1. Structural analysis.

tributes, and common connections. A simple way to do this is to list all the elicited attributes/concepts both vertically and horizontally, as in figure 13–1. Where the row concept precedes the column concept an entry is made in the matrix — that is, where the row is the probe that elicited the column. Figures within the boxes represent the frequency scale data (which can be further simplified to binary data if required). Results can be presented in tree diagrams as in figure 13–2.

The reliability of repertory grid techniques has occasionally been called into question. Reliability can be of two main types: the first of these concerns the reproduction of pertinent constructs by the same individual at time t_2 compared with t_1; the second concerns the comparison of demographically similar groups, comprising different individuals, at different times. In the first instance constructs will be more likely to be dissimilar as the time period between t_1 and t_2 increases. This is neither surprising nor necessarily damaging for the measure. People's way of construing the world changes with experience and as a consequence of major events in life: for example, one's construing of heterosexual relationships is likely to be very different during adolescence than in adulthood, before marriage, and after marriage. Or, if we return to consumer goods, a motor car conjures up very different images for an adolescent male than it does for an older married man. Shorter time periods may also show differences due to changes of mood and of "what's on one's mind." The vagaries of such variance can be compensated by collecting a portfolio of responses for each individual or, more practically, different individuals in different settings and at different times of day.

The second notion of reliability might rest, for example, on whether a sample of 16- to 19-year-olds presents similar constructs about, say, savings and investment, in 1985 as a demographically similar group of different individuals in 1986, and that these constructs were consistently different to those held by the 20- to 24-year-old age groups. It is this broader kind of reliability and patterning that is of central interest to marketers especially when they can concentrate their efforts on specific categories of consumers.

In both reliability examples it has been argued that the reliability of the repertory grid is not reduced by varying results per se provided that these variations can be explained — that is, provided the changes are predictable ones (Fransella and Bannister, 1977).

3.2. Conjoint Measurement

As we have seen, the repertory grid is used to draw up cognitive maps. These maps can be used by advertisers in the design of their campaigns;

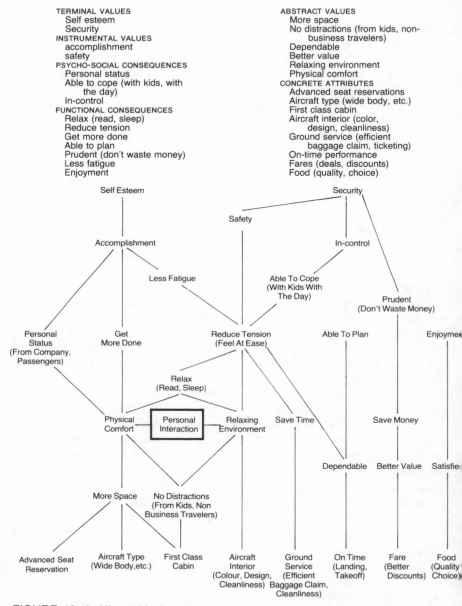

TERMINAL VALUES
  Self esteem
  Security
INSTRUMENTAL VALUES
  accomplishment
  safety
PSYCHO-SOCIAL CONSEQUENCES
  Personal status
  Able to cope (with kids, with
    the day)
  In-control
FUNCTIONAL CONSEQUENCES
  Relax (read, sleep)
  Reduce tension
  Get more done
  Able to plan
  Prudent (don't waste money)
  Less fatigue
  Enjoyment

ABSTRACT VALUES
  More space
  No distractions (from kids, non-
    business travelers)
  Dependable
  Better value
  Relaxing environment
  Physical comfort
CONCRETE ATTRIBUTES
  Advanced seat reservations
  Aircraft type (wide body, etc.)
  First class cabin
  Aircraft interior (color,
    design, cleanliness)
  Ground service (efficient
    baggage claim, ticketing)
  On-time performance
  Fares (deals, discounts)
  Food (quality, choice)

FIGURE 13–2. Hierarchical structure map for hypothetical airline study (reproduced from Gutman and Reynolds, 1983).

"self-confidence" may not be the obvious peg on which to hang an advertising campaign for toothpaste until one learns that an important attribute
of toothpaste is its ability to freshen the breath, laddering to "fresh breath
confidence" and so on. However, repertory grid techniques are rarely used,
in this context, to examine preferences in a way where one could predict
how good A would be chosen over another good B. Conjoint measurement
is aimed at this target.

As before, goods are conceived of as bundles of attributes. But which
attributes are most important in consumer choice? In conjoint analysis,
multiple comparisons between goods are analyzed. The examples of conjoint analysis discussed below are drawn from Green and Wind (1975).

A company has designed a new spot remover for carpets and upholstery.
The company, naturally enough, wants to know what combination of attributes will best favor the success of the product. Management decide on
five attributes: applicator design, brand name, price, a *Good Housekeeping*
seal of approval, and a money-back guarantee. Furthermore, there are
three applicator designs, three brand names, three prices, and the presence
or absence of the endorsement and guarantee. If all possible combinations
were to be tested this would require 108 options — that is,
$3 \times 3 \times 3 \times 2 \times 2 = 108$. Because of practical and cognitive limitations large
numbers of options need to be reduced to something more convenient: in
fact, they can be reduced to orthogonal arrays where all five factors are
balanced. An example of such an array is presented in Figure 13–3 using
only 18 of the 108 possible combinations. The respondent is shown 18
distinct cards that describe the options and is asked to rank them in order
of the likelihood of purchase.

Utility scales for each attribute can be calculated from this ranked data
so as to assess how influential each attribute is in consumers' decisions.
(Details of the calculations involved are presented in Kruskal, 1965.) Computer programs have been designed to calculate the scale values for each
level of each factor in the experimental design in such a way that when
they are added together the *total* utility of each combination will correspond
as closely as possible to the original ranks. The result of this analysis is
presented in figure 13–4. Although the scales range in each case from zero
to one, it will be seen that dichotomous attributes are *not* rated by the
program as either zero or one: for example, the utility rating for the *Good
Housekeeping* seal dimension is put at 0.2 if it is absent and 0.3 if it is
present. The more important an attribute is seen as being in the overall
ratings, the wider the range assigned for the factor on its utility scale: it
can be seen from the histogram at the bottom of figure 13–4 that the
greatest changes in utility relate to package design and price. By combining

Package designs

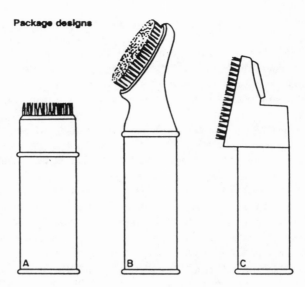

Orthogonal array

	Package design	Brand name	Price	Good Housekeeping seal?	Money-back guarantee?	Respondent's evaluation (rank number)
1	A	K2R	$1.19	No	No	13
2	A	Glory	1.39	No	Yes	11
3	A	Bissell	1.59	Yes	No	17
4	B	K2R	1.39	Yes	Yes	2
5	B	Glory	1.59	No	No	14
6	B	Bissell	1.19	No	No	3
7	C	K2R	1.59	No	Yes	12
8	C	Glory	1.19	Yes	No	7
9	C	Bissell	1.39	No	No	9
10	A	K2R	1.59	Yes	No	18
11	A	Glory	1.19	No	Yes	8
12	A	Bissell	1.39	No	No	15
13	B	K2R	1.19	No	No	4
14	B	Glory	1.39	Yes	No	6
15	B	Bissell	1.59	No	Yes	5
16	C	K2R	1.39	No	No	10
17	C	Glory	1.59	No	No	16
18	C	Bissell	1.19	Yes	Yes	1*

*Highest ranked.

FIGURE 13–3. An orthogonal array of five factors: an example of conjoint measurement (reproduced from Green and Wind, 1975).

the information from figure 13–3 and figure 13–4 the total utility for any given combination of attributes can be arrived at. For example, take the first combination in figure 13–3: U(Packaging, A) = 0.1; U(Brand name, K2R) = 0.3; U(Price, $1.19) = 1.0; U(*Good Housekeeping* seal, No) = 0.2; U(Money-back guarantee, No) = 0.2. Taken together, these attributes score a total utility of 1.8. (The best combination is package B, branded as Bissell, with a price of $1.19, a *Good Housekeeping* seal, and a money-back guarantee.)

In the example described, the attributes were not chosen by the respondents in the experiment. However, there is no reason why the respondents should not choose the attributes — an obvious way to proceed being the preliminary use of repertory grids to uncover the pertinent attributes, followed by conjoint analysis.

3.3. Factorial Studies and Analyses of Variance

A criticism of the conjoint measurement technique (and even in the example described above which required 18 rather than 108 rankings) is that the number of discriminations required of the respondents is too great. Furthermore, the additive model of conjoint analysis underestimates the interactions between attributes and the way they may be traded off, one against another. The paper by Monroe (1976) is taken as an example where respondents are only required to make choices between pairs of goods with differing attribute combinations and where interactions, particularly between price and brand familiarity, are given pride of place. The methodological details of the Monroe study follow.

Preferences were examined for different brands of coffee. The independent variables were: the brand of coffee (whether a distributor or national brand), purchase level (whether the coffee had been purchased recently), familiarity (whether the respondent was familiar with the product but had not purchased it recently), and finally, price differences. Details concerning brand purchasing and familiarity were sought from respondents prior to the purchase proper. In the actual experiments, the respondents, all of whom were women, were asked to compare two brands at a time and to indicate their preferences on a seven point scale ranging from "prefer brand A to brand B very strongly" to "prefer brand B to brand A very strongly." Monroe (1976, pp. 43–44) describes the process as follows:

Each woman made 19 paired comparisons as the price of one of the brands varied systematically. In all cases the first comparison involved no price differences between the brands. Price was then systematically lowered (or raised) by

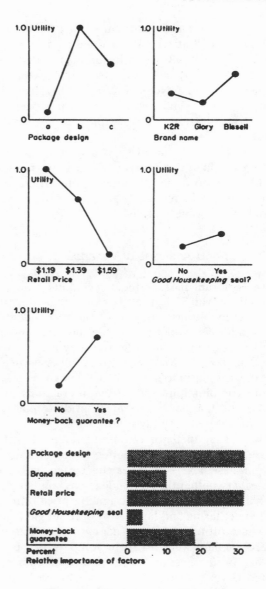

FIGURE 13–4. Results of computer analysis of experimental data used in the example of conjoint measurement (reproduced from Green and Wind, 1975).

a constant amount for nine comparisons for one of the brands; then price was raised (or lowered) by a constant amount from the no-price difference standard for nine more comparisons. The order of the brands, the order of the price manipulations, and the "standard" brand were randomly varied. . . . [P]rice differences ranged from ± 27 cents.

The results were analyzed using an analysis of variance for repeated measures factorial designs (see Winer, 1972). This enabled all possible interactions (as well as main effects) to be calculated. The Neuman-Keuls multiple comparison test was also employed to test the rapidity of preference change as a function of price.

Monroe's experimental results revealed asymmetric preferences due to price differences: brand preferences were more sensitive to price decreases than to price increases. As might be expected, price was found to be a major influence in consumer decisions but the interaction with brand familiarity was striking. When coffee brands were unfamiliar, the women preferred cheaper brands, but these preferences were weaker when price was the only cue available, and many respondents were indifferent. The influence of price was at its strongest when respondents compared brands with which they were equally familiar. Large price differences were required to override familiarity when a familiar brand was compared to an unfamiliar one.

4. Psychological Economics and Experimental Economics Compared

Experimental economics is a flourishing minority interest within economics; a substantial and timely bibliography has been provided by Elizabeth Hoffman (Hoffman and Spitzer, 1985). An experiment reported by Smith in 1962 is a classic example of this genre: it provided the impetus for many others and hence it seems appropriate to provide a brief description of it at this juncture.

Smith was concerned with the validity of the simple competitive model of supply and demand — whether, if supply and demand functions are given, markets produce competitive equilibrium prices and quantities predicted by the model and thereby exhaust all potential profits. The normal supply-and-demand formulation employs the static equilibrium concept, viewing markets as if trades are only allowed in equilibrium, with all trades taking place simultaneously: this insures that in each period during which conditions underlying the supply and demand functions are identical, the same price and quantity are always generated. Economics has traditionally used evidence from purchases as a test of the competitive mechanism and treated these purchases as revealing preferences. However, data so derived are contaminated by the market institutions generating the observed prices: some trades take place out of equilibrium, while it is often to difficult to argue that underlying conditions are not changing also, so reliable inferences are difficult to draw. To overcome these problems, Smith formulated a laboratory experiment parallel to a real market where individual trading could be observed and the influence of market institutions controlled.

In the experiment there were seven buyers and seven sellers, and rather than being consumers and producers they were simply assigned roles as traders in abstract "units." "Buyers" would trade in the units with the experimenter at the end of the experiment in exchange for guaranteed redemption prices and real money in dollars was paid to the subjects. "Sellers," conversely, would have to pay the experimenter specified redemption values for any units they sold in the trading period. The experimenter set different prices for each trader, specifying them on the trader's private payoff sheet. Buyers could make profits by buying below the redemption values that the experimenter had set for them, while sellers could make profits by selling units at prices above the redemption values assigned to them by the experimenter. Subjects were unable to lose money as selling below the redemption price or buying above the redemption prices set by the experimenter were not permitted. figure 13–5 summarizes the experimental design.

The line sloping downwards left to right, the demand function, shows which buyers face which redemption values: for example, the demands of buyer no. 1 (top lefthand) arise from the experimenter's agreement to pay this buyer $5.00 for the first unit purchased, $3.70 for the second and $3.00 for the third; buyers no. 2 through no. 7 each are working with different agreements. The steps on the line sloping upwards left to right, the supply function, indicate the terms on which the sellers can obtain units from the experimenter and hence the prices above which they must sell to make a profit. For example, seller no. 8 (bottom left) must pay $3.20 for the first unit, $4.50 for the second and $5.00 for the third; sellers no. 9 through no. 14 are each trading according to different terms. Assuming the subjects maximize profits, the model predicts that nine or ten trades will be made at the equilibrium price of $4.10 and that total profits will equal the shaded area in figure 13–5.

The results from the experiments showed that after four or five "learning" trials nearly all trades, within a cent or two, were at the equilibrium value.

The study just described is a classic of its type and many, perhaps less

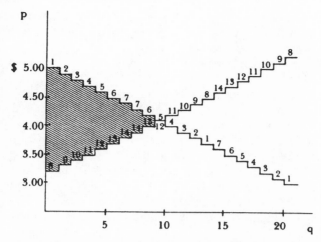

FIGURE 13–5. An example of experimental economics: the experimental design of induced supply-and-demand functions used by Smith (1962).

trivial studies ensued, including the examination of the influence of differing market institutions; these studies are reviewed by Hoffman and Spitzer (1985).

5. A Case for Methodological Pluralism

There is insufficient space to engage in a lengthy methodological debate (and those interested in economic methodology are recommended to consult Caldwell, 1984 and Marr and Raj, 1983). However, in moving toward the conclusion of this chapter, it is necessary to offer suggestions for a way forward. All methods are open to criticism: survey questions and experimental instructions influence the answers given; the quality of subjects' responses can be called into question. But the present author advocates that a behavioral analysis is necessary and desirable as this aids our comprehension of economic and social phenomena. However, this should not be the exclusive frame of reference; rather, a methodological pluralism is recommended. Mainstream economists have proven extremely competent in deriving rigorous models of the economy yet, as always, there is room for improvement. Researchers in psychological economics may lack the formal modeling skills of conventional economists, but there are opportunities for complementary work, especially in attempting to complete what we can call the deductive/inductive circle of the scientific process. (It must also be said that there are other areas where it is difficult if not impossible to envisage a productive liaison between economics, psychology and sociology.)

The methods of experimental economics have commonalities with experimental psychology. In both — and especially when studying human behavior — the reductionist critique is apt. The real world is complex; the experimental setting is one where the experimenter strives to investigate the influence of a restricted number of variables in a controlled environment. The assumption is made that a complex reality is reducible to its constituents. And here, as elsewhere, there are contradictions within the economic discipline itself. The two main ones are: first, that microeconomics is individualistic in that it is based on the assumptions of individual rational actors, yet individuals and small groups are not observed or investigated directly as they are, for instance, in social psychology; second, mainstream economics adheres to the positivistic tradition yet rarely if ever amends its theories in the light of empirical evidence (for a detailed discussion of this contradiction, see Hollis and Nell, 1975). If we put aside the reductionist critique for a moment, it seems at least feasible that experimental economics, and possibly also psychological economics, could contribute to the disentanglement of these contradictions. We are familiar with the notion that good economic models may be based on unrealistic assumptions about individual behavior (cf. Friedman, 1953; Samuelson, 1963, 1964; and Machlup, 1964): it is simply proposed that good models (or perhaps better models) could be developed from more realistic assumptions. However, it must be reiterated that models derived from a behavioral analysis may be of different stuff to deductive generalizations and this is where some of the work in experimental economics may be in error: market models may be good generalizations without the need for "verification" through experimental simulations of the market such as undertaken by Smith (1962). (Similarly, in the context of Katona's work, the measurement of subjective expectations may help in the prediction of aggregate consumer demand, but it does not necessarily follow, at the individual level, that more economically optimistic consumers will consume more, although Pickering, 1977, has produced some supportive cross-sectional data of this type.)

6. Conclusions

This chapter has been concerned with some of the things psychological economists do and how they go about their business. We have concentrated on two main approaches, namely, social survey methods and experimental simulations. The social survey studies have frequently been concerned with macroeconomic phenomena, such as aggregate consumer demand, while experimental studies have concentrated on individual decision-making processes. The instruments used are well tested and the statistical analysis sophisticated. However, here, as elsewhere in the present book, the contribution these studies can make to economics is far from straightforward. The measurements of consumer sentiments and consumer subjective expectations may well be related to and help predict macroeconomic change, but if alternative, purely economic models are shown to be at least equally successful, then why bother to survey respondents in this way? The case is not proven and, to an extent, "You pays your money and takes your choice." It may well be, as some scholars of science have suggested, that competition between alternative theories is not necessarily settled in a "scientific" manner; or, in economic terms, the effort required of economists to learn new skills may not be worth the effort.

The microanalytic studies of choice are on a rather different footing in that often they emerge from normative work in market research and do not aim to offer an alternative explanation for economic consequences; there are no obvious advantages for a market researcher to devise a behavioral model of consumer choice and to test it, or indeed to go beyond the brief provided by clients. However, there have been important developments that may contribute to a future convergence of work on choice by economists and behavioral scientists: an obvious example is Ratchford's (1975) attempt to integrate economic theories of consumer behavior with multiattribute scaling and attitude models, published in an early issue of the avowedly interdisciplinary *Journal of Consumer Research*.

The research program for psychological economics must be directed to empirical studies of individual and social action and theories and hypotheses derived via induction. This is not to propose that such work be atheoretical, as there is always a danger in concluding too much from such evidence; however, the approach seems potentially profitable as too little attention has been placed in recent years on such evidence within economics.

There are some specific areas which the present author considers worthy of future development, namely, experiments that suggest the development of new theory, descriptive studies of decision-making, and the observation of market behavior in situ. In respect of the first area, Hoffman and Spitzer (1985) pick out experimental work concerning real time competitive market processes as particularly likely to lead to the development of new theories. An obvious instance concerns the research efforts of theorists such as Friedman (1984), aimed at developing a dynamic equilibrium model — where allowance is made for a sequence of trades, many of which may be conducted at disequilibrium prices — following the analysis of 20 years of experimental data on double auction markets.

If we are to understand how choosers choose, room must be made for descriptive studies of decision making processes and market behavior in situ. Pinch and Clark (1986) have begun some pioneering work in the latter category, with the aid of tape recordings of the pitches of market traders in action. Although their analysis is sociological, with its associated jargon, there are obvious opportunities for making evidence of this kind more pertinent and of wider appeal and relevance.

The future augurs well for those who believe that a behavioral analysis is worthwhile, not only because it is inherently interesting but because it helps in the resolution of economic problems. Such a resolution requires a new breed of scholar capable of identifying the pertinent and reliable results from behavioral research while at the same time maintaining some of the old values of economic scholarship.

Notes

1. Several other, broader political-economic models have been proposed which take account of fiscal and constitutional structure — for example, Wilensky (1976).

2. An example describing a two question case is given for simplicity. The problem is solved using the following equation:

$$\lambda = P\pi_A + (1 - P)\pi_B$$

where: λ = the proportion of people answering "yes" to either question A or B chosen at random; P is the probability that the sensitive question A about tax cheating is chosen by the random device; $1 - P$ is the probability that the other question B (an innocuous question) is chosen by the random device; π_A is the proportion answering yes to question A (i.e., admitting tax evasion); π_B is the proportion answering yes to question B. The equation cannot be solved as there are two unknowns, namely, π_A and π_B. Consequently the value of π_B is estimated by looking at the responses of a subset of respondents who were provided only with B questions.

14 ECONOMICS AND PSYCHOLOGY: A RESURRECTION STORY

A. W. Coats.

1. The Original Debate and Its Aftermath

Although few historians of economics nowadays view the so-called "marginal revolution" of the 1870s as a complete break with the past, it is still generally seen as an important turning point in the development of the discipline: the beginning of modern professionalized academic economics, and a major paradigm shift which, one recent scholar has persuasively argued, inaugurated a new research program (Fisher, 1986). Central to the achievement of the three major innovators — Jevons, Menger, and Walras — was the formulation and elaboration of a new "subjective" theory of value to supplant the dominant "objective" cost of production theory, which in turn contributed to a fundamental shift of focus from supply-based to demand-based theories of value, production, and distribution (Black, Coats, and Goodwin, 1970). There was, of course, much more to the marginal revolution than this. But for present purposes it will serve as a convenient starting point, for it was followed by a protracted, intense, and complex debate about the relations between economics and psychology which lasted at least until the late 1920s, and which involved many scholars from both disciplines and several different countries.

The controversy was especially vigorous in the United States, where there were strongly marked methodological and doctrinal disagreements. In the course of the discussion three distinct positions emerged: (1) the view that psychology of any kind was irrelevant to economics, since it was exclusively concerned with exchange values or prices irrespective of the motives of those entering into market transactions; (2) the diametrically opposite contention that developments in psychology had so undermined the subjective theory of value that a wholesale reconstruction of the foundations of economics was required; and (3) an intermediate response from those who considered that the new ideas could be assimilated, either wholly or in part, by means of a change in terminology, shifts in theoretical formulation or interpretation, or modifications in theoretical conclusions (Coats, 1976).

In retrospect the most striking feature of this episode is the similarity between the issues in debate at that time and the arguments expressed in the current literature on the relations between economics and psychology, including some of the chapters in this book. Unlike many academic controversies, the earlier debate appeared to be effectively settled by 1930, with victory going to those who rejected all proposals either to abandon the basic "hard core" assumptions of orthodox economic theory or to modify them substantially to take account of psychological theory or research findings. This conclusion accorded both with the post-1870 narrowing of the boundaries of economics (Winch, 1970) and with the broader trend toward the subdivision and compartmentalization of the social sciences. In the process, the central theory of economics was not simply preserved intact: it was reinforced by the more precise specification of its key terms and purged (it was hoped) of subjective psychological residues. (There was also a curious alliance between those who embraced the "objective," and therefore "scientific," behaviorism of J.B. Watson, and Frank H. Knight, who welcomed behaviorism but denied that it was a legitimate psychological theory of human behavior: see Coats, 1976.) The "fundamental assumption," which had so often been identified with the crude and potentially misleading concept of *homo oeconomicus* was depersonalized and expressed in more abstract terms as the concept of rationality or the logic of choice.

During the next two decades or so this conclusion was strongly reinforced by Robbins' famous and influential (albeit controversial) methodological essay, *The Nature and Significance of Economic Science* (1932/1984) and by major developments in the theory of consumers' demand. The basic postulates of economics, Robbins declared, represented "simple and indisputable facts of experience," which required neither theoretical support nor experimental confirmation. They were givens. Although economic theory included an account of the individual's subjective valuations, the rationality assumption entailed no concession to hedonism or any other psychological doctrine. It merely signified consistency of choice. Other economists — some of them highly critical (for example, Hutchison, 1938) — argued that additional, highly restrictive assumptions were also involved, making the foundations of economic analysis purely theoretical and untestable; but this contention did not significantly affect the course of mainstream theory in the ensuing decades.

Also in the 1930s a further step away from conventional marginal utility theory was taken in the Hicks-Allen development of indifference curve analysis, which dispensed with the troublesome concept of cardinal utility, and this was shortly followed by Samuelson's formulation of an operationalist type of "revealed preference" theory which, he claimed, eliminated all nonobservables — such as motivations, introspection, states of mind, etc. — including those presupposed in the Hicks-Allen ordinalist interpretation. For Samuelson, as for many others, this effectively completed the divorce of economics from psychology, fields with which it had been intimately associated in varying degrees ever since the eighteenth century. Yet, as Stanley Wong has persuasively argued, this conclusion was false. Samuelson's successive contributions to this subject were not simply inconsistent; his entire program was methodological, not substantive.

It was launched by Samuelson because ordinal utility theory [Hicks-Allen] was considered methodologically unsatisfactory, not because it was inadequate theoretically or empirically; it was not asserted that the Samuelson Theory (revealed preference theory) offered new insights into consumer behavior (Wong, 1978, p. 127).

In the three decades since it was supposed that Houthakker had "completed" Samuelson's research program (Wong, 1978, p. 2) economists have demonstrated no desire to abandon utility theory. On the contrary, there is a voluminous and highly technical literature on the subject, largely concerned with problems arising from uncertainty and expectations, complications either overlooked or deliberately ignored by earlier generations of economists. However, the development of the expected utility (EU) research program has so far failed to produce results commensurate with the considerable investment of intellectual resources it has attracted. According to a major recent survey of the literature,

. . . the EU model does not offer a rich descriptive theory of problem representation [pace Cross] and will therefore not easily predict new context effects. . . . The failure of EU theory as both a descriptive and predictive model stems from an inadequate recognition of various psychological principles of judgment and choice . . .

which the author illustrates with a variety of examples drawn from recent research (Schoemaker, 1982, p. 548*ff.*; cf. Arrow, 1982, p. 8). He therefore concludes that while the EU model

. . . has yielded deeper insights and more refined questions, both descriptively and normatively . . . its present paradigmatic status (in certain fields) should be questioned. . . . [A]t the individual level EU maximization is more the exception than the rule, at least for the type of decision tasks examined. . . .

and despite its "mathematical tractability" the model lacks "structural validity at the individual level" (Schoemaker, 1982, pp. 530, 550).

Both the critics and the defenders (for example, Gary Becker) agree that utility maximization models may simply generate a "bundle of empty tautologies" rather than a theoretical foundation for predicting behavioral responses to various changes (cf. Rosenberg, 1979). But while the defenders contend that the theory's generality enables the economist to extend his analysis over an ever-widening domain of human affairs, making it the archetypal imperialistic science (Stigler, 1984), some critics view it as a massive misdirection of intellectual energies. To Tibor Scitovsky, for instance, the concept of utility maximization "set back generations of scientific inquiry into consumer behavior, for it seemed to rule out — as a logical impossibility — any conflict between what man chooses to get and what will best satisfy him" (quoted in Schoemaker, 1982, pp. 539–540).

Although the logic of choice approach gained the ascendancy in the post-1930 period, it by no means achieved a complete hegemony. Textbook presentations of utility theory predominated for at least two decades — often accompanied by strenuous denials of all psychological implications — and for some time thereafter they appeared side by side with indifference curves. Moreover in the influential literature stemming from Cambridge, England, under Marshall's powerful shade, no effort was made to exclude references to psychological factors. Admittedly Marshall's followers did not systematically explore his subtle account of the interactions of "wants" and "activities" which was so penetratingly analyzed by the sociologist, Talcott Parsons (1931, 1932). Nevertheless, Ralph Hawtrey's *The Economic Problem* (1926) contains an account of the differences between passive spectators and active participants in enjoyable activities and introduces a suggestive distinction between defensive and creative products, while his extensive writings on monetary topics display a keen awareness of the part played by psychological factors in economic life. Much the same is true of A.C. Pigou's treatment of waves of optimism and pessimism in business cycles, but by far the most widely known examples of this genre are to be found in J.M. Keynes' works, especially his concepts of "animal spirits" and psychological "propensities," and the so-called psychological "law" underlying the relationship between consumption and income (Keynes, 1936, p. 96). Despite his open break with the past, Keynes was quintessentially Marshallian by upbringing and predilection; whereas Hicks, who had learned his advanced economics at the London School of Economics under Robbins' aegis, was primarily influenced by the works of continental economists, such as Pareto, Walras, and the early Austrians. His attempt to dissociate economics from psychology by means of indifference analysis was fully compatible with the view of the original Austrian marginalists (cf. section 3 of chapter 7).

Defenders of classical and neoclassical economics could legitimately claim that neither Keynes' pseudo-psychological "law" nor the innumerable references in economic literature to the psychological "facts" of everyday life called for a surrender, or even major concessions, to those who sought to combine or integrate the two disciplines. Schumpeter, a great historian of economics and a major creative economist in his own right, possibly overstated the case in asserting that "economists have never allowed their analysis to be influenced by the professional psychologists of their time, but have always framed for themselves such assumptions about psychical processes as they thought it desirable to make." Evidently casual empiricism is applied here as elsewhere. However, Schumpeter distinguished sharply between technical or formal economic analysis and what he called "economic sociology" and was much more positive about the latter. Experimental psychology, he contended, did not, but should, interest economists: "the efforts of psychologists to measure physical quantities is not a matter of indifference to any economist who is not lacking in scientific imagination." Behaviorism was an "ideology" that led to meaningless experimentation. It was also programmatic like psychologism, the methodological position that "psychology is really the basis from which any social science must start and from which all fundamental explanation must run." However, Gestalt psychology held significant promise, and Freudian psychology had "vast possibilities" of application to economics and sociology (Schumpeter, 1954, pp. 1058, 27, 797–798, respectively). Here, as always, Schumpeter was open-minded and methodologically eclectic. No doubt he would have welcomed much of the recent active research linking economics and psychology undertaken in the four decades since his death.

2. Double Standards, Prejudice, and Talking at Cross Purposes

Rod Cross' paper in this book (chapter 4) is a copybook example of the combination of methodological prejudices, misunderstandings, and unduly exacting demands that has discouraged many mainstream economists from collaborating effectively with psychologists. Of course, he is quite justified in dismissing as useless "highly abstract discussions of what psychology might have to offer" (section 4, Cross' italics; cf. Schumpeter, 1954, p. 797), but he is far too severe in requiring that economists should consider only those infusions from "psychological theories" (*sic.*) which can either explain existing anomalies in a "non ad hoc fashion," predict "novel facts and other forms of insight," and generate "clear refutable content." Curiously enough, it is the economists' own failure to fulfil these Lakatosian expectations that has been a major focus of complaint in the recent flood of methodological literature, including some of Cross' own strictures on econometrics! (see Cross 1984, pp. 93*ff*, 111*ff*). Why should contributions from psychology be required to live up to these standards? While it may be true that contemporary psychology contains "a welter of conflicting explanations," does this necessarily entail that they are all useless, however difficult it may be to sort the wheat from the chaff? Is the would-be collaborator inevitably condemned to what Cross (section 3) characterizes as "the infinite regress of choosing a psychological theory of choice between competing psychological theories of choice, learning and decision-making"?

Witticisms aside, why should not economists, like others, learn by trial and error what psychologists have to offer them? After all, there are innumerable relevant offerings cited in this book and in the other sources listed in the bibliography. Certainly it would be more convenient — and remarkable — if there were an array of ready-made psychological solutions for the economist's difficulties. Were this so they would surely have been discovered and utilized by now, and there would be no need to appeal for collaboration. The fact that earlier generations of economists have missed opportunities to learn from psychology (Cross' section 1) or to benefit from Shackle's wise insights (section 4; cf. Earl, 1983a, 1986b) need not preclude them from mending their ways in the future. Cross himself welcomes Akerlof's contributions as "piecemeal engineering," implying that Akerlof is not unduly deterred by the fact that interdisciplinary work is still in its early stages and lacking "a set of problems with a natural agenda" (Akerlof, 1984, p. 6, quoted by Cross in section 4) — whatever that is.

Cross' whole approach — where it is consistent — reflects the typical economist's demand for an "integrating theoretical structure" (Hirshleifer, 1985, pp. 61–62, quoted by Cross in section 3), as if it were the sole precondition of useful interactions. In dismissing Bausor's desire for "a richer and more complex characterization of economics than that provided by the Arrow-Debreu general equilibrium model," Cross reflects the economist's preference for generality and simplicity over all other criteria of theory choice (for gentle criticism of the predilection see Hirschman, 1984). But surely the two kinds of approaches can coexist? All that may be required, at least at this stage, is a marginal shift of resources away from theories with "systemwide implications" (Cross' final line) towards more specific "psychological accounts of cognitive process." Indeed this may be unavoidable as economists develop theories about:

> Labor relations, imperfect competition, uncertainty and long-run dynamics [which] encase the decision-maker in a much larger maze than those considered in classical short-run theory. In these areas the economist and the psychologist have numerous common interests in cognitive theory that they have not shared previously (Simon, 1963, p. 709).

Cross demonstrates a curious concern that the infusion of psychology into economics might lead to a loss of "content" — curious, because many observers consider that the discipline already suffers from a lack of substantive content in its more formalized mathematical models (cf. Woo, 1986, Mirowski, 1986), a deficiency that could be remedied by an infusion of empirical content. There is too little prospect of a wave of enthusiasm for interdisciplinary work among economists to warrant the fear that it will radically transform their discipline, undermine its authority, and disturb its present isolation. The principal obstacle to collaborative research is, perhaps, the fundamental difference in style, or even metaphysics, between the two fields. Whereas psychologists tend to look for evidence of behavior and seek to formulate hypotheses to explain it, economists tend to work in the opposite direction, by starting out with formal theory and then considering what modifications might be required to make it applicable to the explanation of specific economic problems (this point was made many years ago: for example, Robinson, 1932, 1933). The very existence of these contrasting approaches suggests that some combination or interaction between the two might prove highly fruitful to both parties. Who knows, it might even encourage "alternative research programs" (Cross' section 5)!

In their fierce determination to protect their theory from refutation by means of what Popper has termed "defensive strategies," economists have retreated further and further into abstract realms that preserve generality at the expense of substantive content. This is no new phenomenon. As far back as 1925 that respected orthodox economist, Jacob Viner, deplored the

> all-too-prevalent methodological fanaticism which prefers the accurate but su-
> perficial to the approximate but fundamental, and which makes adaptability to
> its special technique of investigation, rather than importance, the standard for
> the selection of problems and the delimitation of the scope of inquiry (Viner,
> 1925, p. 659).

In the highly pertinent case of utility theory, for example, George Stigler (himself no radical) remarked, in a classic historical review of the literature, that

> Had specific tests been made of the implications of theories, the unfruitfulness
> of the ruling utility theory as a source of hypotheses in demand would soon
> have become apparent. . . . Not only were such specific implications not sought
> and tested, but there was a tendency, when they appeared to be a threat of an
> empirical test, to reformulate the theory to make the test ineffective (1965, pp.
> 155, 153).

This practice — what Mark Blaug has wittily termed "playing tennis with the net down" — is still widespread, as is clear from his *The Methodology of Economics, or How Economists Explain* (Blaug, 1980).

As A.K. Sen has noted in a recent review of the literature on problems of individual and collective wants and social welfare, the prevalence of purely formal analysis and the willful exclusion of variables that might conceivably provide new information and insights into economic behavior seriously impoverishes economic theory (Sen, 1982, pp. 102–103; cf. Baxter, in this book). According to Tversky and Kahneman, who have done important work in linking economics and psychology, economists have put the hypothesis of rational action "beyond question," so that the burden of proof has been placed "squarely on any alternative analysis of belief and choice. The advantage of the rational model is compounded because no other theory of judgment and decision can ever match it in scope, power and simplicity" (1987, p. 34).

Perhaps the orthodox victory in the earlier phase of debate has proved more inhibiting of the progress of economics than its proponents appreciated.

3. Coming Full Circle?

What of the present state of play? Cross is fully justified in questioning whether current and future attempts to infuse psychology into economics are more likely to be successful (by what criterion?) than were the pre-1930 efforts. More specifically, "Are either the problems faced by theories in economics more severe, or is what psychology has to offer more compelling?" (section 4) than was the case half a century ago. I shall consider these questions in turn, and in both cases offer a strongly affirmative answer.

To judge by the flood of literature on the parlous state of the discipline, economic theory can hardly have been in a more serious condition before 1930. Sample titles, such as: *What's Wrong with Economics?* (Ward, 1972); *The Crisis in Economic Theory* (Bell and Kristol (eds.), 1981); *Economists at Bay, or Why the Experts Will Never Solve Your Problems* (Lekachman, 1976); *Why Economics is Not Yet a Science* (Eichner (ed.), 1983); *Economics and the Real World* (Kamarck, 1983); *Economics in Disarray* (Wiles and Routh (eds.), 1984), all written by recognized economists, either individually or in groups, do not suggest that complacency prevails. This catalogue could easily be supplemented by other book titles and innumerable articles produced by economists with recognized professional credentials. No doubt the collective "self-flagellation" revealed in these works reflects the combination of professional and public concern following the ending of the Keynesian hegemony (c. 1945–1965), and represents a reaction from the collective hubris and exaggerated claims of that era. Moreover, this reaction is partly attributable to recent adverse movements in the economy in a period when economists have given hostages to fortune by playing an increasingly prominent role in public affairs and policy-making.

Many of the pre-1930 criticisms of economic orthodoxy are echoed in recent writings, including the need for: (1) more "realistic" assumptions compatible with observed behavior, and consistent with the findings of other disciplines, including psychology; (2) a shift of focus away from abstract, general theories towards more specific, low- or middle-level empirically grounded theories which should be testable; (3) more systematic empirical research, as a basis for sound empirical generalizations; (4) more dynamic theories, incorporating changes in incomes, tastes, expectations, new commodities, etc.; (5) a broadening of the scope of economic theory, taking account of such influences on economic behavior as habit, custom, social emulation, advertising, etc.; and (6) studies of the influence of market and nonmarket forces on economic and social welfare (cf. Coats, 1976, pp. 49–50).

Doubtless some of these demands are being met, whether by mainstream economists or their critics, and to this extent the discipline may be in better shape than it was 50 years ago. Nevertheless, there are countervailing influences, such as the Friedmanite denial of the relevance of realistic assumptions (which has been widely accepted, notwithstanding severe strictures from numerous methodologists); the undue preoccupation with highly formalistic theory in the training of economists — a sociological as well as an intellectual problem (cf. Earl, 1983c; Woo, 1986); and the dominant influence of general equilibrium models in theoretical economics (Mirowski, 1986). Recent efforts to take account of ignorance and uncertainty in economic life have encountered formidable difficulties. Initial setbacks are only to be expected. Yet, to many qualified observers many economists seem preoccupied with "good games" (Hicks, 1979, p. viii) that have intellectual value but do not enhance their capacity to contribute to the solution of society's pressing problems. Some critics even accuse them of engaging in useless activities equivalent to optimizing the location of deckchairs on the Titanic.

Another prominent feature of recent economics is the tendency to split into warring camps — for example, Keynesians versus Monetarists; or various splinter or dissident groups such as the Austrians, Post Keynesians, New Classicals, Institutionalists (Old and New), Marxists, Sraffians, Radicals, etc. Whether this is a temporary state of affairs is impossible to say. Possibly the current buzzing, blooming confusion is merely the harbinger of a grand new synthesis. As William Baumol observed of the new industrial organization theory of contestable markets: "No uprising by a tiny band of rebels can hope to change an established order and when the time for rebellion is ripe it seems to break out simultaneously and independently in a variety of disconnected centers each offering its own program for the future" (1982, p. 1).

Turning to Cross' second question, "is what psychology has to offer more compelling" than was the case in 1930? — and noting the loaded word "compelling" — one is tempted to respond: can there be any reasonable doubt that 50 years of research into the relations between economics and psychology (including both psychological economics and economic psychology) has added to the corpus of useful theory and empirical result accessible to economists enterprising and open-minded enough to take advantage of it? The substantial bibliography in this book provides a more than adequate starting point. To quote but three examples: 30 years of research in cognitive psychology has immensely enhanced our knowledge of learning and decision-making processes (cf. Simon, 1987); the value of George Katona's even longer series of studies of consumer's attitudes is now much more widely appreciated; and we have recently witness "the behavioral rising in economics' (Gilad, Kaish and Loeb, 1984; see also the two-volume set edited by Gilad and Kaish, 1986). In addition to the inauguration of several new journals concerned with aspects of the relations between economics and psychology, the founding of the Society for the Advancement of Behavioral Economics promises to provide a valuable forum for the exchange of ideas, the coordination of research, the solution of problems of interest to scholars in both fields — possibly in other social sciences also. The proponents of this new movement cite four broad objections to mainstream economic theorizing: (1) a rejection of positivism as the methodological foundation for economic research; (2) a refusal to accept the use of deductive reasoning as a sufficient basis for a (social) science; (3) a marked dislike of static analysis of equilibrium *outcomes* rather than disequilibrium *processes*; and most important of all, (4) a unanimous objection to the *simplistic* economic model of rational agents exhibiting optimizing behavior (Gilad, Kaish, and Loeb, 1984, p. 2, italics in original).

The basic postulates of behavioral economics cited in this manifesto bear a remarkable resemblance to the pre-1930 criticisms of economics cited earlier (Coats, 1976, pp. 49–50; cf. Gilad, Kaish, and Loeb, p. 4). And, exactly like some of the earlier institutionalists, the authors of the new program claim that behavioral economics "is not a field of economics as much as a way of looking at the traditional fields' (Gilad, Kaish, and Loeb, p. 3). Doubtless mainstream economists will dismiss this characterization as an evasion of the responsibility to produce a genuine scientific theory, whereas sympathizers may interpret it as a sensible reluctance to engage in premature generalization.

4. The Revisionists

We live in exciting times. Economics is in a highly unstable and transitional phase, perhaps more so than other social sciences considering that its central structure has so long withstood attack from a motley army of besiegers. No doubt the vast majority of economists adheres to the mainstream theories, but there is a considerable array of contending paradigms and approaches. Revisionists starting from the mainstream are working toward what they call a "new institutional economics" which has certain affinities to and some common sources (such as the work of Herbert Simon) with behavioral economics. According to one spokesman its central themes include the following:

1. Although definitely rational in a true sense, the agent of economic theory is not best conceived as rational in the narrow sense of maximizing within a framework of known alternatives.

2. Economic phenomena are in large measure the result of learning over time by economic agents; economic explanation should thus be a dynamic exercise — dynamic not merely in the sense of dynamic neoclassical models, but in a sense best rendered as evolutionary.
3. The coordination of economic activity is not merely a matter of premediated transactions in markets, but is supported by a wide range of economic and social institutions that are themselves an important topic of theoretical inquiry (Langlois, 1986, pp. 5–6).

As this manifesto suggests, the "new institutionalists" are less critical of the orthodox approach to economic rationality than either the behavioralists or the older generation of American institutionalists — Thorstein Veblen, John R. Commons, Wesley Mitchell, and Clarence Ayres. Nevertheless the differences between the old and new species are less marked than the latter claim, for they have major interests and aims in common, such as: broadening the scope of economics; viewing economic phenomena as processes with a history and a future, rather than as equilibria; emphasizing the interdependence of institutions and economic activity; and making economics a more "evolutionary" discipline, which was Veblen's primary objective. Generally speaking, the new institutionalists attach much less importance to psychology than their pre-1930 precursors. As Simon (1987) has noted, their analyses rely not on rationality assumptions but on "assumptions of informational or other limits on rationality" — that is, on sociological rather than psychological postulates. It is no coincidence that they trace their antecedents, in part, to Menger, who made limited use of psychology in his general theory, while emphasizing the importance of institutions (Runde, in section 3 of chapter 7; Langlois, 1986, pp. 4–5).

5. What Are The Prospects?

It may be both unseemly and hazardous for a historian of economics to engage in futurology. Yet some tentative concluding suggestions about the prospective relations between economics and psychology may be in order. At leat four distinct scenarios can be envisaged.

1. The optimistic view that a new synthesis or paradigm is on the horizon or already here. Thus Scitovsky (1985, p. 19):

> The occasional bits of psychology to be found scattered in the writings of economists can be added up to yield a new, richer framework for economic analysis, capable of explaining many economic problems that are waiting to be explained. All that is needed is an

ingenious young economist to collect the bits and pieces and integrate them into a coherent theory.

Shlomo Maital is even more confident, discussing in some detail the requirements a new paradigm must satisfy (1982, chapter 11, especially p. 262*ff.*), while others explore the broader implications of the "revival of subjectivism" (Wiseman, 1983, especially pp. 87–103, by Coats).

2. The pessimistic view that significant change is either impossible or unlikely given the strength of professional inertia and the pressures to conformity. Supporters of this general position differ markedly in their assessments of the status quo, as is hardly surprising, for despite considerable piecemeal evidence and abundant casual gossip there has been no systematic empirical research on the structure and functioning of the economics profession, even for the United States. Thus the pessimists disagree, for example, about the extent of control over resources and access to influential positions exercised by the discipline's power elite; how far new and prospective recruits are effectively socialized into conformity with the prevailing orthodoxy; the degree of uniformity in graduate training both within and outside the leading schools; the influence of textbooks in disseminating and maintaining established views; and the role of exogenous societal pressures in reinforcing the profession's dominant beliefs and practices. There is a large, scattered, and uneven literature on these matters which it would be misleading to cite selectively and inappropriate to list in detail. However, it is important to appreciate that this literature does not emanate exclusively from dissidents or members of the splinter groups mentioned earlier. Indeed, the state of economics is sufficiently distinctive to attract the attention of scholars concerned with comparative analysis of the sciences (Whitley, 1984).

3. The view that, as on many previous occasions, the economists will make moderate, ad hoc revisions to accommodate some of their critics' objections while preserving intact the existing disciplinary structure, hardcore assumptions, and set of problems. According to two recent Austrian commentators

> There is a "sponginess" to neoclassical economics that enables it to absorb divergent elements around it without ever emphasizing their main points. These fringe ideas become footnotes to which theorists can refer as evidence that they have taken the ideas into account (O'Driscoll and Rizzo, 1985, p. 231).

Or, again, from a "new institutionalist" viewpoint

. . . a major reason for heterdoxy's lack of influence is that many complaints and proposals can be accommodated by slight changes of meaning, treated and accommodated as special case models, or absorbed by broadening the theory somewhat, all with very few ripples. *The fact that prevailing theory defines what are reasonable and sophisticated objections to prevailing theory and what distinguishes appropriate from inappropriate proposals for amendement and reform is another defense.* It is employed primarily when the complaint seems uninteresting and unimportant, but *tends to be used also in cases where the complaint is potentially important but not easily treated by marginal modifications of the theory.* . . .

If the contemporary critics of othodoxy can be accused of not appreciating the importance of a coherent theoretical structure and of underestimating the resiliency and absorptive capacity of prevailing economic orthodoxy, the defenders of orthodoxy can be accused of trying to deny the importance of phenomena with which orthodoxy deals inadequately and at the same time overestimating the potential ability of models within the orthodox framework somehow to encompass these phenomena (Nelson and Winter, 1982, p. 48, italics added).

Of course, neither of these passages is necessarily representative. But taken together they help to suggest why the mainstream classical and neoclassical structure has survived virtually intact for so long, notwithstanding innumerable persuasive and effective attacks, while the second passage contains cogent reasons why the heterodox and orthodox approaches have failed to combine into a synthesis. It is too early to conjecture whether the current revisionist movement from within economics, in response to the behavioral and experimental work in psychology, is likely to change the existing content and structure of economics significantly (Frey, 1986, p. 544). Yet it certainly appears that the resurrection of the movement to bring economists and psychology into close and more fruitful contact is far more promising than its pre-1930 counterpart.

4. If none of the three previous scenarios is correct it may happen that behavioral (or psychological) economics will acquire enough momentum to become a separate quasi-autonomous subdiscipline with its own courses, degrees, training programs, research funds, journals, and societies. This book already indicates that the process is under way, and it seems likely to gather momentum. Indeed it is not unreasonable to foresee that this is but part of a general movement in economics, one may that leave the core of the discipline increasingly isolated and irrelevant to contemporary af-

fairs. This would be compatible with the widespread contemporary view that advanced economic theory and econometrics is becoming simply a branch of applied mathematics, with ever more tenuous links with the real world (for example, Morishima, pp. 51–73, in Wiles and Routh, 1984; Blatt, pp. 166–86, in Eichner, 1983).

To suggest that the resurrection of psychological economics might contribute to the decline and possibly even the death of orthodox economics is a provocative but far-fetched idea. More likely, if one may judge by past experience, is the possibility that the behavioral research program will rejuventate the orthodox tradition without — one hopes — a repetition of the resistance to change that was apparent in the post-1930 era referred to earlier.

15 ON BEING A PSYCHOLOGICAL ECONOMIST AND WINNING THE GAMES ECONOMISTS PLAY

Peter E. Earl

1. INTRODUCTION

For the most part, this book has presented a methodologically-oriented analysis of the development of psychological economics, its tensions and its prospects. Such an orientation promotes the impression that the fate of psychological economics, or indeed any research program, depends essentially on a careful and generally dispassionate assessment of its prospective performance — an assessment heavily dependent on its performance in the past. One is encouraged to conceive of economists as single-minded and humble seekers after truth. In this final chapter the implications of a different line of argument are pursued: the central theme is that the fate of psychological economics is going to be shaped largely, or even — if one is thinking in lexicographic terms — decisively, by whether or not the kinds of research and teaching orientations that it entails are consistent with the career and lifestyle goals of potentially receptive academics. To anticipate how psychological economics may progress toward the year 2000, and to help in its progression, I intend to consider some aspects of the economics and psychology of being a psychological economist. This reflexive approach is one that I first employed in a paper on the curious neglect of the be-

havioral theory of the firm (Earl, 1983c) but, as the title of this chapter
implies, inspiration has also come from Carl Sinderman's (1982) delightful
but deadly serious book *Winning the Games Scientists Play*, a book which
all career-minded economists should read, regardless of whether they share
Eichner's (1983) doubts about the scientific status of economics.

An example may help clarify my underlying theme. Consider a would-
be psychological economist whose aims in life are prioritized, as in the
"behavioral lexicographic" approach to choice: if she believes that to commit herself to such a research and teaching program could very seriously
jeopardize those of her priorities that she ranks higher than ones pertaining
to the ideal style of economics that she would prefer to do, then we would
be unwise to expect her to be an actual convert. This economist is a careerist
and consumer first and an economist second, in contrast to her implicit
treatment by methodologists as an naively lexicographic economic scientist
first and foremost. (That is, according to conventional approaches, she
does not merely set a *target* for her contribution toward the advancement
of economics; she wants to contribute as much as possible given her constraints and she only considers her career and consumption activities when
choosing what kind of economics to do if two or more research programs
tie as apparently *optimal* prospects.) Hence, if it seems as though work as
a psychological economist, in contrast to work of a more mainstream kind,
is insufficiently likely to enable her to reach her desired state as, say, a
Porsche-driving full professor before her thirty-fifth birthday, then so much
the worse for psychological economics.

It is not essential to see choice in behavioral lexicographic terms to make
the case that nonscientific aspects of an economist's life may affect the
kinds of research program that she favors. Suppose such an academic thinks
about her activities in terms of the kinds of tradeoffs that would lend
themselves to depiction on an indifference map. Then her willingness to
make marginal substitutions among the characteristics that different career
plans seem able to help her produce could well be such that she feels she
will do best to use her talents within the mainstream frame of reference,
even if the actual worth of her output is more obviously open to question
(cf. Lancaster, 1966, 1971).

It is important to note that processes of cognition enable career-oriented
scientists to see their material and personal successes as resulting from the
intrinsic worth of the kind of work they have chosen to do, rather than
letting them see that they have chosen their research activities with a view
to potential career and leisure payoffs. Most would find it hard to admit
that they were in academia "for the money": mental processes of cognitive
dissonance reduction will see to this (Festinger, 1957). So long as the

scientific worth of a research program can be debated without it being necessary to concede that logically one or more of its rivals dominates unambiguously, it is possible for a person to tell herself that what she is doing could turn out to be significant and that the nonscientific rewards she reaps are purely incidental benefits. Nor should it be forgotten that it might well be the case that some economists could actually judge psychological economics, rather than a more mainstream approach, as more likely to satisfy their scientific *and* their career and leisure aspirations. In fact, some psychological economists are doing very nicely in career terms, either as a result of or despite their involvement with this mode of research.

The rest of the chapter consists of three main sections. The division of materials between sections 2 and 3 is very much inspired by Kay's (1982) distinction between strategic and tactical decision-making in the theory of the firm: in the former, there is a consideration of the extent to which it may be worth getting involved in psychological economics, given the kinds of other goals that one may have set; in the latter, attention is devoted to recipes for winning the battles that one has decided to fight. Section 4 examines how it may be possible to reduce the costs that research can impose upon *any* academic's mental well-being, but which are likely to be particularly significant for a deviant thinker.

2. Strategic Considerations

In emergent markets, the potential rewards of being a pioneer are enormous if one happens to hit upon a product package that particularly appeals to potentially receptive users. The market for economists is no exception. Problems of information overload raise doubts that most psychological economists will become expert in a wide variety of psychological modes of thinking, so it is to be expected that after initial experimentation over a wide field, a restricted set of approaches will dominate. Star status may await those economists who are among the first to commit themselves to using psychology, and who are the first to work with any of the subsequently favored set of psychological constructs. They may enjoy disproportionately frequent citations and their names, or those of their institutions, or the epithets that they introduce, may come to symbolize entire research methodologies. They may be invited to join editorial boards of journals and speak at conferences, and papers may be commissioned from them. Probably it is not too late to jump on the bandwagon, but anyone thinking of attempting to cast themselves in this sort of role and learn how to act the part might find it useful to consider some of the down-side risks of such a move.

In marketing terms, psychological economics could be seen as a "question mark," a product that is attracting some interest but whose ability to reach the critical mass necessary for takeoff into an eventual broad acceptance is in doubt. At least, this is the pessimistic view that may be taken by those who never cease to be amazed by the widespread ignorance of the thinking behind classic contributions to behavioral economics that are now well over two decades old (for example, Simon, 1959; Cyert and March, 1963); who remember the more recent consternation in the profession when Herbert Simon, "a psychologist," was awarded the 1978 Nobel Prize in economics; or who have had to fight protracted battles even to get approval for a proposal for an interdisciplinary doctoral topic and have found subsequently that when they submitted their work to mainstream journals, referees were prone to object to the whole idea of using psychology, rather than how they used it. Others might assert that the takeoff phase is already in progress, pointing to the proliferation of publications alluded to at the start of chapter 1, and to the growth of a specialist conference circuit.

Although it is clear that it is not impossible for psychologically oriented economists to win good jobs in competition with mainstream theorists and econometricians, it can probably be justifiably claimed that the state of the job market for academic economists presently indicates that it is the risk-loving ambitious young academic who consciously decides to make a big commitment to psychological economics. As far as junior posts are concerned, the stress is on quantitative skills, and usually, on the statistical side, this can be taken to mean expertise in multiple regression methods, rather than the kinds of techniques discussed in chapter 13. For the middle-career academic with a good track record in psychological economics, promoted posts may come up as prospects in the area of economic theory, in departments that have suffered resignations of their more high-flying members. But such a person might well apply only to be told later that "although you were on our short-list, the appointments committee decided to go for people with more mainstream interests and quantitative skills." In the actual case I have in mind, this outcome was not at all surprising, for the department in question wanted staff who would train up their Honors and Masters students so that they could win higher degree places at the Australian National University or in North America: for these students to be able to cope with moves to such institutions they would need to be schooled in, for example, state-of-the-art neoclassical consumer theory and applied consumption analysis, rather than in the state-of-the-art literature on consumer behavior produced in psychological economics. In the minds of most academic economists, behavioral theory and psychological economics are subdisciplinary fringe interests rather than alternative approaches to the core of economics.

Given such a market environment and such attitudes, one might well expect that psychological economics could become somewhat dominated by those who have *already* established their reputations and achieved the rank of full professor through work in the *orthodox* tradition. Once promoted, they can turn their attention to psychology without worrying too much about what other people think. Moreover, their track records as orthodox theorists may also ensure that their changes of course attract considerable attention.

Less well-established scholars who feel attracted to psychological economics would be wise to take note of Kay's (1982, 1984) work on the theory of the firm and pursue a strategy of diversification: for example, do some research in monetary theory and macroeconomics with an eye to keeping up with the conventional literature, but all the while maintain a steady interest in psychological microeconomics. A scholar pursuing such a strategy would be much less vulnerable and much more mobile than one who put all her eggs in the one basket of trying to look at everything from the standpoint of the psychologist and who consequently found it impossible to keep abreast of the more orthodox literature to which she was assembling an alternative. Diversification must, however, be limited, for appointments committees are likely to be much less worried by a person who obviously is only a part-time psychological economist, than they are by someone who does "a little bit of this and a little bit of that" and who therefore may lack depth and commitment to anything in particular. It should also be noted that the particular relatively restrained hedging strategy that has been mentioned would also leave its user in a position sometimes to bring her two main areas of expertise together in a synergistic way, for example in the context of a study of the origins of confidence for investment decisions. (Fascinating use of literature on the psychology of superstition has be made in this area by Gimpl and Dakin, 1984.) Many other "two-pronged" research programs with such potential seem possible.

Even a moderate diversification strategy is not without considerable risks in an age when the name of the game is "publish or perish" and the rewards are tenure or promotion, for psychological economics throws up some publishing dilemmas during its nascent phase. It is not merely the length of one's list of publications that counts but also its composition: a promotions committee, for example, may request that the list supplied by a candidate shall "be annotated by the head of department to indicate (a) which are the more important items, (b) the quality of the publications, and (c) the standing of the journals in which they appeared." Since this directive (taken from a real memorandum) fails to mention books, a possible implication is that the committee may well be unimpressed by them. This could spell danger for a candidate who has found that books are a much more effective means than articles for exploring the case for and experimenting with the use of psychology in economics. Certainly, in the early days of a research program, books have expositional advantages over articles: they permit the exploration of synergistic possibilities, avoiding the need for repeated justifications of points of departure and outlines of new foundations, while providing space to set out diverse elements that lend themselves to integration. In the case of my own research, this approach did win approval in the face of the directive I cited. However, I know from the experiences of others elsewhere that it is unwise to discount the existence of influential academics who actually go even so far as to claim that "a book is worth only one, or less than one, article in a decent journal, since the process of refereeing monographs is much more lax." A final point of caution worth noting in respect of a book-based strategy is that if a reviewer presents a travesty of one's work in a journal, there is normally no right of reply of the kind that exists when someone chooses to comment on an article. (However, misconceptions may sometimes be dealt with in a subsequent work: compare Shefrin, 1985, p. 208, with Earl, 1986b, pp. 233–235, for an example — albeit one that actually in press, anticipating the misconception, even before I had seen the review in question!)

As far as articles are concerned, the problem is that until there is a fairly widespread familiarity with and acceptance of psychological work in economics, it is going to be relatively difficult to win acceptance for it in the prestigious, generalist journals that most economists read as a matter of routine. An embittered cynic might seek to explain this in terms of simple probabilities of acceptance: "The whole thing's a lottery!" (Take the most extreme position and suppose the editorial process is entirely random and that all submissions are of equal quality; then the most difficult journals to publish in are those that are nonspecialist and happen to be rated as prestigious, for they will be the ones to which the most manuscripts are sent in the first instance.) However, a more acceptable explanation is probably that editors of psychology-oriented journals are more likely to know which referees may have some familiarity with the psychological literature that is being used. Hence the referees will be well placed to see what the deviant author is getting at and to comment upon how well the task has been executed. This is in sharp contrast to the position that would face a mainstream referee examining the same paper on behalf of a prestigious, nonspecialist journal. In the latter situation, the task of reporting on a highly unconventional paper will be one that provokes anxiety, and we should therefore expect the referee to err on the side of caution in order to avoid unduly jeopardizing her position as one of the gatekeepers of her science: the review process examines the referee, every bit as much as the paper, so it would not be surprising if she concluded that although some revisions might produce an excellent paper, it would perhaps be better to suggest to the author that it be sent to a journal specializing in its kind of research.

3. Tactics

Given these difficulties, the excellent paper by Akerlof and Dickens (1982) warrants special attention as a model for the design of a career-enhancing piece of work. One takes a particular, well-recognized contribution to psychology that is accessible to the noneconomist and which can easily be related to experiences in everyday life. This puts the referees at ease, while the fact that the kind of psychology in question impinges on some key economic images means that the case for sending it to a widely read and prestigious journal is self-evident. Should such a paper nonetheless be judged unsuitable, it can then be tried in specialist journals.

This tactic looks particularly appealing once we consider the general problems even a receptive economist may be expected to have actually getting to grips with psychology. Here, it is useful to report on some of the things that happened during the preparation of this book. As will already have been apparent from the other chapters, some contributors found the sheer enormity of and lack of consensus in the psychology literature quite intimidating. It was difficult to know where to start and which approaches to take seriously if one simply plunged head-first into the psychology section of one's library. One contributor asked, desperately, "What's the psychology equivalent of Samuelson?" Another went directly to one of his psychology colleagues for advice. The advantages of having a spouse with a training in psychology were clear. Some contributors needed assistance because they were the first in their departments to turn their attention in the direction of psychological economics: this meant that their libraries did not stock journals such as the *Journal of Economic Psychology* and the *Journal of Economic Behavior and Organization*, and hence they were unsure which papers might be worth chasing up on interlibrary loans. Others had been trying for months to get library subscriptions started for such journals, but found this impossible because of funding cutbacks: it became apparent that there were advantages in serving as a departmental library liaison officer.

The existence of books such as the present one and those edited by Gilad and Kaish (1986) and MacFadyen and MacFadyen (1986) may help in the future to reduce the startup costs of becoming a psychological economist, especially through their bibliographies. The latter will point to the existence of important edited collections and monographs as well as to which journals outside the economics mainstream might be particularly useful, either as sources or as resting places for output. Economists previously may have been less inclined than psychologists to make use of collections of abstracts or publications such as *Current Contents*: certainly the empirical nature of much of modern psychology has made it essential for the practicing clinician routinely to try to keep abreast of the latest work, simply to safeguard the welfare of her patients. To the extent that economists move in the direction of a behavioral approach, it becomes a methodological requirement that they should be similarly aware of pertinent empirical findings. The greater the commitment of a journal to this approach, the more its editors and referees will view ignorance of such work as reprehensible.

With the psychological literature and concepts firmly under control, attention should be turned to how to package what one has to offer. Whenever research output deviates substantially from conventional modes of thinking, its reception can be greatly dependent on its presentation, and some presentations will appeal to some audiences more than others: for instance, I found Neil Kay's (1984) critique and attempted reorientation of the standard theory of the firm full of devastating wit and beautifully pointed examples, but its method of attack clearly worried Hey (1984). Like the behavioral theorist of the firm, the psychological economist may find it useful to note the distinction that modern clinical psychologists draw between aggressive and assertive modes of behavior when they are trying to help patients improve their abilities to cope with life (see Alberti and Emmons, 1982). The clinical psychologists' message is easy enough to state, but takes some practice to follow: changes in style in my own work (contrast Earl, 1983a, with Earl, 1986b) owe much to it, but my transition from an over-aggressive to an assertive style is, I fear, still in process.

The clinical psychologist might illustrate the distinction to a patient by taking the example of a person who has a newish consumer durable that has become defective and has to be taken back to the shop from which it was purchased. The aggressive customer would typically enter the store in an obvious fit of rage, immediately demanding to see the manager, all the while making very little eye contact with any of the staff she encountered. The assertive customer would enter, head-high, and say, calmly but firmly, "This has ceased to work, but I've had a read of the warranty and I think you may be able to get it fixed for me at the manufacturer's expense. Could you check on this for me, please?" If a person tries to "keep her cool" rather than "getting uptight and emotional," and shows she has "done her homework" carefully before coming to the conclusion that is probably going to be inconvenient for the person she has to confront, then her chances of a fair hearing and an amenable response are greatly enhanced: a hostile person can seem difficult to reason with and calm down, and therefore seems much more of a threat to the person she is confronting.

The lesson from this should be that there is a world of difference between, on the one hand, aggressively announcing one's commitment to using psychology in a strident, hostile tone that seems to reflect a basically paranoid and defensive position (in this context, the expectation that neoclassical readers will make no attempt to listen open-mindedly to one's claims) and, on the other hand, assertively and calmly presenting an outline of the pro's and con's of doing economics in the chosen area with and without psychological foundations, stating precisely the methodological case for a preference for the former approach. A publisher might well accept — and attempt to market as "controversial" — a book which could easily be construed as if it proclaimed that those economists who avoid psychology are a bunch of idiots or charlatans. However, the positive contribution it sought to offer would stand a much better chance of getting a carefully considered hearing if its author started out by reporting her own surprise at the new insights and issues that arose as a result of experimenting to see what psychology might offer to an economist.

If the scope of a piece of work is fairly narrowly defined, it should be possible largely to avoid having to confront mainstream thinkers over basic methodological differences. The tactic here is to begin by preaching the "horses for courses" case for methodological pluralism so persuasively argued by Loasby (1976): for example, it can be noted that, like a small car, a neoclassical economic model may be very economical to use, yet just because such a car is brilliant as an urban vehicle, no one would seriously urge that it be considered an adequate vehicle for getting about in rugged outback terrain, for economy is of precious little use if one is bogged down in mud and sand, and unable to cover the ground that it would be possible to traverse in a thirsty and, in urban terms, cumbersome jeep. Whatever one's partiality to the use of psychology in economics, one should not set out seeming to wish to reject outright the orthodox approach; rather, one should explicitly recognize that abstractions are necessary in any model-building activity and, while they can permit insights, they limit the range of phenomena that it is possible to address. Having made this point, one can then note that so far it does not appear to have been the case that the orthodox methodology has been particularly instructive in the narrow, but nonetheless important, context one has in mind, despite its widely recognized powers elsewhere. If previous attempts in the context are as limited or flawed as one suspects, then referees will be less inclined, and indeed will find it harder, to challenge the piece of work: it is not claiming that because the orthodox methodology is deficient in a particular context, questions should be raised about its more general worth.

The tactic of choosing a well-defined area that is out of bounds to the conventional research program, or that is one in which psychological economics leads to conspicuously different conclusions, also has the advantage that referees will not be able to object to the work by claiming that it is merely another but less convenient way of explaining familiar results. This objection is one that psychological economists will often encounter when they submit research that deals with more basic areas of economic interest. (I speak from experience: see Earl, 1986b, p. 285.) In the latter context, they should guard against it in anticipation by making a point that should be obvious but is often missed by those referees who prefer to bury their heads in the sand. Once again, it is a point that can be made with the aid of a transportation analogy, as follows. It may be the case that presently several methods exist for me to get to a particular destination, and that one of these is particularly convenient. However, if none of them can be guaranteed to be wholly reliable, owing to the possibility of breakdowns, bad weather, industrial disruptions, and so on, then I would be foolish not to acquire some knowledge of how to use what presently seem less appealing ways of getting to my destination. It could also be added that experience with different methods may lead to a heightened appreciation of the limitations and advantages of each method, and hence to an improved ability to anticipate the contexts in which particular methods could be downright misleading, rather than just inconvenient to use.

Finally, under the tactics heading, we come to the issue of the teaching of psychological economics and how it might effectively be promoted. According to Kuhn (1962), one of the distinguishing features of "normal" as opposed to "revolutionary" science is that it has found its way into the textbooks. On these terms, for example, rational expectations are now, for better or worse, part of normal economic science. Not so psychological economics, though there are some encouraging signs, such as the reprinting of Thaler's (1980) paper in the book of readings edited by Breit and associates (1986). The closest we so far have, to my knowledge, is *The*

Economic Mind (Furnham and Lewis, 1986), which is a review concerned more with economic psychology than than psychological economics (on this distinction, see comments by Lewis in section 1 of chapter 13) and is aimed more at academics than undergraduate students. Such a lack of suitable textbooks is a major barrier to the teaching of specialist courses in psychological economics, and presently any proposals that may be written are unlikely to be well received by publishers owing to the lack of an obvious market: we have a double bind to overcome before psychological economics can become part of normal economic science. Someone has got to take the initiative, and the associated risk, before the circle can be broken and the time for this may not yet be ripe.

One scenario by which one might envisage the necessary change would be as follows. First, a psychological economist in a resource-rich university succeeds in getting a specialist final year option set up. To overcome her students' demands for course materials she insures that the library creates an extensive photocopy package of key articles and portions from books and hands out fairly detailed, longhand synopses of her own lectures. Each year, these lecture summaries get longer and longer, as she inserts points of clarification and updates them to take account of recent developments. It is then but a short step to move in the direction of a full-blown book by arranging to have the perfected, integrated, and properly detailed summaries produced by the university printing department for sale at cost-price to her class. The fact that she has produced the package on a personal computer and a Laserwriter means that she is able to persuade a publisher to take the risk of having it properly printed, for wide distribution, from the camera-ready copy that she can provide: by eliminating typesetting costs she has substantially reduced the costs of poor sales.

In the scenario just outlined, the phrase "resource-rich university" was a key element. As long as present pressures on resources in many universities continue, prospects for the introduction of specialist courses in psychological economics do not look good, except in cases where departments are dominated by practicing psychological economists who can simply out-gun their more conventional colleagues when it comes to a vote. In this environment, perhaps the best prospects arise in faculties where staffing numbers are related to student enrollments, and a case can be made that such courses could serve as a profitable means for stealing student enrollments from psychology departments that allow students some option units in their degrees. A variation on the theme is to promote the creation of joint economics/psychology degree structures. Otherwise, however, the psychological economist may need to adopt more subversive measures to get the message across. One approach is to press the case for the introduction of marketing and other business-oriented courses for which student demand is likely to be high and yet which can provide excellent vehicles for putting forward psychological economics. (In the case of business policy courses, it is possible to present not merely the psychology of the firm but also, if one is so inclined, the "new institutional" transactions cost economics, for which it might otherwise prove difficult to find a slot — cf. Earl, 1984.) It may also be possible to include limited psychological inserts in many preexisting courses without causing trouble with a head of department who insists, for example, that "We must cover the mainstream ideas properly in order that our students can cope with a graduate program elsewhere." For example, the potential relevance of work on noncompensatory decision heuristics can be shown to a money and banking class when attempts are being made to analyze debates about portfolio substitutability among the assets and liabilities of rival financial institutions.

Those whose real desire is to follow Loasby's philosophy that people should have several perspectives at their disposal will, of course, not be satisfied unless they can teach a complete parallel program of psychological economics alongside the mainstream material that they are expected to teach. The only way to do this without cutting down the number of topics covered seems to me to entail passing the burden to the students: one can use the lectures as vehicles for discussing psychological economics and provide extensive handouts as backup material; meanwhile, one can insist that students work through a conventional text by themselves or with their friends, with tutorials being used for sorting out problems. Students may well resist such moves as attempts to force them to learn twice as much, or because, after years of being fed highly deterministic mono-paradigm tuition that smoothed over differences between rival methodologies, they are unsettled by the idea that it might be useful to have several different paradigms at their disposal. To pass to the students the burden of cramming a quart into a pint pot certainly requires an adjustment of student expectations, but I, for one, have never been able to see the point of spending scarce lecturing time trying to convey material that was much better articulated in textbooks through which students could work at their own pace.

4. Avoiding Burnout

Needless to say, I make no claim that the preceeding sections have presented a foolproof set of recipes for success as a psychological economist in today's highly competitive academic environment. In addition to making choices of research modes, projects, and target audiences, the psychological economist needs some recipes for ensuring that research is not an unduly stressful process, not an activity that leads to a tendency to cry out at the end of the day, "Why do I bother? It's just not worth it!" This kind of condition is increasingly becoming recognized and labeled as "burnout" (see Diamond, 1986): most of us probably suffer from it on occasion but I know of no economists who, like clinical psychologists, get together for monthly anti-burnout dinners. Most of us can probably also readily recognize cases of the polar extreme, namely what is coming to be known as rustout, which could well arise in some cases from desperate moves to escape from a burnout trap. Rustout seems to afflict those who have decided to try to avoid stress as far as possible via strategic choices of their environments, or who have chosen untaxing routines to cope with potentially stressful environments — as in the case of "spoonfed" students who are able to achieve passes by exploiting their tutors rather than by developing their own problem-solving skills and discovering how well they can do on their own if they try. At the risk of mixing metaphorical terminology, one might say that people who suffer from rustout are prone to turn into "deadwood" and fail to realize their full potential.

Obvious kinds of events prone to produce feelings of burnout include rejection letters pertaining to carefully crafted articles and books, or crises during the research process that at first sight seem insurmountable. Such setbacks will be particularly distressing if they come as surprises: if they have been previously imagined as possibilities, the chances are that the academic has given some advance thought to ways of dealing with them, should they eventuate. Hence before sending pieces off for review, or before seriously commencing work on a new project, the psychological economist would be wise to pause and think of — and even write down — a list of possible outcomes, and consider to what extent the new piece of work or her own skills seem capable of standing up as barriers to imagined counter-desired possibilities (for example, "Could I cut this article down in size by a third if they insisted on it, as indeed they might given that it started out merely as a comment on X's paper?"). The active use of one's imagination at this stage may not only mean one is mentally prepared for unwanted outcomes, it may also result in time being saved because thoughts about possible limitations provoke one to take preemptive corrective measures. However, it is important to avoid going too far in this direction: just as the unduly conceited economist is likely to discover that life is full of unpleasant surprises, so the overly modest one with a vividly pessimistic imagination may end up producing very little in the way of finished work owing to spending too much time trying to produce "bullet-proof" research designs and written-up output. A certain amount of bravado is a necessary component of the successful psychological economist's personality. One of the keys to avoiding academic burnout is to experiment with a view to finding a happy medium in allocating one's time between planning, researching and writing-up. It is probably wise to recognize that, timewise, it may be more efficient to rely on other minds for advice on how finally to polish up output into a publishable form, while remembering that too early a submission is much less likely to inspire referees to make constructively critical comments.

When a counter-desired possibility — previously imagined or otherwise — eventuates, quite how devastating an experience it entails will depend on how its implications have been construed: a person may choose to construe an event in any way that she wishes, but some ways of seeing things can be much more dysfunctional than others. There is a world of difference between seeing, say, a rejection letter as indicating that one will never be able to reach the heights to which one has been aspiring in the profession or as if the domination of the established orthodoxy is going to be impossible to crack, and as seeing it as a means for enabling oneself to improve the quality of one's exposition and integrate one's work better with the existing literature and thereby make it amenable to a wider audience. (This latter construction does not also have to imply that one should be prepared to be putty in the hands of referees and feel obliged to try to accommodate *every* point they have raised: for example, quite often it is necessary to be assertive in the face of referees arguing for insertions that reflect their own particular "hobby-horses" but which would mainly serve to distract boundedly rational readers from the main point of the particular piece of work.) A striking illustration of what can happen when an academic economist has made all manner of personally significant images contingent on the acceptance of his work is evident in Phelps-Brown's biographical memoir on Roy Harrod: in 1928 Harrod suffered a serious nervous breakdown after a misunderstanding led Frank Ramsey to write a highly adverse report for the *Economic Journal* on his pioneering article on what we know nowadays as the marginal revenue curve (see Phelps-Brown, 1980, p. 9). The work of Dryden (1984) and Ellis and Grieger (1977) on rational-emotive therapy (RET) is something that most academics, particularly fledgling ones, could do well to read as a means of changing their ways of construing things and hence of helping them take academic life in their stride rather than letting it get on top of them.

The social nature of an academic economist's workaday lifestyle is something which mainstream economists probably take for granted, without even necessarily recognizing the significance of social interaction as a means toward the prevention of burnout. When the publications race is going badly, one needs enormous reserves of self-confidence to avoid loss of morale if one keeps from others the news of the latest rejection letter. The same may be said about the earlier stages of research whenever departures are being made from standard modes of thought: can so many neoclassical lemmings be missing the point as they continue down channels that to the deviant thinker look full of disaster potential? In most cases, personal self-confidence is buttressed by some form of social support group. Members of these groups may help each other avoid burnout purely by sharing opinions in an essentially tribal manner, without necessarily being able to offer conclusive philosophical demonstrations of rightness. They may or may not be able to offer academically influential connections, though obviously, in seeking to understand the development of psychological economics, it would be foolish to ignore the possible contribution of these connexions.

Such support groups can take many forms, and the forms they do take for an individual may vary with that person's career circumstances. Every psychological economist should note the admirable efforts of Professor Amitai Etzioni of George Washington University in initiating the creation of a formal Network for the Advancement of Socio-Economics, which includes a number of psychologists on its founding council. But for most people, it may be enough that they have one or two colleagues engaged in similar kinds of research, or people in other institutions with whom they have an affinity and with whom they can correspond and meet at conferences. Members of a psychological economists' support group may even be entirely orthodox economists who enjoy debating methodological issues or who share similar career frustrations despite their different areas of interest (for example, a mutual horror over a forest of "deadwood" that seems to stand between themselves and the higher rungs of academia).

Any psychological economist who fails to take steps to build up a new kind of support system is very likely to find it traumatic to move from a highly supportive environment to one in which her colleagues turn out to be largely surprised and mystified by the kind of research she does and the teaching she wishes to pursue. For anyone contemplating a move between such different working environments, it could prove wise to recognize that local affinities may take a good deal of time to reveal themselves, and that for the first few weeks or months in the new environment time might be very usefully spent trying to establish new contacts through correspondence with fellow thinkers and by participating at conferences. However, in respect of the latter suggestion, it must be added that a newly relocated psychological economist may well feel much less of a "fish out of water" at gatherings of psychologists, than at economists' conferences that offer no special sessions in this area and whose organizers make no attempt to provide participants with a ready means by which they might be able to locate participants with interests similar to their own. The relatively inexperienced young scholar should not generally feel intimidated about taking the initiative in writing to more senior scholars whose work has proved inspirational; often the reaction will be a very pleasant surprise, including letters expressing more encouraging views about the state of the discipline, information about new developments of special interest, copies of as-yet-unpublished papers, and even invitations to serve as a visiting seminar/conference speaker or prepare papers for volumes similar to the present one. The young scholar should not forget that senior academics themselves usually need support systems and that there can be few things more guaranteed to make them believe their research efforts have been worthwhile than news that they have won yet more converts: no wonder they are often so reciprocally supportive, even if their seniority means that they are overloaded with administrative duties!

5. Concluding Thoughts

It would not be at all surprising if some readers construed this chapter as often having deserved the more light-hearted title of "Confessions of a Psychological Economist," and some may have also worried about the dangers of generalizing from individual cases. I hope my use of actual experiences (of myself or others) will be excused because of the role such information may play as a pointer to what can, at least sometimes, happen if particular commitments are made. However, it would probably assist the future development of psychological economics if some of the remarks in this closing chapter were seen as a somewhat tongue-in-cheek examination of how academic economists do, or should, operate. Its author certainly never *planned* to become a psychological economist; he just found himself bound up in the activity with too much fascination to worry (initially) about the possible consequences of such a preoccupation. Economists who have kept well clear of psychology would have us all believe that decisions are usefully to be seen as if they emerge from a careful consideration of the possible sequels to rival courses of action. Yet the economics profession is such that if potential psychological economists *did* bother to stop and think like this, rather than getting themselves swept along by events or choosing on the basis of "animal spirits," then prospects for psychological economics could be severely limited owing to the comparative riskiness of such research. Most of the previous chapters in this book have, I hope, served to indicate that if this did happen, the outcome could justifiably be construed as a severe case of market failure.

BIBLIOGRAPHY

Note: numbers in brackets at the end of each entry refer to the chapter(s) in which citation occurs.

Adams, J.S. (1965) Inequity and social exchange. In Berkowitz, L. (ed.), *Advances in Experimental Social Psychology*, vol. 2. New York and London: Academic Press (9).

Addison, J.T. (1974) Productivity bargaining: the externalities question. *Scottish Journal of Political Economy* 21: 123–142 (9).

Addison, J.T. and Burton, J. (1984) The sociopolitical analysis of inflation. *Weltwirtschaftliches Archiv* 120: 90–119 (9).

Agassi, J. (1969) Unity and diversity in science. In Cohen, R. and Wartofsky, M. (eds.), *Boston Studies in the Philosophy of Science, 4*. New York: Humanities Press (11).

Agassi, J. (1975) Institutional individualism. *British Journal of Sociology* 26: 144–155 (3).

Aitken, S. and Bonneville, L. (1980) *A General Taxpayer Opinion Survey*. Washington, DC: CSR (13).

Akerlof, G.A. (1984) *An Economic Theorist's Book of Tales*. Cambridge: Cambridge University Press (4, 5, 14).

Akerlof, G.A. and Dickens, W.T. (1982) The economic consequences of cognitive dissonance. *American Economic Review* 72: 307–319 (3, 13, 15).

Akerlof, G.A. and Yellen, J.L. (1985a) Can small deviations from rationality make significant differences to economic equilibria? *American Economic Review* 75: 708–720 (3).

Akerlof, G.A. and Yellen, J.L. (1985b) A near-rational model of the business cycle with wage and price inertia. *Quarterly Journal of Economics, Supplement* 100: 823–838 (5).

Alberti, R.E. and Emmons, M.L. (1982) *Your Perfect Right: A Guide to Assertive Living* (4th edition). San Luis Obispo, CA: Impact Publishers (15).

Alcaly, R.E. and Klevorick, A.K. (1970) Judging quality by price, snob appeal and the new consumer theory. *Zeitschrift fur Nationalekonomie* 30: 53–64 (10).

Alchian, A.A. (1950) Uncertainty, evolution, and economic theory. *Journal of Political Economy* 58: 211–221 (5).

Alderfer, C.P. (1972) *Existence, Relatedness and Growth: Human Needs in Organizational Settings*. New York: Free Press (9).

Allais, M. (1953) Le comportement de l'homme rational devant le risque: critique des postulats et axioms de l'ecole americaine. *Econometrica* 21: 503–546 (4).

Allingham, M. and Sandmo, A. (1972) Income tax evasion: a theoretical analysis. *Journal of Public Economics* 1: 323–338 (13).

Alter, M. (1982) Carl Menger and Homo Oeconomicus: some thoughts on Austrian theory and methodology. *Journal of Economic Issues* 16: 149–160 (7, 8).

Annable, J.E. (1977) A theory of downward-rigid wages and cyclical unemployment. *Economic Inquiry* 15: 326–344 (9).

Arrow, K.J. (1959) Toward a theory of price adjustment. In Abramovitz, M. (ed.), *Allocation of Economic Resources*. Stanford: Stanford University Press (4).

Arrow, K.J. (1963) Utility and expectation in economic behavior. In Koch, S. (ed.), *Psychology: A Study of a Science, Volume 6, Investigations of Man as a Socius — Their Place in Psychology and the Social Sciences*. New York: McGraw-Hill (2).

Arrow, K.J. (1970) *Essays in the Theory of Risk-Bearing*. New York, Elsevier (2).

Arrow, K.J. (1982) Risk perception in psychology and economics. *Economic Inquiry* 20: 1–9 (3, 4, 14).

Arrow, K.J. and Hahn, F.H. (1971) *General Competitive Analysis*. San Francisco: Holden-Day, Inc. (4).

Atkinson, R.L., Atkinson, R.C. and Higard, E.R. (1983) *Introduction to Psychology*. New York: Harcourt Brace Jovanovitch (9).

Azariadis, C. (1981) Self-fulfilling prophesies. *Journal of Economic Theory* 25: 380–396 (5).

Baumol, W.J. (1982) Contestable markets: an uprising in the theory of industry structure. *American Economic Review* 72: 1–13 (14).

Baumol, W.J. and Quandt, R.E. (1964) Rules of thumb and optimally imperfect decisions. *American Economic Review* 54 :23–46 (5, 6).

Bausor, R. (1982) Time and the structure of economic analysis. *Journal of Post Keynesian Economics* 5: 163–179 (2).

Bausor, R. (1984) Toward a historically dynamic economics: examples and illustrations. *Journal of Post Keynesian Economics* 6: 360–376 (2).

Bausor, R. (1985) The limits of rationality. *Social Concept* 2: 66–83 (2).

Baxter, J.L. (1973) Inflation in the context of relative deprivation and social justice. *Scottish Journal of Political Economy* 20: 263–282 (9).

Baxter, J.L. (1980) A general model of wage determination. *Bulletin of Economic Research* 32: 3–17 (9).

Bayton, J.A. (1958) Motivation, cognition, learning — basic factors in consumer behavior. *Journal of Marketing* 22: 282–289 (10).

Becker, G.S. (1976) *The Economic Approach to Human Behavior*. Chicago: University of Chicago Press (5).

Bell, D. and Kristol, I. (eds.), *The Crisis in Economic Theory*. New York: Basic Books (14).

Bell, D.E. (1982) Regret in decision making under uncertainty. *Operations Research* 30: 961–981 (5).

Bell, D.E. (1985) Disappointment in decision making under uncertainty. *Operations Research* 33: 1–27 (5).

Berkson, W. and Wettersten, J. (1984) *Learning From Error*. La Salle, Il: Open Court (3).

Binswanger, H.P. (1981) Attitudes towards risk: theoretical implications of an experiment in rural India. *Economic Journal* 91: 867–890 (5).

Birner, J. (1985) Review of Boland, L.A. (1982) *Foundations of Economic Method*. *British Journal for the Philosophy of Science* 36: 215–21 (4).

Black, R.D.C., Coats, A.W. and Goodwin, C.D.W. (eds.), *The Marginal Revolution in Economics*. Durham, NC: Duke University Press (14).

Blatt, J. (1983) How economists misuse mathematics. in Eicher, A.S. (ed.), *Why Economics is not yet a Science*. Armonk, NY: M.E. Sharpe, Inc. (6).

Blanchard, O.J. and Summers, L.H. (1987) Hysteresis and the European unemployment problem. National Bureau of Economic Research, reprinted in Cross, R. (ed.), *Unemployment, Hysteresis and the Natural Rate Hypothesis*. Oxford: Blackwell (4).

Blaug, M. (1980) *The Methodology of Economics: or How Economists Explain*. Cambridge: Cambridge University Press (7, 14).

Blume, L.E., Bray, M.M. and Easley, D. (1982) Introduction to the stability of rational expectations equilibrium. *Journal of Economic Theory* 26: 313–317 (3, 5).

Blume, L.E. and Easley, D. (1982) Learning to be rational. *Journal of Economic Theory* 26: 340–351 (5).

Boehm, S. (1982) The ambiguous notion of subjectivism: comment on Lachmann. in Kirzner, I. M. (ed.), *Method, Process and Austrian Economics: Essays in Honour of Ludwig von Mises*. Lexington: D.C. Heath and Company (7).

Boehm-Bawerk, E. (1889/1973) *Value and Price: An Extract*. Illinois: Libertarian Press (7).

Boland, L.A. (1978) Time in economics vs. economics in time: the "Hayek Problem". *Canadian Journal of Economics* 11: 240–262 (7).

Boland, L.A. (1979) Knowledge and the role of insitutions in economic theory. *Journal of Economic Issues* 8, 957–972 (11).

Boland, L.A. (1981) On the futility of criticizing the neoclassical maximization hypothesis. *American Economic Review* 71: 1031–6 (3, 5).

Boland, L.A. (1982) *The Foundations of Economic Method*. London: George Allen and Unwin (3, 11).

Boland, L.A. (1986) *Methodology for a New Microeconomics: The Critical Foundations*. Boston: Allen & Unwin (1, 3).

Boland, L.A. and Newman, G. (1979) On the role of knowledge in economic theory. *Australian Economic Papers* 18: 71–80 (8).

Boulding, K.E. (1972) Human settlement and the quality of life. In Strumpel, B., Morgan, J.N. and Zahn. E. (eds.), *Human Behavior in Economic Affairs: Essays in Honor of George Katona*. New York: Elsevier (9).

Bourne, F.S. (1963) Different kinds of decisions and reference group influence. In Bliss, P. (ed.), *Marketing and the Behavioral Science*. Boston: Allyn and Bacon (10).

Bower, G.H. (1975) Cognitive psychology: an introduction. In Estes, W.K. (ed.), *Handbook of Learning and Cognitive Processes*, vol. 1. Hillsdale, NJ: Lawrence Erlbaum (3).

Bower, G.H. and Hilgard, E.R. (1981) *Theories of Learning* 5th edition. Englewood Cliffs, NJ: Prentice-Hall (3).

Braverman, H. (1986) *Labor and Monopoly Capital: The Degradation of Work in the Twentieth Century*. New York: Monthly Review Press (1).

Bray, M.M. (1982) Learning, estimation, and the stability of rational expectations. *Journal of Economic Theory* 26: 318–339 (5).

Brehmer, B. (1980) In one word: Not from experience. *Acta Psychologica* 45: 223–241 (3).

Breit, W., Hochman, H.M. and Saueracker, E. (eds.) (1986) *Readings in Microeconomics*. St Louis, Missouri: Times Mirror/Mosby (15).

Brennan, G. and Buchanan, J. (1981) The normative purpose of economic "science": rediscovery of an eighteenth century method. *International Review of Law and Economics* 1: 155–166 (12).

Brennan, G. and Buchanan, J. (1984) Voter choice: evaluating political alternatives. *American Behavioral Scientist* 28: 185–201 (12).

Brennan, G. and Lomasky, L. (1984) Inefficient Unanimity. *Journal of Applied Philosophy* 1: 151–163 (12).

Brennan, G. and Lomasky, L. (1985) The impartial spectator goes to Washington: toward a Smithian theory of electoral behavior. *Economics and Philosophy* 1: 189–212 (12).

Brown, W. and Sisson, K. (1975) The use of comparisons in workplace wage determination. *British Journal of Industrial Relations* 13: 23–53 (9).

Burton, J. and Addison, J.T. (1977) The institutionalist analysis of wage inflation: a critical appraisal. *Research in Labor Economics* 1: 333–376 (9).

Caldwell, B.J. (ed.) (1984a) *Appraisal and Criticism in Economics*. Boston: Allen & Unwin (13).

Caldwell, B.J. (1984b) Praxeology and its critics: an appraisal. *History of Political Economy* 16: 363–379 (7).

Caldwell, B.J. (1986) Review of O'Driscoll, G.P. and Rizzo, M. J. (1985) *The Economics of Time and Ignorance. Southern Economic Journal* 52: 1185–6 (8).

Chamberlin, J.R. (1976) A diagrammatic exposition of the logic of collective action. *Public Choice* 26: 59–74 (12).

Chipman, J.S. (1960) The foundations of utility. *Econmetrica* 28: 193–224 (10).

Chomsky, N. (1957) *Syntactic Structures. The Hague: Mouton and Company (2).*

Chomsky, N. (1965) *Aspects of the Theory of Syntax.* Cambridge, MA: M.I.T. Press (2).

Chomsky, N. (1975) *Reflections on Language.* New York: Pantheon Books (2).

Citrin, J. (1979) Do people want something for nothing?: public opinion on taxes and government spending. *National Tax Journal* 32 (supplement): 113–129 (13).

Claxton, G. (1980) Cognitive psychology: a suitable case for what kind of treatment? In Claxton, G. (ed.), *Cognitive Psychology.* London: Routledge and Kegan Paul (3).

Coats, A.W. (1976) Economics and psychology: the death and resurrection of a research programme. In Latsis, S.J. (ed.), *Method and Appraisal in Economics.* Cambridge: Cambridge University Press (1, 4, 5, 14).

Coats, A.W. (1983) The revival of subjectivism in economics. In Wiseman, J. (ed.), *Beyond Positive Economics?* London: Macmillan (1, 14).

Coddington, A. (1975) Creaking semaphore and beyond: a consideration of Shackle's *Epistemics and Economics. British Journal for the Philosophy of Science* 26, 151–163 (7).

Coddington, A. (1982) Deficient foresight: a troublesome theme in Keynesian economics. *American Economic Review* 72: 480–487 (2).

Coddington, A. (1983) *Keynesian Economics: the Search for First Principles.* London: George Allen and Unwin (1, 4, 7).

Cohen, L.J. (1979) On the psychology of predictions: whose is the fallacy? *Cognition* 7: 385–407 (3).

Cohen, L.J. and Axelrod, R. (1984) Coping with complexity: the adaptive value of changing utility. *American Economic Review* 74: 30–42 (3).

Coughlin, R. (1980) *Ideology, Public Opinion and Welfare Policy.* University of California (Berkeley): Institute of International Studies (13).

Cox, J.R. and Griggs, R.A. (1982) The effects of experience on performance in Watson's selection task. *Memory and Cognition* 10: 496–502 (3).

Crocker, J. (1982) Biased questions in judgment of covariation studies. *Personality and Social Psychology Bulletin* 8: 214–220 (3).

Cross, J.G. (1980) Learning to search. *Journal of Economic Behavior and Organization* 1: 197–221 (3).

Cross, J.G. (1983) *A Theory of Adaptive Economic Behavior.* Cambridge: Cambridge University Press (3, 5, 6).

Cross, R. (1982) *Economic Theory and Policy in the UK.* Oxford: Martin Robertson (1).

Cross, R. (1984) Monetarism and Duhem's thesis. in Wiles, P. and Routh, G. (eds.), *Economics in Disarray.* Oxford: Blackwell (14).

Cross, R. and Allan, A. (1987) On the History of Hysteresis. In Cross, R. (ed.),

Unemployment, Hysteresis and the Natural Rate Hypothesis. Oxford: Blackwell (4).

Cullis, J. and Lewis, A. (1985) Some hypotheses and evidence on tax knowledge and preferences. *Journal of Economic Psychology* 6: 271–287 (13).

Cyert, R.M. and March, J.G. (1963) *A Behavioral Theory of the Firm*. Englewood Cliffs, NJ: Prentice-Hall (15).

Debreu, G. (1959) *Theory of Value*, Cowles Foundation Monograph 17. New Haven: Yale University Press (2).

DeCanio, S. J. (1979) Rational expectations and learning from experience. *Quarterly Journal of Economics* 93: 47–57 (5).

De Meza, D. and Dickinson, P.T. (1984) Risk preferences and transactions costs. *Journal of Economic Behavior and Organization* 5: 223–236 (5).

Diamond, C.T.P. (1986) Avoiding "burnout" and "rustout": a dependency grid study of teacher stress. In Bell, R., Costigan, J. and Reddy, P. (eds.), *Collected Papers of the 3rd Australasian Personal Construct Psychology Conference, 1986*. Melbourne: Lincoln Institute of Health Sciences (15).

Dow, A. and Dow, S.C. (1985) Animal Spirits and Rationality. In Lawson, T. and Pesaran, H. (eds.) *Keynes' Economics: Methodological Issues*. Armonk, NY: M.E. Sharpe, Inc. (2).

Dow, S.C. and Earl, P.E. (1982) *Money Matters: A Keynesian Approach to Monetary Economics*. Oxford: Martin Robertson (9).

Dryden, W. (1984) *Rational-Emotive Therapy: Fundamentals and Innovations*. London: Croom Helm (15).

Duesenberry, J.S. (1949) *Income, Saving and the Theory of Consumer Behavior*. Cambridge, MA: Harvard University Press (9, 10).

Dunlop, J.T. (1957) The task of contemporary wage theory. In Taylor, G.W. and Sisson, F. C. (eds.), *New Concepts in Wage Determination*. New York: McGraw-Hill (9).

Earl, P.E. (1983a) *The Economic Imagination: Towards a Behavioural Analysis of Choice*. Brighton: Wheatsheaf (2, 3, 7, 9, 14, 15).

Earl, P.E. (1983b) The consumer in his/her social setting: a subjectivist view. In Wiseman, J. (ed.), *Beyond Positive Economics?* London: Macmillan (3, 7, 8).

Earl, P.E. (1983c) A behavioral theory of economists' behavior. In Eichner, A.S. (ed.), *Why Economics Is Not Yet a Science*. Armonk, NY: M.E. Sharpe, Inc. (1, 6, 14, 15).

Earl, P.E. (1984) *The Corporate Imagination: How Big Companies Make Mistakes*. Armonk, NY: M.E. Sharpe, Inc. (15).

Earl, P.E. (1986a) A behavioral analysis of demand elasticities. *Journal of Economic Studies* 13: 20–37 (3, 7).

Earl, P.E. (1986b) *Lifestyle Economics: Consumer Behaviour in a Turbulent World*. Brighton: Wheatsheaf (2, 3, 7, 9, 12, 14, 15).

Earl, P.E. (1986c) Review of L.A. Boland (1986) *Methodology for a New Microeconomics*. *Economic Journal* 96: 1134–1135 (1).

Earl, P.E. and Kay, N.M. (1985) How economists can accept Shackle's critique of economics without arguing themselves out of their jobs. *Journal of Economic Studies* 12: 34–48 (1, 2).

Eaton, H.O. (1930) *The Austrian Philosophy of Values*. Norman: University of Oklahoma Press (8).

Ebbesen, E.B. and Konecni, V.J. (1980) On the external validity of decision-making research: what do we know about decisions in the real world. In Wallsten, T.S. (ed.), *Cognitive Processes in Choice and Decision Behavior*. Hillsdale, NJ: Lawrence Erlbaum (3).

Eckstein, O. and Wilson, R.A. (1962) The determination of money wages in American industry. *Quarterly Journal of Economics* 76: 379–414 (9).

Edgren, G., Faxen, K. and Odhner, C. (1969) Wages, growth and the distributon of income. *Swedish Journal of Economics* 71: 133–160 (9).

Edwards, W. (1955) The prediction of decisions among bets. *Journal of Experimental Psychology* 50: 201–214 (5).

Edwards, W. (1968) Conservatism in information processing. In Kleinmuntz, B. (ed.), *Formal Representation of Human Judgment*. New York: Wiley (3).

Eichner, A.S. (1983) Why economics is not yet a science. *Journal of Economic Issues* 17: 507–520 (14, 15).

Einhorn, H.J. (1980) Learning from experience and suboptimal rules in decision making. In Wallsten, T.S. (ed.), *Cognitive Processes in Choice and Decision Behavior*. Hillsdale, NJ: Lawrence Erlbaum (3).

Einhorn H.J. and Hogarth, R.M. (1981) Behavioral decision theory: processes ofjudgment and choice. *Annual Review of Psychology* 32: 53–88 (3).

Einhorn, H.J. and Hogarth, R.M. (1985a) Ambiguity and uncertainty in probabilistic inference. *Psychological Review* 92: 433–461 (5).

Einhorn, H.J. and Hogarth, R.M. (1985b) Probable cause: a decision making framework. Working paper, Graduate School of Business, Center for Decision Research, University of Chicago (3).

Ellis, A. and Grieger, R. (eds.) (1977) *Handbook of Rational-Emotive Therapy*. New York: Springer (15).

Ellsberg, D. (1961) Risk, ambiguity, and the Savage axioms. *Quarterly Journal of Economics* 75: 643–669 (5).

Elster, J. (1983) *Sour Grapes*. Cambridge: Cambridge University Press (2).

Elster, J. (1984) *Ulysses and the Sirens* (rev. edition). Cambridge: Cambridge University Press (3, 6).

Endres, A.M. (1984) Institutional elements in Carl Menger's theory of demand: comment. *Journal of Economic Issues* 18: 897–904 (8).

Estes, W.K. (1972) Research and theory on the learning of probabilities. *Journal of the American Statistical Association* 67: 81–102 (5).

Evans, J. St B.T. (1980) Thinking: experimental and information processing approaches. In Claxton, G. (ed.), *Cognitive Psychology*. London: Routledge and Kegan Paul (3).

Eysenck, M.W. (1984) *A Handbook of Cognitive Psychology*. London: Lawrence Erlbaum (3).

Festinger, L. (1957) *A Theory of Cognitive Dissonance*. New York: Harper & Row (15).

Feyerabend, P.K. (1970) Consolations for the specialist. In Lakatos, I. and Musgrave, A. (eds.), *Criticism and the Growth of Knowledge*. London: Cambridge University Press (3).

Fischhoff, B. and Beyth-Marom, R. (1983) Hypothesis evaluation from a Bayesian perspective. *Psychological Review* 90: 239–260 (3).

Fishbein, M. and Ajzen, I. (1975) *Belief, Attiitude, Intention and Behavior*. Reading, MA: Addison-Wesley (3, 9).

Fisher, R. (1985) Taxes and expenditures in the US: public opinion surveys and incidence analysis compared. *Economic Inquiry* 23: 525–550 (13).

Fisher, R. (1986) *The Logic of Economic Discovery: Neoclassical Economics and the Marginal Revolution*. Brighton: Wheatsheaf (14).

Foster, N., Henry, S.G.B. and Trinder, C. (1984) Public and private sector pay: a partly disaggregated study. *National Institute of Economic and Social Research Economic Review*: 63–73 (9).

Fransella, F. and Bannister, D. (1977) *A Manual for the Repertory Grid Technique*. London: Academic Press (13).

Freud, S. (1950) *The Interpretation of Dreams*. Translated by A. A. Brill. New York: The Modern Library (2).

Freud, S. (1953) *A General Introduction to Psychoanalysis*. Translated by J. Riviere. New York: Pocket Books (2).

Freud, S. (1960) *The Ego and the Id*. Translated by J. Riviere. New York: W.W. Norton, Inc. (2).

Friedman, B. M. (1979) Optimal expectations and the extreme information assumptions of "rational expectations" macromodels. *Journal of Monetary Economics* 5: 23–41 (5).

Friedman, D. (1984) On the efficiency of experimental double auction markets. *American Economic Review* 74: 54–72 (13).

Friedman, M. (1953) The methodology of positive economics. In Friedman, M. (ed.), *Essays in Positive Economics*. Chicago: University of Chicago Press (5, 13).

Frydman, R. and Phelps, E.S. (eds.) (1983) *Individual Forecasting and Aggregate Outcomes: "Rational Expectations" Examined*. Cambridge: Cambridge University Press (5).

Furnham, A. and Lewis, A. (1986) *The Economic Mind: The Social Psychology of Economic Behaviour*. Brighton: Wheatsheaf, and New York: St Martins Press (1, 13, 15).

Georgescu-Roegen, N. (1954) Choice, expectations and measurability. *Quarterly Journal of Economics* 68: 503–534 (9).

Georgescu-Roegen, N. (1966) *Analytical Economics: Issues and Problems*. Cambridge, MA: Harvard University Press (9).

Georgescu-Roegen, N. (1968) Utility. *International Encyclopaedia of the Social Sciences*, vol. 16. pp. 236–67, Crowell: Collier-Macmillan (8, 9).

Gilad, B. and Kaish, S. (eds.) (1986) *Handbook of Behavioral Economics (Volume A: Behavioral Microeconomics; Volume B: Behavioral Macroeconomics)*. Greenwich, CT: JAI Press, Inc. (1, 14, 15).

Gilad, B. Kaish, S. and Loeb, P.D. (1984) From economic behavior to behavioral economics: the behavioral uprising in economics. *Journal of Behavioral Economics* 13: 1–22 (14).

Gilhooly, K.J. (1982) *Thinking: Directed, Undirected and Creative*. London: Academic Press (3).

Gimpl, M.L. and Dakin, S.R. (1984) Management and magic. *California Management Review* 27: 125–136 (15).

Gintis, H. (1974) Welfare criteria with endogenous preferences: the economics of education. *International Economic Review* 15: 415–430 (2).

Gjerdingen, D.H. (1983) The Coase theorem and the psychology of common-law thought. *Southern California Law Review* 56: 711–760 (12).

Gordon, J.R. (1983) *A Diagnostic Approach to Organizational Behavior*. Boston: Allyn and Bacon (9).

Gordon, R.J. (1981) Output fluctuations and gradual price adjustment. *Journal of Economic Literature* 19: 493–530 (9).

Grandmont, J. (1977) Temporary general equilibrium theory. *Econometrica* 45: 535–72 (2).

Green, J. (1977) The non-existence of informational equilibria. *Review of Economic Studies* 44: 451–464 (5).

Green, P. and Wind, Y. (1975) New ways to measure consumers' judgements. *Harvard Business Review* 53 (July/August): 107–117 (13).

Grossman, S.J. and Stiglitz, J.E. (1980) On the impossibility of informationally efficient markets. *American Economic Review* 70: 393–408 (5).

Grubb, E.L. and Grathwohl, H.L. (1967) Consumer self-concept, symbolism and market behavior: a theoretical approach. *Journal of Marketing* 31: 22–27 (10).

Gutman, J. (1982) A means-end chain model based on consumer catgorization processes. *Journal of Marketing* 46: 60–72 (7, 13).

Gutman, J. and Alden, S.D. (1985) Adolescents' cognitive structures of retail stores and fashion consumption: a means-end chain analysis of quality. In Jacoby, J. and Olson, J.C. (eds.), *Perceived Quality.*, Lexington, MA: D.C. Heath (for New York University Institute of Retail Management) (7).

Haines, W.W. (1982) The psychoeconomics of human needs: Maslow's hierarchy and Marshall's organic growth. *Journal of Behavioral Economics* 11: 97–121 (9).

Hall, R.E. (1978) Stochastic implications of the lifecycle-permanent income hypothesis. *Journal of Political Economy* 86: 971–87 (6).

Haltiwanger, J. and Waldman, M. (1985) Rational expectations and the limits of rationality: an analysis of heterogeneity. *American Economic Review* 75: 326–40 (3).

Hands, W. (1985) Karl Popper and economic methodology. *Economics and Philosophy* 1: 83–99 (3).

Harvey, J.H., Town, J.P. and Yarkin, K.L. (1981) How fundamental is the "fundamental attribution error"? *Journal of Personality and Social Psychology* 40: 346–349 (3).

Harvey, J.H. and Weary, G. (1984) Current issues in attribution theory and research. *Annual Review of Psychology* 35: 427–59 (3).

Hastie, R. (1984) Causes and effects of causal attribution. *Journal of Personality and Social Psychology* 46: 44–56 (3).

Hawtrey, R.G. (1926) *The Economic Problem*. London: Longmans (14).

Hayakawa, B. and Venieris, Y. (1977) Consumer interdependence via reference groups. *Journal of Political Economy* 83: 599–615 (11).

Hayek, F.A. (1937) Economics and knowledge. *Economica* 4: 33–54 (5, 7).

Hayek, F.A. (1952) *The Sensory Order*. London: Routledge & Kegan Paul (1, 7).

Hayek, F.A. (1952/1979) *The Counter-Revolution of Science*. Indianapolis: Liberty Press (7).

Hayek, F.A. (1973) The place of Menger's *Grundsatze* in the history of economic thought. in Hicks, J.R. and Weber, W. (eds.), *Carl Menger and the Austrian School of Economics*. Oxford: Clarendon Press (8).

Hayek, F.A. (1976) Carl Menger, introduction to Menger, C. (1871/1976) *Principles of Economics*. New York: New York University Press (7).

Hayes-Roth, F. and Waterman, D. (1978) *Pattern Directed Inference Systems*. New York: Academic Press (6).

Heijdra, B.J. and Lowenberg, A.D. (1986a) Duhem-Quine, Lakatos, and research programmes in economics. *Journal of Interdisciplinary Economics* 1: 175–187 (5).

Heijdra, B.J. and Lowenberg, A.D. (1986b) The neoclassical research program: some Lakatosian and other considerations. Unpublished paper (5).

Henle, M. (1962) On the relation between logic and thinking. *Psychological Review* 69: 366–378 (3).

Herzberg, F., Mausner, B. and Singerman, B.B. (1959) *The Motivation to Work*. New York: Wiley (9).

Hey, J.D. (1981) *Economics in Disequilibrium*. New York: New York University Press (2).

Hey, J.D. (1982) Search for rules of search. *Journal of Economic Behvior and Organization* 3: 65–81 (6).

Hey, J.D. (1983a) Towards double negative economics. In Wiseman, J. (ed.), *Beyond Positive Economics?* London: Macmillan (3).

Hey, J.D. (1983b) Whither uncertainty? *Economic Journal, Conference Papers* 93: 130–139 (5).

Hey, J.D. (1984) Unshackling economics. *Scottish Journal of Political Economy* 31: 202–208 (15).

Hey, J.D. (1986) A pilot experimental investigation into optimal consumption under uncertainty. In Maital, S. (ed.), *Applied Behavioral Economics*. Amsterdam: North-Holland (6).

Hey, J.D. and Dardanoni, V. (1987) A preliminary analysis of a large-scale experimental study of optimal consumption under uncertainty. Springer-Verlag lecture notes (ed. W. Albers) (6).

Hicks, J.R. (1946) *Value and Capital* (2nd edition)., Oxford: Clarendon Press (2).

Hicks, J.R. (1979) *Causality in Economics*. New York: Basic Books (2).

Hirsch, F. (1977) *Social Limits to Growth*. London: Routledge and Kegan Paul (9).

Hirschman, A.O. (1984) Against parsimony: three ways of complicating some categories of economic discourse. *American Economic Review, Papers and Proceedings* 74: 89–96 (14).

Hirschman, E.C. and Holbrook, M.B. (eds.) (1981) *Symbolic Consumer Behavior*. Ann Arbor: Association for Consumer Research (10).

Hirschman, E.C. and Holbrook, M.B. (1982) Hedonic consumption: emerging concepts, methods and propositions. *Journal of Marketing* 46: 92–101 (10).

Hirshleifer, J. (1985) The expanding domain of economics. *American Economic Review* 75: 53–68 (4, 5, 14).

Hirshleifer, J. and Riley, J.G. (1979) The analytics of uncertainty and information: an expository survey. *Journal of Economic Literature* 17: 1375–1421 (4).

Hoffman, E. and Spitzer, M.L. (1985) Experimental law and economics: an introduction. *Columbia Law Review* 85: 991–1036 (5, 13).

Hogarth, R.M. (1981) Beyond discrete biases: functional and dysfunctional aspects of judgmental heuristics. *Psychological Bulletin* 90: 197–217 (3).

Hogarth, R.M. and Kunreuther, H. (1985) Ambiguity and insurance decisions. *American Economic Review, Papers and Proceedings* 75: 386–390 (5).

Hollis, M. and Nell, E. (1975) *Rational Economic Man*. Cambridge: Cambridge University Press (13).

Houthakker, H.S. (1961) The present state of consumption theory. *Econometrica* 29: 704–40 (10).

Hunt, M. (1982) *The Universe Within*. Brighton: Harvester Press (6).

Hutchison, T.W. (1938) *The Significance and Basic Postulates of Economic Science*, reprinted 1965. New York: Augustus M. Kelley (14).

Hutchison, T.W. (1981) *The Politics and Philosophy of Economics: Marxians, Keynesians and Austrians*. Oxford: Blackwell (7).

Hyams, S. (1972) The index of consumer sentiment and economic forecasting — a reappraisal. In Strumpel, B, Morgan, B. and Zahn, E. (eds.), *Human Behavior in Economic Affairs*. New York: Elsevier (13).

Ironmonger, D.S. (1972) *New Commodities and Consumer Behaviour*. Cambridge: Cambridge University Press (12).

Jahoda, M. (1982) *Employment and Unemployment: A Social-Psychological Analysis*. Cambridge: Cambridge University Press (1).

James, W. (1890) *The Principles of Psychology*. New York: Henry Holt & Co. (8).

Johnson-Laird, P.M. (1983) *Mental Models*. Cambridge: Cambridge University Press (3).

Johnston, W.M. (1972) *The Austrian Mind: An Intellectual and Social History*. Berkeley: University of California Press (8).

Jung, C.G. (1959) *Archtypes and the Collective Unconscious: Volume 9 of Collected Works*. Translated by R.F.C. Hull. New York: Bollingen (2).

Jung, C.G. (1964) *Man and his Symbols*. New York: Dell (2).

Jungermann, H. (1983) Two camps on rationality. In Scholz, R.W. (ed.), *Decision Making under Uncertainty*. Amsterdam: North-Holland (5).

Juster, T. (1981) An expectational view of consumer spending prospects. *Journal of Economic Psychology* 1: 87–105 (13).

Kahneman, D., Slovic, P. and Tversky, A. (eds.) (1982) *Judgment Under Uncertainty: Heuristics and Biases*. Cambridge: Cambridge University Press (3, 4, 5).

Kahneman, D. and Tversky, A. (1979) Prospect theory: an analysis of decision under risk. *Econometrica* 47: 263–291 (3, 4, 5, 6).

Kahneman, D. and Tversky, A. (1982a) Judgment under uncertainty: heuristics and biases. In Kahneman, D., Slovic, P. and Tversky, A. (eds.), *Judgment Under Uncertainty: Heuristics and Biases*. Cambridge: Cambridge University Press (5).

Kahneman, D. and Tversky, A. (1982b) Subjective probability: a judgment of representativeness. In Kahneman, D., Slovic, P. and Tversky, A. (eds.), *Judgment Under Uncertainty: Heuristics and Biases*. Cambridge: Cambridge University Press (3, 5).

Kalman, P.J. (1968) Theory of consumer behavior when prices enter the utility function. *Econometrica* 36: 497–510 (2, 10).

Kamarck, A.M. (1983) *Economics and the Real World*. Oxford: Blackwell (14).

Kassarjian, H.H. and Robertson, R.T. (eds.) (1965) *Perspectives in Consumer Behavior*. Glenview, IL: Scott, Foresman (10).

Katona, G. (1953) Rational behavior and economic behavior. *Psychological Review* 60: 307–18 (10).

Katona, G. (1960) *The Powerful Consumer*. New York: McGraw-Hill (9).

Katona, G. (1967) Anticipations statistics and consumer behavior. *American Statistician* 21: 12–13 (13).

Katona, G. (1975) *Psychological Economics*. New York: Elsevier (9, 13).

Katona, G. (1977) *Psychological Analysis of Economic Behavior*. Westport: Greenwood Press (13).

Katz, E. (1957) The two-step flow of communication: an up-to-date-report on an hypothesis. *Public Opinion Quarterly* 21: 70–82 (10).

Katz, E. and Lazarsfeld P.F. (1955) *Personal Influence*. Glencoe: Free Press (10).

Kay, N.M. (1982) *The Evolving Firm*. New York: St. Martins Press (2, 15).

Kay, N.M. (1984) *The Emergent Firm: Knowledge, Ignorance and Surprise in Economic Organization*. London: Macmillan (15).

Kelley, H.H. (1967) Attribution theory in social psychology. *Nebraska Symposium on Motivation* 15: 192–238 (3).

Kelley, H.H. (1972) Attribution in social interaction. in Jones, E.E. et al. (eds.), *Attribution, Perceiving the Causes of Behavior*. Morristown, NJ: General Learning Press (3).

Kelley, H.H. and Michela, J.L. (1980) Attribution theory and research. *Annual Review of Psychology* 31: 457–501 (3).

Kelly, G.A. (1955) *The Psychology of Personal Constructs*. New York: W.W. Norton and Company, Inc. (1, 2, 3, 5, 7, 9, 13).

Kelly, G.A. (1963) *A Theory of Personality*. New York: W.W. Norton and Company, Inc. (2, 7).

Keynes, J.M. (1931) Economic possibilities for our grandchildren. In Keynes, J. M. (ed.), *Essays in Persuasion*. London: Macmillan (10).

Keynes, J.M. (1936) *The General Theory of Employment, Interest and Money*. London: Macmillan (9, 10, 14).

Kinsey, K. (1985) *Theories and Models of Tax Cheating*. Chicago: American Bar Federation (13).

Kirzner, I.M. (1976a) *The Economic Point of View*. Kansas City: Sheed and Ward, Inc. (7).

Kirzner, I.M. (1976b) On the method of Austrian economics. In Dolan, E. G. (ed.), *The Foundations of Modern Austrian Economics*. Kansas City: Sheed and Ward, Inc. (7).

Kirzner, I.M. (1978) *Competition and Entrepreneurship* (paperback edition). Chicago: University of Chicago Press (7).

Kirzner, I.M. (1979) *Perception, Opportunity and Profit*. Chicago: University of Chicago Press (2, 7).

Kirzner, I.M. (1982) Uncertainty, discovery, and human action: a study of the entrepreneurial profile in the Misesian system. In Kirzner, I.M. (ed.), *Method, Process and Economics: Essays in Honour of Ludwig von Mises*. Lexington: D.C. Heath and Company (7).

Kirzner, I.M. (1985) Review of O"Driscoll, G.P. and Rizzo, M.J. (1985) *The Economics of Time and Ignorance. Market Process*. 3: no. 2 (7).

Kish, L. (1965) *Survey Sampling*. New York: Wiley (13).

Klayman, J. (1984) Learning from feedback in probabilistic environments. In Borcherding, K., Brehmer, B., Vlek, C., and Wagenaar, W.A. (eds.), *Research Perspectives on Decision Making Under Uncertainty*. Amsterdam: North-Holland (5).

Knowles, K.G.J.C. and Robinson, D. (1962) Wage rounds and wage policy. *Bulletin of the Oxford University Insitute of Economics and Statistics* 24: 269–329 (9).

Koertge, N. (1975) Popper's metaphysical research program for the human sciences. *Inquiry* 19: 437-462 (3).

Koertge, N. (1979) The methodological status of Popper's rationality principle. *Theory and Decision* 10: 83–95 (3).

Kotler, P. (1965) Behavioral models for analyzing buyers. *Journal of Marketing* 29: 37–45 (10).

Kruskal, J.B. (1965) Analysis of factorial experiments by estimating monotone transformations of the data. *Journal of the Royal Statistical Society — Series B* 27: 251–263 (13).

Kuhn, T.S. (1962) *The Structure of Scientific Revolutions*. Chicago: University of Chicago Press (15).

Lachmann, L.M. (1976) From Mises to Shackle: an essay on Austrian economics and the kaleidic society. *Journal of Economic Literature* 14: 54–62 (7).

Lachmann, L.M. (1977) *Capital, Expectations and the Market process*. Kansas City: Sheed, Andrews and McMeel, Inc. (7).

Lachmann, L.M. (1978) Carl Menger and the incomplete revolution of subjectivism. *Atlantic Economic Journal* 6: 57–59 (8).

Lachmann, L.M. (1979) The recent controversy concerning equilibriation. *Austrian Economics Newsletter*, Fall (7).

Lachmann, L.M. (1982) Mises and the extension of subjectivism. in Kirzner, I.M. (ed.), *Method, Process and Austrian Economics: Essays in Honour of Ludwig von Mises*. Lexington: D.C. Heath and Company (7).

Lachmann, L.M. (1984a) George Shackle's place in the history of subjectivist thought. Paper prepared for the George Shackle Conference, University of Surrey, 7–8 September 1984 (7).

Lachmann, L.M. (1984b) Der Markt ist kein Uhrwerk. *Frankfurter Allgemeine Zeitung*, November 24 (7).

Lachmann, L.M. (1985) Review of O''Driscoll, G.P. and Rizo, M.J. *The Economics of Time and Ignorance. Market Process* 3, Fall (7).

Lachmann, L.M. (1986) *The Market as an Economic Process*. Oxford: Basil Blackwell (7).

Lakatos, I. (1970) Falsification and the methodology of scientific research programmes. In Lakatos, I. and Musgrave, A. (eds.), *Criticism and the Growth of Knowledge*. London: Cambridge University Press (3, 5).

Lancaster, K.J. (1966) A new approach to consumer theory. *Journal of Political Economy* 74: 132–157 (10, 15).

Lancaster, K.J. (1971) *Consumer Demand: A New Approach*. New York: Columbia University Press (9, 13, 15).

Langlois, R.N. (1982) Austrian economics as an affirmative science: comment on Rizzo. In Kirzner, I.M. (ed.), *Method, Process and Austrian Economics: Essays in Honour of Ludwig von Mises*. Lexington: D.C. Heath and Company (7).

Langlois, R.N. (ed.) (1986) *Economics as a Process: Essays in the New Institutional Economics*. Cambridge: Cambridge University Press (14).

Latsis, S.J. (1976) A research programme in economics. In Latsis, S.J. (ed.), *Method and Appraisal in Economics*. Cambridge: Cambridge University Press (3, 7).

Lazer, W. (1964) Life-style concepts and marketing. In Greyser, S. A. (ed.) *Towards Scientific Marketing*. Chicago: American Marketing Association (10).

Leibenstein, H. (1950) Bandwagon, snob and Veblen effects in the theory of consumers' demand. *Quarterly Journal of Economics* 65: 183–207 (10).

Leibenstein, H. (1966) Allocative efficiency vs. X-efficiency. *American Economic Review* 56: 392–415 (1).

Leibenstein, H. (1976) *Beyond Economic Man*. Cambridge, MA: Harvard University Press (1, 9).

Leibenstein, H. (1979) A branch of economics is missing: micro-micro theory. *Journal of Economic Literature* 17: 477–502 (5).

Lekachman, R. (1976) *Economists at Bay: or Why the Experts Will Never Solve Your Problems*. New York: McGraw-Hill (14).

Levi, I. (1985) Illusions about uncertainty. *British Journal for the Philosophy of Science* 36: 331–340 (5).

Levi, I. (1986) The paradoxes of Allais and Ellsberg. *Economics and Philosophy* 2: 23–53 (4).

Levine, D.P. (1977) *Economic Studies: Contributions to the Critique of Economic Theory*. London: Routledge and Kegan Paul (2).

Levine, D. P. (1978) *Economic Theory, Volume 1*. London: Routledge and Kegan Paul (2).

Levine, D.P. and Levine, L.S. (1975) Social theory and social action. *Economy and Society* 4: 162–193 (2).

Levinson, H.M. (1960) Postwar movements of prices and wages in manufacturing industries. In *Study of Employment, Growth and the Price Level*, Joint Economic Committee, Study Paper 21. Washington, D.C.: United States Congress (9).

Levy, S.J. (1959) Symbols by which we buy. In Stockman, L.H. (ed.), *Advanced Marketing Efficiency*. Chicago: American Marketing Association (10).

Lewis, A. (1982) *The Psychology of Taxation*. Oxford: Martin Robertson (13).

Lewis, A. and Cullis, J (1987) Preferences, economics and psychology and the psychology of economic preferences. *Journal of Behavioral Economics* (forthcoming) (13).

Lippman, S.A. and McCall, J.J. (1981) The economics of uncertainty: selected topics and probabilistic methods. In Arrow, K.J. and Intriligator, M.D. (eds.), *Handbook of Mathematical Economics*, vol. I. Amsterdam: North-Holland (5).

Little, I.M.D. (1949) A reformulation of the theory of consumer. behaviour. *Oxford Economic Papers* 1 (new series): 90–99 (10).

Little, I.M.D. (1957) *A Critique of Welfare Economics* (rev. edition). Oxford: Oxford University Press (12).

Littlechild, S.C. (1979) Comment: radical subjectivism or radical subversion? In Rizzo, M.J. (ed.), *Time, Uncertainty, and Disequilibrium*. Lexington: D.C. Heath and Company (7).

Littlechild, S.C. (1982) Controls on advertising: an examination of some economic arguments. *Journal of Advertising* 1: 25–37 (7).

Littlechild, S.C. (1983) Subjectivism and method in economics. In Wiseman, J. (ed.), *Beyond Positive Economics?* London: Macmillan (7).

Loasby, B.J. (1976) *Choice, Complexity and Ignornace*. Cambridge: Cambridge University Press (12, 15).

Loasby, B.J. (1982) Economics of dispersed and incomplete knowledge. In Kirzner, I.M. (ed.), *Method, Process and Austrian Economics: Essays in Honour of Ludwig von Mises*. Lexington: D.C. Heath and Company (7).

Loasby, B.J. (1983) Knowledge, learning and enterprise. In Wiseman, J. (ed.), *Beyond Positive Economics?* London: Macmillan (3, 7).

Loasby, B.J. (1986) Organization, competition, and the growth of knowledge. In Langlois, R.N. (ed), *Economics as a Process: Essays in the New Institutional Economics*. Cambridge: Cambridge University Press (5).

Loomes, G. and Sugden, R. (1982) Regret theory: an alternative theory of rational choice under uncertainty. *Economic Journal* 92: 805–824 (5, 6).

Loomes, G. and Sugden, G. (1986) Disappointment and dynamic consistency in choice under uncertainty. *Review of Economic Studies* 53: 271–282 (5).

Lopes, L.L. (1982) Doing the impossible: a note on induction and the experience of randomness. *Journal of Experimental Psychology: Learning and Cognition* 8: 626–636 (3).

Lowenberg, A.D. and Heijdra, B.J. (1985) Equilibrium notions in macroeconomics: an historical approach. Unpublished paper (5).

Lucas, R.E. Jr. (1981) Understanding business cycles. In Lucas, R. E. Jr. (ed.), *Studies in Business-Cycle Theory*. Cambridge, MA: The MIT Press (5).

Lutz, M.A. and Lux, K. (1979) *The Challenge of Humanistic Economics*. Menlo Park, CA: Benjamin/Cummings Publishing (9).

Lydall, H.F. (1976) Theories of the distribution of earnings. In Atkinson, A. B. (ed.), *The Personal Distribution of Incomes*. London: Allen and Unwin (1).

MacFadyen, A.J. and MacFadyen, H.W. (eds.) (1986) *Economic Psychology: Intersections in Theory and Application*. Amsterdam: North-Holland (1, 15).

Machina,M. J. (1982) "Expected utility" analysis without the independence axiom. *Econometrica* 50: 277–323 (4, 5, 6).

Machina, M.J. (1983a) Generalized expected utility analysis and the nature of observed violations of the independence axiom. In Stigum, B.P. and Wenstop, F. (eds.), *Foundations of Utility and Risk Theory with Applications*. Dordrecht: D. Reidel (5).

Machina, M.J. (1983b) The economic theory of individual behavior toward risk: theory, evidence and new directions. IMSSS Technical Report no. 433 (6).

Machlup, F. (1964) Professor Samuelson on theory and realism. *American Economic Review* 54: 733-736 (13).

Maddala, G.S. (1977) *Econometrics*. Tokyo: McGraw-Hill Kogakusha (5).

Maital, S. (1982) *Minds, Markets and Money*. New York: Basic Books (14).

March, J.G. (1978) Bounded rationality, ambiguity, and the engineering of choice. *Bell Journal of Economics* 9: 587–608 (3).

Markowitz, H. (1952) The utility of wealth. *Journal of Political Economy* 60: 151–158 (5).

Marr, W. and Raj, B. (eds.) (1983) *How Economists Explain*. Lanham: University Press of America (13).

Marshall, A. (1890 [1920, 8th edition]) *Principles of Economics*. London: Macmillan (9, 10).

Maslow, A. (1954) *Motivation and Personality*. New York: Harper and Row (9).

Mason, R.S. (1981) *Conspicuous Consumption*. Farnborough: Gower Press (10).

McCarthy, W.E.J., O'Brien, J.S. and Dowd, V.G. (1975) *Wage Inflation and Wage Leadership: A Study of the Role of Wage Bargains in the Irish System of Collective Bargaining*. Dublin: Economic and Social Research Institute (9).

McCrohan, K. (1982) The use of survey research to estimate trends in non-compliance with federal income taxes. *Journal of Economic Psychology* 2: 231–240 (13).

McLelland, D. (1961) *The Achieving Society*. Princeton, NJ: Van Nostrand (9).

Mehra, Y.P. (1976) Spillovers in wage determination in U.S. manufacturing industries. *Review of Economics and Statistics* 58: 300–312 (9).

Menger, C. (1871/1976) *Principles of Economics (Grundsatze)*. New York: New York University Press (7, 8, 9).

Menger, K. (1973) Austrian marginalism and mathematical economics. In Hicks, J.R. and Weber, W. (eds.), *Carl Menger and the Austrian School of Economics*. Oxford: Clarendon Press (6).

Miller, E. (1975) Status goods and luxury taxes. *American journal of Economics and Sociology* 34: 141–154 (10).

Mirowski, P. (1986) *The Reconstruciton of Economic Theory*. Boston: Kluwer (14).

Mises, L. (1949/1966) *Human Action*. Chicago: Contemporary Books, Inc. (7).

Mises, L. (1957/1981) *Theory and History: An Interpretation of Social and Economic Evolution*. CT: Arlington House Publishers (7).

Mitchell, D.J.B. (1980) *Unions, Wages and Inflation*. Washington, DC: Brookings Insitution (9).

Monroe, K. (1976) The influence of price differences and brand familiarity on brand preferences. *Journal of Consumer Research* 3: 42–49 (13).

Morgan, J.N. (1978) Multiple motives, group decisions, uncertainty, ignorance and confusion: a realistic economics of the consumer requires some psychology. *American Economic Review Papers and Proceedings* 68: 58–63 (9).

Morishima, M. (1984) The good and bad uses of mathematics. In Wiles, P. and Routh, G. (eds.), *Economics in Disarrary*. Oxford: Blackwell (14).

Moser, K. and Kalton, G. (1971) *Survey Methods in Social Investigation*. London: Heinemann Educational Books (13).

Muth, J.F. (1961) Rational expectations and the theory of price movements. *Econometrica* 29: 315–335 (5).

Neisser, U. (1976) *Cognition and Reality*. San Francisco: W.H. Freeman (3).

Nelson, R.R. and Winter, S.G. (1982) *An Evolutionary Theory of Economic Change*. Cambridge, MA: Harvard University Press (1, 14).

Newell, A. (1973) You can't play twenty questions with nature and win. in Chase, W. G. (ed.), *Visual Information Processing*. New York: Academic Press (3).

Newell, A. and Simon, H.A. (1972) *Human Problem Solving*. Englewood Cliffs, NJ: Prentice-Hall (3, 6).

Newman, G. (1972) Institutional choices and the theory of consumer behavior. Unpublished MA thesis, Simon Fraser University (11).

Nisbett, R.E., Krantz, D.H., Jepson, C. and Kunda, Z. (1983) The use of statistical heuristics in everyday inductive reasoning. *Psychological Review* 90: 339–363 (3).

Nisbett, R.E. and Ross, L. (1980) *Human Inference: Strategies and Shortcomings of Social Judgement*. Englewood Cliffs, NJ: Prentice-Hall (3).

Norman, D.A. (1981) Twelve issues for cognitive science. in Norman, D. A. (ed.), *Perspectives on Cognitive Science*. Norwood, NJ: Ablex (3).

O'Driscoll, G.P. and Rizzo, M. (1985) *The Economics of Time and Ignorance*. Oxford: Blackwell (7, 14).

O'Higgins, M. (1981) Aggregate measures of tax evasion: an assessment. *British Tax Review* 5: 286–302 (13).

Olson, J. and Reynolds, T. (1983) Understanding consumers' cognitive structures: implications for advertising strategy. In Percy, L. and Woodside, A. (eds.), *Advertising and Consumer Psychology*. Lexington, MA: Lexington Books (13).

Olson, M. (1965) *The Logic of Collective Action*. Cambridge, MA: Harvard University Press (12).

Parsons, T. (1931) Wants and activities in Marshall. *Quarterly Journal of Economics* 45: 101–140 (14).

Parsons, T. (1932) Economics and sociology: Marshall in relation to the thought of his time. *Quarterly Journal of Economics* 46: 316–347 (14).

Pasinetti, L.L. (1981) *Structural Change and Economic Growth*. Cambridge: Cambridge University Press (4).

Payne, J.W. (1976) Task complexity and contingent processing in decision making: an information search and protocol analysis. *Organizational Behavior and Human Performance* 16: 366–387 (3).

Payne, J.W. (1982) Contingent decision behavior. *Psychological Bulletin* 92: 382–402 (3).

Phelps-Brown, E.H. (1980) Sir Roy Harrod: a biographical memoir. *Economic Journal* 90: 1–33 (15).

Piaget, J. (1970) *Psychology and Epistemology*. Translated by A. Rosin. New York: The Viking Press (2).

Piaget, J. (1981) *The Development of Intelligence*. Translated by M Piercy and D.E. Berlyne. Totowa, NJ: Littlefield, Adams (2).

Pickering, J.F. (1977) *The Acquisition of Consumer Durables*. London: Associated Business Programmes (13).

Pickering, J.F. (1984) Purchasing expectations and the demand for consumer durables. *Journal of Economic Psychology* 5: 342–352 (13).

Pinch, T. and Clark, C. (1986) The hard sell. *Sociology* 20: 169–191 (13).

Pitz, G. and Sachs, N.J. (1984) Judgment and decision: theory and application. *Annual Review of Psychology* 35: 139–163 (3).

Plott, C.R. (1982) Industrial organization theory and experimental economics. *Journal of Economic Literature* 20: 1485–1527 (6).

Pollak, R.A. (1970) Habit formation and dynamic demand functions. *Journal of Political Economy* 78: 745–763 (2).

Pollak, R.A. (1977) Price dependent preferences. *American Economic Review* 67: 64–75 (10).

Popper, K.R. (1961) *The Poverty of Historicism*. London: Routledge and Kegan Paul (3).

Popper, K.R. (1965) *The Logic of Scientific Discovery* New York: Harper and Row (3).

Popper, K.R. (1968) *Conjectures and Refutations*. New York: Harper and Row (3).

Popper, K.R. (1972) *Objective Knowledge*. London: Oxford University Press (3).

Popper, K.R. (1976) The logic of the social sciences. In Adorno, T.W. et al. (eds.) (translated by G. Adey and D. Frisby), *The Positivist Dispute in German Sociology*. New York: Harper and Row (3).

Radner, R. (1982) Equilibrium under uncertainty. In Arrow, K.J. and Intriligator, M.D. (eds.), *Handbook of Mathematical Economics*, vol. II. Amsterdam: North-Holland (5).

Ratchford, B.T. (1975) The new economic theory of consumer behavior: an interpretive essay. *Journal of Consumer Research* 2: 65–75 (13).

Rawls, J. (1971) *A Theory of Justice.* Cambridge, MA: Harvard University Press (9).

Reder, M. (1947) *Studies in the Theory of Welfare Economics.* New York: Columbia University Press (10).

Remenyi, J.V. (1979) Core demi-core interaction: toward a general theory of disciplinary and subdisciplinary growth. *History of Political Economy* 11: 30–63 (1).

Restle, F. (1962) The selection of strategies in cue learning. *Psychological Review* 69: 329–343 (3).

Reynolds, T.J. and Gutman, J. (1983) Developing images for services through means-end chain analysis. In Berry, L.L., Shostack, G.L. and Upah, G.D. (eds.), *Emerging Perspectives in Service Marketing.* Chicago: American Marketing Association (13).

Reynolds, T.J. and Gutman, J. (1984) Laddering: extending the repertory grid methodology to construct attribute-consequence-value hierarchies. In Pitts, R. and Woodside, A. (eds.), *Personal Values and Consumer Psychology.* Lexington, MA: D.C. Heath (13).

Reynolds, T.J. and Jamieson, L.F. (1985) Image Representations: an analytic framework. In Jacoby, J. and Olson, J.C. (eds.), *Perceived Quality.* Lexington, MA: D.C. Heath (13).

Robbins, L. (1932/1984) *An Essay on the Nature and Significance of Economic Science.* London: Macmillan (7, 14).

Robinson, J.V. (1932) *Economics is a Serious Subject.* Cambridge: W. Heffer and Sons (14).

Robinson, J.V. (1933) *The Economics of Imperfect Comptition.* London: Macmillan (14).

Rosenberg, A. (1979) Can economics explain everything? *Philosophy of the Social Sciences* 9: 509–529 (14).

Ross, A.M. (1948) *Trade Union Wage Policy.* Berkeley and Los Angeles: University of California Press (9).

Ross, A.M. (1957) The external wage structure. In Taylor, G.H. and Pierson, F. (eds.), *New Concepts in Wage Determination.* New York: McGraw-Hill (9).

Ross, L. (1977) The intuitive psychologist and his shortcomings. In Berkowitz, L. (ed.), *Advances in Experimental Social Psychology*, vol. 10. New York: Academic Press (3).

Rosser, M.J. (1977) A behavioural approach to welfare economics. Lanchester Polytechnic, Department of Economics Staff Seminar Discussion paper No. 19, December, 1–28, Coventry, United Kingdom (12).

Rothbard, M.N. (1976) Praxeology: the methodology of Austrian economics. In Dolan, E.G. (ed.), *The Foundations of Modern Austrian Economics.* Kansas City: Sheed and Ward (7).

Runciman, W.G. (1966) *Relative Deprivation and Social Justice.* Henley, England: Routledge and Kegan Paul (9).

Russell, T. and Thaler, R. (1985) The relevance of quasi rationality in competitive markets. *American Economic Review* 75: 1071–1082 (5).

Sahlin, N.E. (1983) On second order probabilities and the notion of epistemic risk. In Stigum, B.P. and Wenstop, F. (eds.), *Foundations of Utility and Risk Theory with Applications*. Dordrecht: D. Reidel (5).

Samuelson, P.A. (1955) Diagrammatic exposition of a theory of public expenditure. *Review of Economics and Statistics* 37: 350–356 (12).

Samuelson, P.A. (1963) Problems of methodology — discussion. *American Economic Review Papers and Proceedings* 53: 231–236 (13).

Samuelson, P.A. (1964) Theory and realism: a reply. *American Economic Review* 54: 736–739 (13).

Sanford, A.J. (1985) *Cognition and Cognitive Psychology*. London: Weidenfeld and Nicolson (3).

Sargan, J.D. (1971) A study of wages and prices in the U.K., 1949–1968. In Johnson, H.G. and Nobay, A.R. (eds.), *The Current Inflation*. London: Macmillan (9).

Schall, L.D. (1972) Interdependent utilities and Pareto optimality. *Quarterly Journal of Economics* 86: 19–24 (10).

Schewe, C.D. (1973) Selected social psychological models for analyzing buyers. *Journal of Marketing* 37: 31–39 (10).

Schoemaker, P.J.H. (1982) The expected utility model: its variants, purposes, evidence and limitations. *Journal of Economic Literature* 20: 529–563 (3, 4, 5, 6, 14).

Schumpeter, J.A. (1954) *History of Economic Analysis*. Oxford: Oxford University Press (4, 8, 14).

Schustack, M.W. and Sternberg, R.J. (1981) Evaluation of evidence in causal inference. *Journal of Experimental Psychology: General* 110: 101–120 (3).

Schutz, A. (1967) *The Phenomenology of the Social World*. Evanston, IL: Northwestern University Press (8).

Schutz, A. (1970) *Reflections on the Problem of Relevance*. New Haven: Yale University Press (8).

Schutz, A. (1971) *Collected Papers I: The Problem of Social Reality*. The Hague: Martinus-Nijhoff (8).

Scitovsky, T. (1945) Some consequences of the habit of judging quality by price. *Review of Economic Studies* 12: 100–105 (10).

Scitovsky, T. (1976) *The Joyless Economy*. New York: Oxford University Press (11).

Scitovsky, T. (1985) Psychology by economists. Unpublished paper prepared for eighth annual Middlebury Conference on Economic Issues, October (14).

Scott, R.H. (1972) Avarice, altruism, and second party preferences. *Quarterly Journal of Economics* 86: 1–18 (10).

Selten, R. (1983) Towards a theory of limited rationality: some remarks of the symposium's impact on economic theory. In Scholz, R. W. (ed.), *Decision Making under Uncertainty*. Amsterdam: North-Holland (5).

Sen, A.K. (1982) Rational fools: a critique of the behavioral foundaitons of economic theory. In Sen, A.K. (ed.), *Choice, Welafre and Measurement*. Oxford: Blackwell (14).

Shackle, G.L.S. (1955) *Uncertainty in Economics*. Cambridge: Cambridge University Press (2).

Shackle, G.L.S. (1969) *Decision, Order, and Time* (2nd edition). Cambridge: Cambridge University Press (2).

Shackle, G.L.S. (1972) *Epistemics and Economics*. Cambridge: Cambridge University Press (5, 7).

Shackle, G.L.S. (1974) *Keynesian Kaleidics*. Edinburgh: Edinburgh University Press (2).

Shackle, G.L.S. (1983) Professor Kirzner on entrepreneurship. *Austrian Economics Newsletter* 4: 7–8 (7).

Shapiro, H.T. (1972) The index of consumer sentiment and economic forecasting. In Strumpel, B., Morgan, J.N. and Zahn, E (eds.), *Human Behavior in Economic Affairs*. New York: Elsevier (13).

Shefrin, H. (1985) Review of P.E. Earl (1983) *The Economic Imagination*. *Journal of Economic Behavior and Organization* 6: 206–209 (15).

Siebert, W.S. and Addison, J.T. (1981) Are strikes accidental? *Economic Journal* 91: 389–404 (1).

Simon, H.A. (1959) Theories of decision-making in economics and behavioral sciences. *American Economic Review* 49: 253–83 (3, 7, 9, 12, 15).

Simon, H.A. (1963) Economics and psychology. In Koch, S. (ed.), *Psychology: A Study of a Science, Volume 6, Investigations of Man as a Socius — Their Place in Psychology and the Social Sciences*. New York: McGraw-Hill (14).

Simon, H.A. (1976) From substantive to procedural rationality. In Latsis, S.J. (ed.), *Method and Appraisal in Economics*. Cambridge: Cambridge University Press (4, 5, 7).

Simon, H.A. (1978) Rationality as process and as product of thought. *American Economic Review* 68: 1–16 (3).

Simon, H.A. (1979) Rational decision making in business organizations. *American Economic Review* 69: 493–513 (3, 5, 9).

Simon, H.A. (1981) Cognitive science: the newest science of the artificial. In Norman, D.A. (ed.), *Perspectives on Cognitive Science*. Norwood, N.J: Ablex (3).

Simon, H.A. (1984) On the behavioral and rational foundations of economic dynamics. *Journal of Economic Behavior and Organization* 5: 35–55 (3).

Simon, H.A. (1987) Behavioral economics. In Eatwell, J., Milgate, M. and Newman, P. (eds.), *The New Palgrave*. New York: Stockton Press (14).

Simon, H.A. and Hayes, J.R. (1976) The understanding process: problem isomorphs. *Cognitive Psychology* 8: 165–190 (3).

Sinderman, C.J. (1982) *Winning the Games Scientists Play*. New York: Plenum Press (15).

Skinner, B.F. (1972) *Beyond Freedom and Dignity*. New York: Vintage Books (2).

Skinner, B.F. (1976) *About Behaviorism*. New York: Vintage Books (2).

Slovic, P., Fischhoff, B. and Lichtenstein, S. (1977) Behavioral decision theory. *Annual Review of Psychology* 28: 1–39 (3).

Smith, V.L. (1962) An experimental study of competitive market behavior. *Journal of Political Economy* 70: 111–137 (13).

Smith, V.L. (1982) Microeconomic systems as an experimental science. *American Economic Review* 72: 923–955 (5).

Snyder, M. and Swann, W.B. (1978) Hypothesis testing processes in social interaction. *Journal of Personality and Social Psychology* 36: 1202–1212 (3).

Solow, R.M. (1979) Alternative approaches to macroeconomic theory: a partial view. *Canadian Journal of Economics* 12: 339–355 (9).

Solow, R.M. (1980) On theories of unemployment. *American Economic Review* 70: 1–11 (5, 9).

Sommers, M.S. (1964) Product symbolism and the perception of social strata. In Greyser, S.A. (ed.), *Towards Scientific Marketing*. Chicago: American Marketing Association (10).

Steedman, I. and Krause, U. (1986) Goethe's Faust, Arrow's impossibility theorem and the individual decision taker. In Elster, J. and Hylland, A. (ed.), *Foundations of Social Choice Theory*. Cambridge: Cambridge University Press (12).

Steers, R.M. and Porter, L.W. (1979) *Motivation and Work Behavior*. New York: McGraw-Hill (9).

Stigler, G.J. (1948) Review of P.A. Samuelson's *Foundations of Economic Analysis*. *Journal of the American Statistical Association* 43: 603–605 (10).

Stigler, G.J. (1961) The economics of information. *Journal of Political Economy* 69: 213–225 (5).

Stigler, G.J. (1965) *Essays in the History of Economics*. Chicago: University of Chicago Press (14).

Stigler, G.J. (1984) Economics: the imperial science? Scandinavian Journal of Economics 86: 301–313 (14).

Stigler, G.J. and Becker, G.S. (1977) De gustibus non est disputandem. *American Economic Review* 67: 76–90 (2, 5, 11, 12).

Stitch, S.P. and Nisbett, R.E. (1980) Justification and the psychology of human reasoning. *Philosophy of Science* 47: 188–202 (3).

Strumpel, B., Morgan, J.N. and Zahn, E. (eds.) (1972) *Human Behavior in Economic Affairs*. New York: Elsevier (1).

Streissler, E. (1972) To what extent was the Austrian school marginalist? *History of Political Economy* 4: 426–441 (8).

Sugden, R. (1986) New developments in the theory of choice under uncertainty. *Bulletin of Economic Research* 38: 1–24 (5).

Svenson, O. (1979) Process descriptions of decision making. *Organizational Behavior and Human Performance* 23: 86–112 (3).

Thaler, R. (1980) Towards a Positive Theory of Consumer Choice. *Journal of Economic Behavior and Organization* 1: 39–60 (5, 15).

Thurow, L.C. (1983) *Dangerous Currents: The State of Economics*. New York, Oxford University Press (9).

Tobin, J. (1972) Inflation and unemployment. *American Economic Review* .62: 1–8 (9). Tobin, J. and Dolbear, F.T. (1963) Comments on the relevance of psychology to economic theory and research. In S. Koch (ed.), (1963) *Psychology: A Study of a Science, Volume 6, Investigations of Man as a Socius — Their Place in Psychology and the Social Sciences*. New York: McGraw-Hill (2).

Trevithick, J.A. (1976) Money wage inflexibility and the Keynesian labour supply function. *Economic Journal* 86: 327–332 (9).

Tschirgi, J.E. (1980) Sensible reasoning: a hypothesis about hypotheses. *Child Development* 51: 1-10 (3).

Turner, H.A. and Jackson, D.A.S. (1970) On the determination of the general wage level: a world analysis; or "unlimited labour forever." *Economic Journal* 80: 827–849 (9).

Tversky, A. (1972) Elimination by aspects: a theory of choice. *Psychological Review* 79: 281–299 (3).

Tversky, A. and Kahneman, D. (1974) Judgment under uncertainty: heuristics and biases. *Science* 185: 1124–1131 (3).

Tversky, A. and Kahneman, D. (1987) Rational choice and the framing of decisions. In Hogarth, R.M. and Reder, M.W. (eds.), (1987) *Rational Choice: The Contrast Between Economics and Psychology*. Chicago: University of Chicago Press (14).

Vanden Abeele, P. (1983) The index of consumer sentiment: predictability and predictive power in the EEC. *Journal of Economic Psychology* 3: 1–17 (13).

Van Raaij, W.F. (1985) Attributions of causality to economic actions and events. *Kyklos* 38: 3–19 (3).

Veblen, T. (1899) *The Theory of the Leisure Class*. New York: Macmillan (10).

Vickers, D. (1978) *Financial Markets in the Capitalist Process*. Phildelphia: University of Pennsylvania Press (2).

Vickers, D. (1985) On relational structures and non-equilibrium in economic theory. *Eastern Economic Review (2)*.

Viner, J. (1925) The utility concept in value theory and its critics. *Journal of Political Economy* 33: 636–659 (14).

Walras, L. (1874/1954) *Elements of Pure Economics*. Translated by W. Jaffee. Chicago: Richard. D. Irwin (4).

Ward, A. and Pickering, J.F. (1981) Preliminary testing of the explanatory power of the EEC consumer attitudes survey in the the UK. *Applied Economics* 13: 19–34 (13).

Ward, B. (1972) *What's Wrong with Economics?* New York: Basic Books (14).

Warneryd, K. and Walerud, B. (1982) Taxes and economic behavior: some interview data on tax evasion in Sweden. *Journal of Economic Psychology* 2: 187–211 (13).

Warr, P.B. (1983) Work, jobs and unemployment. *Bulletin of the British Psychological Society* 36: 305–311 (1).

Wason, P.C. (1960) On the failure to eliminate hypotheses in a conceptual task. *Quarterly Journal of Experimental Psychology* 12: 129–140 (3).

Wason, P.C. and Johnson-Laird, P.N. (1972) *Psychology of Reasoning*. London: B.T. Batsford (3).

Waterman D.A. and Newell, A. (1971) Protocol analysis as a task for artificial intelligence. *Artificial Intelligence* 2: 285–318 (6).

Weintraub, E.R. (1985) Appraising general equilibrium analysis. *Economics and Philosophy* 1: 23–37 (2).

Wells, G.L. and Harvey, J.H. (1977) Do people use concensus information in making causal attributions? *Journal of Personality and Social Psychology* 35: 279–293 (3).

Whitley, R. (1984) *The Intellectual and Social Organization of the Sciences*. Oxford: Clarendon Press (14).

Wieser, F. (1929) Das Wesen und der Hauptinhalt der Theoretischen National-oekonomie. *Gesammelte Abhandlugen*, Verlag von J.C.B. Mohr (Paul Siebeck) Tubingen (7).

Wilensky, H. (1976) *The New Corporatism, Centralization and the Welfare State*. Beverly Hills: Sage (13).

Wiles, P. and Routh, G. (eds.) (1984) *Economics in Disarray*. Oxford: Blackwell (14).

Williams, R. and Defries, L. (1981) The roles of inflation and consumer sentiment in explaining Australian consumption and savings patterns. *Journal of Economic Psychology* 1: 105–120 (13).

Winch, D. (1970) Marginalism and the boundaries of economic science. In Black, R.D.C., Coats, A.W. and Goodwin, C.D.W. (eds.), *The Marginal Revolution in Economics*. Durham, NC: Duke University Press (14).

Winer, B.J. (1972) *Statistical Principles in Experimental Design*. New York: McGraw-Hill (13).

Winter, S.G. (1964) Economic "natural selection" and the theory of the firm. *Yale Economic Essays* 4: 225–272 (3, 5, 6).

Winter, S. G. (1971) Satisficing, selection, and the innovating remnant. *Quarterly Journal of Economics* 85: 237–261 (5).

Wong, S. (1978) *The Foundations of Paul Samuelson's Revealed Preference Theory*. London: Routledge and Kegan Paul (14).

Woo, H.K.H. (1986) *What's Wrong with Formalization in Economics?* Newark, CA: Victoria Press (14).

Wood, A.J.B. (1978) *A Theory of Pay*. Cambridge: Cambridge University Press (9).

Woods, W.A. (1960) Psychological dimensions of consumer decisions. *Journal of Marketing* 24: 15–19 (10).

Zarnowitz, V. (1985) Recent work on business cycles in historical perspective. *Journal of Economic Literature* 23: 523–580 (3).

INDEX